THE NIGHT SKY
OF THE LORD

Alan Ecclestone

THE NIGHT SKY
OF THE LORD

Darton, Longman & Todd
London

First published in Great Britain in 1980 by
Darton, Longman & Todd Ltd
89 Lillie Road
London SW6 1UD

© 1980 Alan Ecclestone

ISBN 0 232 51397 X ⟶ 20027735

Printed in Great Britain by
The Anchor Press Ltd and bound by
Wm Brendon & Son Ltd, both of Tiptree, Essex

296

For
Catherine, Rachel, Richard, Joanna, Andrew, Stephen, Daniel,
Rosalind, Simon, and their generation

Errata

p. 31, l. 28 (also in Bibliography and Index): *for* Paul Vellacot *read* Herbert Butterfield.

p. 228, l. 3: the correct title of W. Ullmann's book is *Medieval Foundations of Renaissance Humanism.*

Contents

it's about a cat
bigger than Bulgakov's, east
of Jeoffry in the night sky of the Lord;
it stalks like plague along the grass,
fathering history on our post-diluvial age.

Peter Porter, *Cat's Fugue*

and that the cat
Who really laid it on us
is his Dad.

Lawrence Ferlinghetti,
Sometime during Eternity

1.   A Time To Speak

1

'Rush down the plenitude, and you shall see
Isaiah counting famine on this lee.'

Hart Crane, *The Bridge.*

'One does not expect novel cards when playing so traditional a game;
it is the hand that matters.'

I. A. Richards, *Principles of Literary Criticism*

A poem or even a single line of poetry needs more than one man's lifetime in which to yield its meaning. Not only what the poet intended but the reverberations of what he wrote, which come echoing from the circumstances of other times, are full of meaning for us now. Whispering or bellowing in our ears they surge around our lives today, and tomorrow will beat upon other shores. Now, when the night sky of the Lord is upon us, we must ask as did Isaiah long ago: 'What of the night?' (Isaiah 21.2.)

This book is a personal reflection on living at this time. It lacks, and this must constantly be kept in mind, first-hand experience of much to which it refers. I have been, like millions more, shielded from the terrible evils of the world by the accident of being born and living in relatively peaceful, stable England. Nevertheless the suffering and the horrors that others have known and still face are part of the world in which I live. To speak of one world or one human life is to admit that the diminishments of others, their griefs and pains, cannot go unregarded by me or others, save at the cost

1

of coarsening and degrading that shared life. We cannot sleep off
the anguish of mankind.

I am concerned then with an attempt to stay awake, to look as
honestly as I can at today's and tomorrow's world, to think out
how best to pray, speak and act with others in it. A great many
worlds, like Chinese boxes, are hidden within it. The significance
of very many will elude us while the problems they create crowd
in upon us. The choices we have may be very small but we must
make those we can. Religion, philosophy, politics, are fields in
which we may do so. It is true that the choices we must now make
are made in circumstances so largely novel and swiftly changing
that beliefs, traditions, concepts of the past not only offer little
help but may even hinder us in the attempt. Yesterday's map of
this human enterprise may prove to be more misleading than we
dare think. Each of us, even so, must do what he can to make
sense of the journey.

I write as a Christian and as one still in heart and mind a parish
priest, and therefore I write for the 'all sorts and conditions of
men' (Book of Common Prayer) among whom I have spent my
life. Some of them go to church but the majority do not. Some of
them play an active part in public affairs but most of them don't.
A number of them are expert in the technology and scientific work
which is rapidly altering the world-conditions in which we live.
The majority must somehow learn to acquire the skills with which
to run a home, sustain a marriage, bring up children, earn a living,
be good neighbours, and gain some sense of values to lend meaning
to their lives. As one among them I share these common problems
and hopes.

Not one of us can hope to know anything but a fragment of the
vast body of knowledge that now accrues to mankind, that now
helps men to solve the problems that have beset them in the past,
but also adds its own quota of perils hitherto inconceivable. To
the experts and scholars in many fields, therefore, I hope this book
will acknowledge its debt. I am even now moved to ask, like
Padraic Pearse's 'Fool', 'Was it folly or grace?' that led me to enter
these fields at all. That I have often been mistaken, blind and
presumptuous in so doing is likely enough. Such faults may warn

others and point the way forward to more adequate, wiser dealing with what has to be faced.

Some recognized starting point from which to look out on that other land is needed. Some clue or compass to give direction to our thought is called for. I have chosen to find this starting point in one complex and difficult question which has been, is and will go on being for years to come important in our world. It is that concerning the relations of Christians and Jews, or, even more broadly, that of the world's treatment of the Jews. If it seems strange at first to attach such great importance to this, I can only hope in the course of the book to show good and sufficient reasons for so doing.

My choice has not wholly been dictated by the thought that some kind of reparation is owed to the Jews, as indeed more people are ready to admit than would have done so forty years ago. I believe that where underlying attitudes are not changed old habits will reassert themselves. A new pamphlet[1] published by the National Front repeats the charges and calumnies made against the Jews in much the same language that the Nazis used a generation ago. We have therefore to make a more deliberate effort to examine the springs of such manifestations of hatred. We must learn to see the ramifications of what might appear at first sight to be a sectarian matter. We must resist the temptation to be too perplexed or irritated by some present-day aspects of the manifestations of this hatred to want to go on thinking and praying about it. We must see that what is involved is a matter of life and death for the civilized world. It concerns not only Jews, but all mankind.

This is a large claim to make. It requires us to look closely at and to weigh up the bearing of the Jewish question upon all the hopes and purposes that men cherish for tomorrow's world, to examine closely how human history is to be understood, how nations are to be seen and served, ethical standards to be respected, and human relationships enabled to become more mature. There are no blue-prints for any of these things in this book, but there

---

1. *Spearhead.* Quoted in a *Times* article by W. Frankel in 1978.

are some questions raised about both the willingness on our part
to face them and the ways in which we might set about it.

It is as material to be used in praying that I would first of all
wish the book to be read. We must come to the subject in a way
that involves our whole nature. Max Plowman once wrote (in
Bridge into the Future) about Truth as 'that which makes more than
an intellectual correspondence within one'. He went on to say:
'unless I am moved all of a piece for deeper reasons than I can
explain, my intellectual assent is so superficial as to be worthless.'
I do not think that we have been helped either to approach social-
political matters or to pray about them with the totality of spiritual
concentration that they demand. Unless we can learn to pray
'moved all of a piece' we can scarcely hope to attain the seriousness
of purpose that the gravity of the problem calls for. We shall not
redeem the evils of past misdoing nor lay any foundations of
lasting worth for future living unless that prayer grasps and offers
to God, bravely, the deepest things that are involved. The declaration that finally emerged from Vatican II on the Jews was not
something to be proud of. It was rather a warning that more
penitence, more charity, more courage, more ample generosity of
spirit was needed if the real renewal of Christian life was to be
helped to grow. The wrong kind of worldliness was at work.

I am well aware that for many reasons this is a difficult plea to
make. Prejudices stored in the human mind spring to action at
the mention of the Jews. It is hard to talk sanely about them.
Fantasies, speculations, ignorant gossip, all combine to withstand
any bids for truth. Behind the rubbish of today's foul speech lie
nineteen hundred years of hostility between the Christian and
Jewish faiths. Pride, persecution, envy, cruelty, fear, lack of charity, ignorance, want of imagination, and, today, some sense of
guilt, make heavy the burden of this divorce. The Jews themselves
often make it more difficult still, for their wounds are raw and
they see no reason to hide them. They know that men are quick
to absolve themselves as well as ready to hate those whom they
have wronged. Confronted by such bitter perversities we must
learn to pray:

Because the depths
Are clear with only death's
Marsh-light, because the rock of grief
Is clearly too extreme for us to breach:
Deepen our depths,
And aid our unbelief.

                    (David Gascoyne, *De Profundis*)

More learned, more eloquent, more profound pleas on the subject
than I could hope to make have been made already, and my
indebtedness to them will everywhere be obvious. Nevertheless I
count it a matter of personal obligation to try to reinforce attention
to the Jewish problem.

There is a further preliminary question to be faced. Does this
Jewish problem affect the lives of ordinary men and women? What
is so special about it? Many people either rarely meet a Jew or have
any reason to feel concerned about them. Jews will continue to be
an entertainer's joke, the subject of some scurrilous story, the
paste-board villains of a folktale brought up to date. There are
now more obvious, possibly more vulnerable alien ethnic groups
in our society than Jews. West Indians, East-African Asians, Ben-
galis, Pakistanis, Sikhs, present other targets. Why single out the
Jews?

I have no desire to minimize the importance of the community-
relations problem affecting the many peoples now living in the
great cities of the industrialized world. In England we have as yet
hardly begun to tackle the issues raised by the pluralistic society.
But the case of the Jews is different from that of all others. It is,
in the first place, a longstanding problem. It has nineteen centuries
of history behind it. So protracted a failure in human relations
must spring from exceptional difficulties. In the second place, the
problem is not a racial but a religious one, even if the majority of
the citizens of this country are largely indifferent to it. It touches
not a denominational issue but the spiritual infrastructures of
society. The Jew does not seek to proselytize, does not ask for
special favours, but by his presence he obstructs a general slide
into religious indifference on the one hand and by a resolute non-

conformity challenges the assumptions of society on the other. Whether remaining obstinately separate or determinedly seeking assimilation he has therefore always aroused disquiet. Laurens van der Post has written of this age-old problem in his novel *The Seed and the Sower*. He speaks of 'the mass instincts to seize an excuse for pulling down the very thing that they themselves have need of elevating', and of those who appear to be predestined to bear the suffering that this brings because they 'personify most clearly the singularity that has to be humiliated and sacrificed'. The Jew has been throughout history that humiliated brother.

It is this aspect of anti-semitism – religious anti-semitism – which has to be kept in mind. Paradoxically it has been brought to the attention of modern man by one who most resolutely endeavoured to exclude the religious element entirely from his work. Yet Freud also admitted that despite his contempt for 'sacred frenzies' he had never lost a feeling of solidarity with the Jewish people[1]. Psychoanalysis was Jewish in his opinion because it expressed the freedom to pursue the truth about human nature unhindered by dogmas and superstitions. The Jew in his obstinate singularity invaded the areas which the mass-instincts of the non-Jewish world would rail off. He was hated because he told men things about themselves which they did not care to know.

Two things therefore make the Jewish question of personal concern for us. The first of these arises from the share which each of us has in the shaping of what is said and done in the world. Here each of us bears some witness to truth or betrays it. Indifference or unthinking acquiescence in things as they are or as we suppose them to be, even our silence at critical times, contributes to what takes place. As I re-read today a short booklet by Charles Singer, *The Christian Approach to the Jews*, written in 1937, a plea addressed in the first instance to the International Missionary Council, and through that body to all Christians, I know now that his words, painful to read in the aftermath of these critical years, did not reach me. They did not alert me to the gravity of what was then being done in the heart of Europe. 'As a result of hesitation, of timidity,

1. See M. Robert, *From Oedipus to Moses*, p.41.

of delay,' wrote Dr. Singer, 'we have seen submerged in Europe that common feeling which was believed to be characteristic of our modern world, so that events which would have outraged Christendom in the last century, or even a few years ago, pass now almost unnoticed.' I know now that my Christianity was too ill-informed and insensitive, too shallow and dull of vision, to recognize that what was said and done to the Jews was of supreme importance to mankind.

Secondly, my starting-place is not an idea but an event, an event of such a monstrous character that it threatens the annulment of all things human. That event is the Holocaust, the planned murder of the Jews of Europe put in hand by the Hitlerite régime a generation ago.[1]

That event is not to be set apart as a freakish phenomenon of the past. On the contrary it must be seen, if it is to be truly understood, as inextricably bound up with certain features of European life, its history and culture. It is rooted in things in which all of us have been participants, in things which are at work in us today. For that reason the Holocaust must not be pushed out of mind, nor must I simply read books or watch television programmes about it. This may be my one real chance of learning what the crucifixion of Jesus Christ didn't bring home to me, of learning to pray in a way unattempted before.

It is the wider significance that must therefore be faced. The Jewish problem, of which the Holocaust is but one episode, planned indeed as the final episode, touches all levels of the spiritual as well as the social and political life of Europe. It does so, not only because the Hebraic element of its culture has been of supreme importance in the moulding of its moral and spiritual characteristics, but also because Judaism continues to represent a religious understanding of life distinct from the conceptualizations and compromises into which the Christian religion has been drawn. Our job is to see the event in relation to the Biblical view of

1. 'In each generation, one event more than any other makes this lesson, (that we ought to care for the other) especially pertinent, as it gives it a character specific to that age. For this century I believe this event is the extermination of the European Jews in the gas chambers . . . ' Bruno Bettelheim, *Encounter*, Dec. 1978.

human history to which both faiths subscribe, and this history in the light of the event itself. It is not an event in the past, but one which stands squarely across our path like the angel confronting Balaam's ass. Our job is an integral part of the demand being made on men at this time to transform the life of Europe and the whole world, not simply to give adequate scope for science and technology or to secure full employment, but to bring into being the kind of society which promises a more adequately human life to mankind as a whole. The demand is above all a demand for greater imagination. The state, the church, the family, the school, the arts, the person, all these are due for reshaping and radical overhaul if we take seriously what the Holocaust implies.

Jews form a very small minority group among the world's peoples. We might justly speak of them even so not only as amongst the world's most imaginative peoples but as a cause of imagination among others. Judaism is in essence a search for reality in human life; a radical, ruthless, confident attempt to come to the truth of our human condition. It has possessed itself of an enormous corpus of traditional religious usage, as extensive as life itself, against which minds like that of Freud declared war, but as Marthe Robert has pointed out, in *From Oedipus to Moses*, even Freud found Judaism 'worthy of respect not only because of its mission or potential mission as an upholder of reason in its battle against mythology and superstition, but also because it is timelessly imbued with meaning and with the joy of life and because it is wise'. It is both personal in intention and universal in scope. It is ready at times to criticize all titles to authority such as men delight to acquire, to subject all traditions to iconoclastic demands.

The history of Judaism in nineteenth century Europe, during which time it produced the most impressive array of the world's intellectual leaders, was marked with tensions, particularly in Germany, that threatened to destroy the traditional patterns of Jewish behaviour. Not only within their ranks but in their relations with contemporary society Jews were involved in endless debate about the practice and outlook of their faith in the context of the contemporary world. There were many who opted, with varying degrees of cynicism, for 'conversion' and assimilation, believing that, in

Heine's words,[1] it was 'an entrance ticket into European culture'. There were others who attempted reforms which would bring Judaism into line with the social and cultural life around them. Such men endeavoured to reshape the patterns of worship, to rethink the questions of rabbinic authority and communal autonomy, to subject the whole corpus of law to continuous searching criticism. They could be openly contemptuous of the mass of Jews whose observance of traditional religious ceremonies and 'babbling array of their prayers "made them" just like the riff-raff of other religious groups'. There were times when both sides were constrained to appeal to the police to check their opponents' behaviour.

Judaism is not to be thought of as a 'monolithic' structure, but as a lively tension between timeless obligation to serve God and instant awareness of changing demands. It has been summed up as constituting unceasing interrogation. For both Jews and Christians, being alive to God must mean being sensitive to the fact that his questions are being put to them. It is a function of the Spirit as Jews and Christians have known it to enter searchingly into man's house, and there to put questions, now like a breath and now like a wind, to try all things that it finds there, to question their fitness to endure. The process in our own night-sky is of near gale-force winds.

It is a delusion to suppose that the disturbing questions will, if ignored, go away, if suppressed be forgotten, or that by hiding ourselves like naked Adam we can escape them. It is no less delusive to expect that we shall get comforting answers to our own questionings. To live with our uncertainties is not simply a necessary part of our education at all levels; it is the very truth of faith. To endure the sifting process of interrogation is the hallmark of discipleship.

It is now thirty years or more since Europe began to learn the bare facts of the evil design of the Holocaust in all its enormity. How much has been learned from the facts, is the question we must ask. The bare re-iteration of them is not enough. It can be counter-productive, involving us in sterile discussions – as to

1. Quoted in J. Carlebach, *Karl Marx and the Radical Critique of Judaism.*

whether, for instance, Hitler was personally responsible for ordering the destruction of the Jews. The real issue is more demanding.
For a very long time the Christian churches not only accustomed
themselves to not asking questions about a great many aspects of
life and human behaviour, but discouraged those who felt moved
to do so. The record of the treatment of such inquirers is bad and
bloody. All too often advances in knowledge and social behaviour
have had to be made in the teeth of the opposition of the defenders
of orthodoxy. Questioning itself was feared and resented, submission and silence approved. Throughout human history it has been
thought wrong to ask the question 'Where is thy brother? (Genesis
4.9)

Yet ask it we must if we are to learn to be human. 'Hitler will
be defeated:' wrote Namier in 1941, 'and yet, unless the Jewish
problem is faced in the light of history and with a courageous
realistic approach, it will continue to poison our lives and the
minds of non-Jews.' Some real effort has been made to face it.
Christian leaders and scholars have come together with Jews.
Groups praying for new understanding between the two faiths
have long been at work. A statement reporting a seminar held in
Holland in 1978 attended by Christians of many denominations
declared. that 'only in overcoming anti-semitism will a true ecu-
menical unity be found, because the people of God and the covenant of God with his people cannot be divided. We are bound
together with the Jewish people in this covenant.' Christians have
been invited to join in synagogue services on the Day of Atonement in London, and the Council for Christian-Jewish understanding made special appeals for the prayers of Christians as the 1979
Camp David conversations between the Arabs and Israelis began.

Nevertheless I feel uneasy about Namier's words. It is difficult
to find evidence of a realistic approach to the Jewish problem or
to show how it has affected the learning processes of the churches
in Britain. To too many people Auschwitz is simply a deplorable
event in the past. It does not initiate purposeful action today.

Should it do so? The answer that this book endeavours to make
is that failure or unwillingness on the part of the churches to give
it a primary importance indicates both insensitivity and a lack of

imagination that bodes ill for the life of the world in the years ahead. To neglect it is to lose a great opportunity to learn from and along with Jews what it was that went sour in relations between the two faiths long ago, why the cleavage persisted and grew more prolific of hatred, why at all times the Jew has been held unwelcome in Christian society, and how in the mercies of God reconciliation might come about. Old habits die hard. The whole matter can so easily be relegated to the margins of Christian concern instead of becoming a spur to immediate action. Nothing less than a profound change of heart and mind, more thorough-going than most Christians have yet felt expected of them, can help them to begin to see its bearing upon the whole witness and work of the Church in the world.

Eyes must be opened. The elucidation of human experience must become a primary job in prayer. We know now how easily men may falsely see canals on Mars when minded to do so, with what like facility they may fail entirely to see things that disturb their presuppositions. The blindness that once overcame Israel at a crit-ical moment in her history is not likely to be a failing of that nation alone. Again and again we see men as things, as objects rather than persons. Words such as: 'nobody was hurt, only two or three niggers got killed' are used. The experience of true community and the loving interpenetration of persons in unified life cannot even begin until we are able to see each other properly. How much do we want to see? How ready are we to learn the bitter truth in the remark 'You have mistook me all the while'? Men and women as husbands and wives, peoples and nations the world over, have suffered because of these mistakes. One day the price of such failure may bankrupt mankind.

I am far from suggesting that the world's troubles would end were Christians and Jews to begin to see each other in a wholly new light. Responsible living today must be concerned with all the nations, their needs and hopes, with the economic and political problems of all of them, with the symbolism of art and science as well as that of religion, with the formative process in which tech-nology and social organization must play an increasingly influential part. There is nonetheless a special relationship between these two faiths, a kinship which may not be disavowed, a conception of the nature of human life, a history which is now interwoven with the fate of the world, and which must be acknowledged if the next forward steps are to be taken. For both, the recognition of this relationship is already an urgent matter. To be indifferent to it is to misread the message of our beclouded skies. European man has learned from the Jews in awkward but deliberate fashion to live towards the future with confidence; he has now to learn from the Jewish faith what it means to live today. It is here and now that he finds himself in darkness, a darkness that threatens to betray him to hatred ¿f himself and life, to lead him to self destruction because he is naked and afraid. He has once again to learn from the Jew that today is the day that the Lord hath made. Today he must stand in the hidden God's presence.

Certain things stand out which demand the attention of heart and mind:

1. Anti-semitism, which has stained the history of Christendom and which has thereafter been become universal must be acknowledged and understood.

2. Anti-Jewish theology in its various forms must be overhauled and replaced by a wholly new pattern of thinking. These forms range from the appropriation by Christians of all they deemed spiritually valuable, while Judaism was rejected as a 'failed religion', to outright efforts to detach Jesus Christ from the Jewish people.

3. The recovery of the Hebraic understanding of the creation and of the nature of human life by Christians must become a priority.

4. The religious significance of Jesus must be newly conceived and presented to the world with the help which a new relationship between Jews and Christians can give.

5. The problems posed by the existence of the State of Israel must be seen as pointers to world relations and to national developments in the future. They are more than domestic issues of the Middle East.

These points call for a searching re-appraisal of the traditional understanding of both faiths. They require a more honest admission of faults in the past, more critical concern to know why they

happened. They also demand new attention to the damaging effects
of the faults written into our history. They likewise raise questions
about the future. What would consitute genuine acts of penitence
on the part of Christians for the wrongs done to the Jews? What
changes of attitude on the part of the Christian Church are called
for if the process of re-education is seriously undertaken? What reshaping of worship and of our understanding of God is needed
from both if together they are to contribute to a more adequate
guidance of mankind in the future? Religions are not commonly
marked by alacrity in welcoming change. Their function has been
protective rather than exploratory and adventurous. But both the
Jewish and Christian faiths are attuned to another note. 'Today if
ye will hear His voice' brings both to a moment, one and infinite,
that may disclose new heaven and earth, and summons Christian
and Jew to set out to find them.

2

'But I've gotta use words when I talk to you.'
                              T. S. Eliot, *Fragment of an Agon*

   The Holocaust, the organized attempt to exterminate the Jews
of Europe undertaken by the Nazi regime, is our point of departure. That event is now embedded in Europe's history, the extermination camps are located on Europe's map. The documentation
of the operation is pitilessly precise. The whole enterprise can be
played down, ignored, lamented or disputed, but it cannot be
erased from Europe's life. In focussing attention upon it I have no
wish to isolate it from the Turkish massacres of the Armenians or
Stalin's murder campaigns, conducted over some twenty years
against all who opposed his will. Conniving at genocide has stained
the history of almost all the great nations of the world today. But

this particular event may help us to understand better the forces that have led men to join in such murderous acts.

It can do so first because it brings us face to face with the seemingly harmless but irrational aspects of our rejection of our fellow human beings. Unlike the 'nigger' or the 'red', the Jew needs no distinction of colour or political views to make him an object of malice. The label is all that is needed. Good for a joke in quiet times, the Jew can become the enemy in our midst as soon as the social and economic conditions grow hard. He is then the alien who cheats and fleeces the poor, the parasite and the subverter of ordered life. When things go wrong 'The Jew is underneath the lot.'[1] He is 'the shadow' in everyman's life. On the Jew self-hatred and irrational fears can be projected.

How the Jews came to earn that reputation demands much patient study of ourselves as well as of the Jews. Great Jews like Marx and Freud and Kafka have helped us to set about this. We should miss the significance of the question were we to suppose, for example, that it had died with the dead of the camps or been thrust abroad to become the Arab-Jew conflict. Already attempts are being made to belittle or deny what happened, to exculpate the men responsible for it. Already the newspapers speak of renewed desecration of the graveyards of Jews in parts of Europe, of synagogues bombed in France, of Jews in London suburbs molested, of Russian Jewry harassed daily, of violence against Jews in Argentina and other parts of the world. Pamphlets naming Jews as enemies of the people have appeared in Britain. While the Arab-Israeli conflict contributes to it, it does not entirely account for the anti-semitic drive.

We must note the fact that anti-semitism is older than the Christian faith. Haman's hatred of Mordecai and his people shows its classical precedent. Nevertheless it is a shameful feature in Christian history, and has not always been regarded as of great importance. It is no part of my purpose, to use Acton's words, 'to convert history into a frightful monument of sin', but rather to try to use it as a key to self-understanding today. Indifference to the past can

---

1. T. S. Eliot, 'Burbank with a Baedeker, Bleistein with a cigar.'

case-harden us to the present. Only by bringing into the light the operation aptly named 'Night and Fog' can we hope to set our sights towards healthier relationships in the future.

To grow indifferent to the memories is not enough. In all the busy rewriting of the liturgical prayers of the established church that has gone on these last twenty years no prayer has been put forth for general use by Christians comparable to that which appears in the Forms of Prayer for Jewish Worship produced by the Reform Synagogues of Great Britain: 'We remember our six million dead, who died when madness ruled the world and evil dwelt on earth. We remember those we knew, and those whose very name is lost. . .'. Dare we say, 'of course, you would expect the Jews to remember them', and leave it at that?

Perhaps we had grown too used to leaving it at that, too uncritical, too ill-informed about the past, to recognize the evil intensity of anti-semitism at work in our contemporary world. Britain during the nineteenth century was involved in international questions but not greatly moved to inquire what common or singular factors were at work in the brutal pogroms in Russia and Poland, in the cruelties that were practised in Roumania, in the conventional anti-semitism of the German upper classes, or the passions aroused by the Dreyfus affair in France.

What is clear, looking back, is that these things were not marked or felt sufficiently sharply by the nervous system of the body we call, perhaps a little too glibly, the Body of Christ – the Christian Church – to occasion pain or alarm.

The insensibility that was shown by masses of Christians to the fate of the Jews must prompt not only the question; 'After Auschwitz, what?' but also compel us to ask 'Why Auschwitz at all?' Such interrogation goes to the foundation of European society. It compels us to admit that, despite its indebtedness to Christian ideals and institutions, it sustained a life marked through the centuries by barbarity and by the callous ill-treatment of weak and defenceless people. Its schools, its laws, its prisons, its mines and mills were far from honouring in practice Him whose nature was revealed most chiefly in His mercy and pity. Nor had the Church been distinguished by a sustained and resolute endeavour to make mercy and pity the guide-lines of public behaviour. 'In spite of its saints, mystics and martyrs,' writes F. C. Happold, 'the history of the Christian Church is a sorry one. It is far too much the story of intolerance, persecution and bigotry, of inquisitions, torture and burning, of "images of God" which had little resemblance to the loving Father or to Our Lord Jesus Christ.' The Holocaust is not to be separated from the long record of the persecution of heretics, the burning of witches, the torture of prisoners, the starving of peasants and artisans, the massacre of minorities, and the slower but equally anguish-producing insensitive treatment of women and children that went on at all times.

Christian spirituality has dwelt much on the sufferings of Jesus Christ on the Cross. Whether it has done so wisely and with true compassion is open to question. Crude acquaintance with suffering is not the best education of the spirit. Crude images of the crucifixion and no less crude hymnology expressing doctrines of atonement could only blunt sensibility. Von Hugel once counselled his niece to refrain from reading Dante's *Inferno* in the early stages of her education, not because he wanted to shield her from the realities of life but because he wanted her to meet them only when prepared by a long process of spiritual training to deal understandingly with them. That kind of restraint has not been widely observed. Our own times have witnessed an extreme desire to abolish any reticence in the public presentation of all forms of human behaviour. The impact of this on emotional life and on standards of value has not been deeply considered.

The Jewish question takes on renewed importance when we consider how the Holocaust is to be kept in the minds of this generation. Neither supposedly neutral documentation of it nor versions which bring it within the purview of entertainment can help. The Nazis were not unwilling to film their methods of dealing with victims. Lacking a sense of awe and a common acceptance of human relationships the viewers and readers confronted by scenes dealing with the most fundamental regions of life are exposed to brutal and cynical exploitation. The Moors Murder tapes were no more than a Do-It-Yourself kit of that genre, whose most hideous triumph lay in the elimination of all sense of shame.

The post-Auschwitz world is engaged with the problem of how to create a more adequate principle of integration for 20th century society, a principle that affords an ethical and aesthetic framework for human life and restores the illumination and awe, once given by the numinous element in religion, to modern man. For the moment confusion reigns. Joseph Heller's *Catch 22* put it briefly that 'so many monstrous events were occurring that he was no longer positive which events were monstrous and which were really taking place'.

It is therefore a major concern of the spiritual education of our time that we face the fact of Auschwitz. To Peter Cauchon's question in the Epilogue to Shaw's *St Joan*, 'Were not the sufferings of our Lord Christ enough for you?', we must for our generation answer No. Our meditations on the Passion of Christ were not sufficient to awaken us to the realities of a world in which anti-semitism flourished. To set our faces in another direction we have to see ourselves as participants in it. We came on the scene after centuries of acquiescence in evil things had prepared for this Final Operation. We were in some sense already conditioned to be insensitive to it. If now we are moved to try to do better we need to make all the use we can of the work of men like Viktor Frankl, Bruno Bettelheim and others who used their time in the camps not simply to survive but also to understand what was being revealed there of human behaviour. Their analysis is of supreme importance to the shaping of a relevant spirituality for our time and to our understanding of what lay behind the evil things then released. 'I am absolutely convinced,' wrote Frankl later, in his introduction to *The Doctor and the Soul*, 'that the gas-chambers of Auschwitz, Treblinka and Maidenek were ultimately prepared not in some Ministry or other in Berlin, but rather at the desks and in the lecture-halls of nihilistic scientists and philosophers.' To that judgment we may well have to add the more ambiguous contributions of historians and theologians.

In the meanwhile we are faced by the question of our own fitness to learn, our preparedness to wait in the dark, our will to endure in faith. I turn elsewhere for a clue to what it involves. The famous conversion of Saul of Tarsus helped to shape a whole cultural epoch. His own words describing it are stark and revealing. The light and the darkness were scarcely divided. Something we have come to call conversion or being born again is happening to the man struck down upon the earth upon his back and lifting up empty arms in Caravaggio's picture. Is it total surrender, total victory, or both? He is a man in labour, in travail with his own rebirth. His is the illumination of a death, the ecstasy of consummated love. In the moment when that which he thought he had was stripped from him, when the light itself plunged him into darkness, when purpose dissolved into waiting, this empty-handed man was possessed of new being.

We cannot command such times but we can learn something of what they reveal, whether on the road to Damascus or Treblinka. They are likely to come, as the Jewish prophets warned long ago, as days of darkness rather than of light, of humiliation rather than exaltation. Illumination and humiliation are bound up together. They come in the darkness of ordinary daylight, the daylight of this post-Auschwitz world. They commit us as they committed Paul to the process of rebirth. Nothing less will do.

Meanwhile the shadow cast by the rejection of Judaism carried to such lengths both by the Christian Church and by the secular state falls across our world. Mere artificial light will not help us. Only the most resolute setting before ourselves of the things which have been done, partly in the name of the Church and partly because the Church was too enfeebled to protest, can help us to find our way now. There has been no lack of diagnoses of our sick society. There has been some readiness to admit that amongst the contributory factors to that malaise the decline in the strength of traditional religion has played an important part. Our civilization has for a considerable time been dominated by the advances in science and technology which divert attention from the more difficult and disturbing problems of man's inner life. The expansion of knowledge and the refinement of skills have not been accompanied by growth in mature relationships and by greater discrimination in styles of life. The result is a loss of meaningful living.

Revival of religious concern will come. What matters most is the character or nature of it. One crucial aspect of this I take to be a complete change in the relations between Christians and Jews in the future. Both have suffered deeply, though in different ways, from the estrangement of the past. For Jews life has been restricted by brutal enforcement of subjection to 'Christian' dictation:

> By the torture, prolonged from age to age,
> By the infamy, Israel's heritage,
> By the Ghetto's plague, by the garb's disgrace,
> By the badge of shame, by the felon's place,
> By the branding tool, the bloody whip,
> And the summons to Christian fellowship.
>   (R. Browning, 'Holy Cross Day')

For Christians the losses have been equally grave. For many centuries men have used words that hailed the crucified rejected Son of Man as their Lord and Master; yet in his name and their doctrinal pronouncements of it they have put their brothers to death with unspeakable cruelties. They filled their churches with pictures and statues of Him but failed to see Him in the person of the despised and ill-treated stranger. They talked much of His Incarnation, of His sharing our flesh and blood, of the dignity that He thus had given to the least of men and women, but they traded in flesh for profit as long as they could and degraded those who were weak and unable to resist them. With unctuous pride they talked of the freedom He had bought for them with his life while they thrust the Jew aside and kept working men in servitude of body and mind. They repeated the great commandments of the Bible and spat upon those of their neighbours marked out with a yellow spot or David's star. They sought the power and wealth of the world and forgot the warning of the Epistle of James, that most Jewish book of the New Testament, that such things would consume them like fire. She who had sat crowned upon the seven hills has yet to render account for her stewardship.

It is not only in terms of a task neglected or sins committed that the matter is to be seen. It is with the future of mankind that we are really concerned, with the future of two faiths whose business it is to point men in hope to God. To do so the Church will need to learn much from those who have trodden the harder way for so long and who have maintained their faith under grievous oppression. Only so can it hope to use the resources God gave it to accomplish its mission. 'Who knows,' wrote Anne Frank, 'it might even be our religion from which the world and all peoples learn good, and for that reason and that reason only do we have to suffer now.'[1]

1. Quoted in *Forms of Prayer for Jewish Worship* (Reform Synogogues of Great Britain, 1977'.

2. A Time To Question

'Faced with renewed persecution, one asks oneself again how the Jew came to be what he is and why he has drawn upon himself this undying hatred.'

Sigmund Freud, *Letter to Arnold Zeig, September 30th, 1934*.

'Even now, Moses the Prophet, and Moses and Son the clothiers, do not discriminate themselves with a clearness I should desire at times. My error was soon found out and corrected.

"There, I declare now", said my Mother, when I betrayed my misconception, "if that child hasn't got 'old of the idea that Moseses is Moses."

'I referred the matter to Porky Owls, who derided me for not knowing the difference. The former, he pointed out, were Jews and would go to Hell; and the latter was an Israelite and would go to Heaven, being in the Bible.'

William de Morgan, *Joseph Vance*

To ask the right questions has long been seen to be the foundation of all fruitful advances in knowledge. To hear what questions are put to us has marked true wisdom. It is our business, as men and women who are concerned to grow to our full stature, to be alive to such questioning by God and man. We must sort out what questions we should ask and hear, cease asking foolish ones, and in no way flinch from those that are rightly searching; we must distinguish those that call for a solution from those that need only answers, and dwell patiently with those that await revelation.

There are also occasions when all questions melt into one; when to ask 'Who is this?' is all that seems left to do; when to hear the words 'Will ye also go away?' determines commitment for life. From the literature of the Holocaust we derive many questions,

21

not all of them patient of answers. We learn much about the ultimate questions. For example, reading Viktor Frankl's work we may learn that 'How am I to survive?' could not well be answered except in terms of 'What meaning do I attach to my survival?'

Let us begin with questions raised by the event itself. Why did the Holocaust come about? What prompted men to plan and carry out such enormities of murderous cruelty, combining careful attention to the details of organization with uninhibited brutality and calculated sadistic purpose? What end did it really serve? Why did millions of Germans acquiesce in its operation? Throughout the pages of *Mein Kampf* the Jews are described as the great enemies of the German people and of Aryan culture, masters at once of international finance and of the Bolshevik revolutionary plots. Hitler tells us that 'once when I was walking through the inner city I suddenly came across a being in a long caftan with black side-locks. My· first thought was: Is that a Jew?' Not a human being, it seems, but a Jew, a creature of diabolical nature. But does even the glimpse of a mythological horror help us to understand what Himmler meant when, addressing his lieutenants in October, 1943, he described the gassing of over five million such Jews as 'an unwritten and never-to-be-written page of glory'?

We could of course turn to the Jewish population of Germany and Austria to ask how they understood their situation. Did the victims themselves know why it took place? Many of the older generation proudly called themselves German and not until after 1918 did they begin to discover afresh their Jewishness as a significant thing. 'Having been educated in Germany,' writes Nahum Goldmann, born in Lithuania, 'I was a German patriot. Besides, for Jews the whole world over it was a simple matter: Tsarist Russia was the worst enemy of Jews and Jewry, the Germans were against Russia, so we were pro-German.' Numbers of others made mixed marriages with Christians or decided that Christianity was more helpful to them and parted company, as they thought, with Judaism. While not disclaiming their Jewish origin, many intellectuals endeavoured to disassociate themselves wholly from the religious parochialism of the synagogues. At what stage did such men begin to realize that nothing but death awaited them in their German Fatherland and why? Did many foresee, for example, when Walter Rathenau was murdered in 1922, that Jewry itself was marked down for destruction? We know too that as the Hitler regime got under way the emigration of educated Jews increased, but what of the rest? Did they still hope that persecution would stop short of the final operation or that world opinion would bring pressure to bear on Germany's rulers to relieve their lot?

In the neighbouring states of Poland, Hungary and Roumania a longstanding anti-semitism was rife; we could ask how far this had helped to build up the traditions of brutal exclusion and inhuman acts which the Nazis were to continue. In the outside world Britain, France and the United States played a leading part; we must ask how informed they were about what was being done, how much people wanted to know the facts or were anxious to act when they did. How much of the truth did the Vatican and the church leaders throughout the world know? Or was it that more urgent political, economic and military problems crowded out attention to the plight of the Jews? Had Europe paid close enough attention to the post-war mind of Germany to be able to judge what was taking place?

These questions inspire scores of others, and numerous books have been written about them. Some of these examine the consequences of the Versailles Treaty, the economic, political and ideological conditions of the defeated Germans. They dwell on the weakness of the Weimar Republic, the internal dissensions of German life, the bitter and cynical mood of the cultural scene, exemplified in the life of Berlin. Others ask: 'why did humanistic traditions and models of conduct prove so fragile a barrier against political bestiality? What of Germany's great religious concern? Had the First World War and its aftermath, the senseless carnage of Verdun and the Somme, the credit-collapse and unemployment, so benumbed the spiritual vitality of millions that they could offer no real resistance to outrageous acts?

The more closely we study the movement of international affairs, the more we are conscious how little able political leaders were in those years to secure a control of affairs. Too many false clues, too many crossed purposes were to engage and divert attention. 'Many questions remain almost taboo.' They involve the political and military authorities in charge. They raise issues of international relations over which it is still felt desirable to draw veils. It is evident that neither before, during or since the war have Jews been of deep international concern. Worldwide publicity of the part the churches played or did not play in respect of the fate of Jews, or statesmen's decisions that might have saved some of them, has not been welcomed. Despite all the flood of literature that has appeared, the inquiries remain curiously inconclusive. Perhaps we should still ask Why?

Today when the postwar operations – the returning of expatriate Russians to certain death in the Soviet Union or the handling of boatloads of illegal immigrants into Palestine – have become better known, investigations reveal a callous unimaginative treatment of human lives that is hard to face. The events are too near and the shame is too painful. No-one relishes the thought that his words may be quoted to indicate that he helped these vile things to come about. We can re-read today the declaration of the Church Presidents and Bishops of Saxony, Meckleburg, Schleswig-Holstein, and other parts of Germany, made in December 1941; this affirms that 'indisputable documentary evidence' proved that 'the Jews are responsible for this war in its world-wide magnitude,' and demands that 'the severest measures should be taken against the Jews, and that they should be expelled from all German countries'. No good purpose is served by drawing men's attention only to this declaration. Are we not all involved?

I want for this reason to shift the approach to the question of why the Holocaust happened to an entirely personal basis. There were in Germany and elsewhere great numbers of men who were determined for various reasons to destroy the Jews. They were able to do so because in an infinitely complex web of events and circumstances they gained the power and opportunity to do it. Somewhere in those circumstances millions of unimportant people like myself were involved. We made up the world in which the Holocaust happened. To ask why it did take place means asking how much or how little we understood what was going on or being done in our name by others. If the answer to the question shows that I and millions like myself were ignorant of the realities of the world in which we lived, so grossly ignorant that the Holocaust could take place in it without our being at least fore-warned, it will at least serve to make clear that there was something lacking from our spiritual education. If the job of the Church, for example, is to bring men to the truth, however ugly that truth may prove to be, then it is our concern to ask how far people like myself, members of the churches, learned the truth about our civilized life in Europe to any responsible extent. If we lived in a cushioned protected world of unreal things, our citizenship and our churchmanship were both touched by that unreality. Part of the answer to the question may be that my contribution was ignorance not just of immediate events but of longstanding human relations and centuries of misdoing. The charges that are made against the leaders of the Churches are grave indeed. It is not my purpose to accuse them, but to look at my own remote and yet real complicity in it.

To do so means starting with questions of a quite different kind and seemingly far removed from the grim event. They were shaped and put to me by my circumstances; born in an industrial English city in the first decade of this century, growing up in a working-class home, getting further education by scholarships, sensing the strains of war and unemployment, joining a church and a political party, marrying and raising a family, training to be a teacher and getting ordained. In and through all these things I shared in the ignorance and the knowledge, the politics and the religion, which had their bearing upon the Holocaust, even though in the first twenty years of my life I remember meeting only one Jew, a dignified, lonely and courteous old man.

In the somewhat narrow setting of English life, my most press-ing concerns were those of my livelihood, my relations with my family and parochial life. They represented no more than the tip of an iceberg of anxiety never far from the surface. The pressure or menace of circumstances came from too many various, ill-defined or largely unknown sources to be understood and faced with confidence. The political, economic and cultural movements of the day reach people's attention in a confused, distorted condition, in the crude simplifications of newspaper headlines, screen flashes or the quotable comments of leading men. The quotations are made to do duty for knowledge. Personalities count for more than principles, emotional appeals move men more than facts. In the over-dramatization that is used to secure attention to things of the past or to present the mediations by which the past was not only turned into the present but continues to change the present, can never be easy to grasp. Our society differs from that which has gone before; it multiplies the factors that contribute to its shaping, and it suggests that we know how they work. My questioning, such as it was, had to start at that level. When I put it together and ask what home and my parents' outlook, the schools and the teachers I had, the church and the university I knew, the newspapers and books I read, the friends I made and the work I did, contributed to my understanding of a world in which the Holocaust was in preparation, I cannot now be anything but dismayed. What I learnt bears no more real relation to the facts than the little flags on a wall map of the 1914–1918 western front which had indicated what we thought was going on there.

It was not that the questions were not asked. They were different from those of the scientist or the lawyer; more akin to those of the artist. At their best they were a kind of resistance movement, rejecting the easier answers and living with nagging doubts. I looked only at the smokeladen air of an industrial city and at the squalid factories and mean streets that bounded the existence of those who lived and worked in them. It was a Lowry landscape whose familiar filthy rivers were images of its eddying life. Into what sea would they one day pour their waters?

The resistance to these boundaries was very strong in my parents' lives and I added my own inquiry, set going and sustained by the study of history at school and university. I am conscious today that much of what I gained was the formulation of views – the Whig interpretation of history in its various forms – and that there was all too little wrestling with optical illusions and packaged beliefs. Learning to think historically and to understand even a little of the interplay of the half-seen and often contradictory movements of men's minds and feelings is a much heavier task. More perplexing still is the deployment of historical insights towards the conditions in which one lives. Straying one day as a schoolboy into a public lecture given by Henry Clay to students of the Workers Educational Association in a back-street room, I began to attempt to make this connection. I cannot claim to have been realistic or unprejudiced in my efforts to do so. I see these efforts now as a flickering needle wavering upon the scale of human unawareness of the reality of the world. One day it would jump to register an event that put humanity itself in doubt.

Nevertheless this historical questioning, such as it was, turned my attention to the Church. I came to it with my father's imaginative sense of its beauty, my mother's resistance to its pretentiousness and her dismay at its failings, my own adolescent romantic belief in God. It was not very difficult to see that the Church in that Lowry landscape, whatever else it might be elsewhere, offered chiefly moments of withdrawal from the harsher conditions of life and work. An enclave in a world becoming indifferent to it, it enabled some few to keep alive a warmer, more personal experience of human community than could be found elsewhere. The churches and chapels still nourished some features of the Judaeo-Christian faith, still linked the lives of their members by scriptural words to Israel's prophets and the disciples of Jesus. But attrition was plainly at work. These churches made less and less of an impact on thoughts and feelings that were not connected with devotional matters. Whether a church was 'High Church' or 'Low' was as much as most people probably knew of its calling. Around them an urbanized population grew up, a disinherited proletariat of Christian faith, that knew them only by name. It was not at all likely that the fate of the Jews in Europe would be felt as a sharp concern. It would have been possible to guess what would happen if to the active antagonism of German or French anti-semites had been added the indifference or ignorance of English churchmanship.

How had it come about? How consciously did men in these churches address themselves to the multiform problems that the contemporary world thrust upon them? That voices of warning, like that of John Neville Figgis, were raised in pre-1914 days is

clear. It is no less true that the impact of the First World War
aroused in many hopes and desires to reground the Church in the
nation's life and to establish a spiritual leadership there. The
changes they brought about stopped a long way short of the issues
that had to be faced. The Life and Liberty Movement, Copec, the
revision of the Prayer Book, world missionary work, were evidence of good faith. What was missing was a prophetic insight
that would give a different dimension to all such efforts. When in
The Idea of History Collingwood speaks of history as 'imaginative
effort to know the nature of man', he speaks of what was so largely
missing from the way the Church looked at its task. It did not see
men and the times in any revealing light. The salvation-truth that
it had been commissioned to teach did not reach men where they
were because the imaginative leap needed to establish relations
with them was not made. When the Church of England emerged
from the Second World War the document it produced, entitled
Towards the Conversion of England showed its small capacity to
attempt the effort. It was an unlikely soil to nourish any great
concern for Germany's Jews.

Yet the question remained: From whom else could one expect
this concern? The culture and civilization of Europe was what
Christianity had managed to make out of Greek and Roman and
Hebrew materials, however its guidance of this civilization had
weakened and grown indecisive in modern times. The Church was
my father and mother. The problems of its condition were not to
be solved by disavowing it but by working as best one could in
its ranks. The choice that I made was to seek ordination in the
priesthood of the Church of England, to work out my answers to
the questions I faced as a pastor and teacher among the people
whose life I shared with faith in God.

Looking back on that choice, and in part at the time, I realized
that like most of my peers I came to it with very little real knowledge of myself, mankind, the world and the Church. My education was always a lap behind the conditions to which I had come.
What mattered most now was the kind of training I might hope
to get for the work I had undertaken to do. It consisted chiefly in
reading some part of the vast mass of writing about God, the

Church, its doctrines, worship and spirituality which made up the substance of theological instruction. So huge a field, embracing all that mattered most to God and man, had perforce to be reduced to a few recognizable plots. The training, if it could be called this, was not designed to consider closely how any of this impinged upon the lives of those for whom it was intended to be a gospel, or even to turn the questioning process nearer home. It was assumed that a Church so long at work in this field knew what men and their needs were, and could meet them with God's grace and truth channeled in the traditional forms. For most aspirants to holy orders the Church itself would be sufficiently venerable and authoritative to be the answer. Why else seek ordination in it? In the aftermath of the 1914–1918 war and in the successive crises of an exhausted Europe the relevance of much of the life-style of the Church was not immediately obvious, but a beginner in such august surroundings is not well placed to raise objections. He has first to listen and ponder and pray. Theological fashion, a lively bait at any time, was then dominated by the impressive work of Barth. The labyrinth of theology is in any case daunting enough to make most entrants glad to seize hold of whatever threads are offered for guidance.

'At twenty', wrote Julian Green, 'I believed in my elders' answers. I thought they knew. Now that I myself am an elder, when people come to me full of questions, I don't know what to answer.' I have found Green's *Diaries* helpful because he retained the ability to go on asking questions throughout his life. He understood that there is no final answer to human problems and that the search and labour for provisional answers must be renewed day after day. What I found most lacking from my introduction to theology was what has been called 'radical amazement' that prevents 'god-talk' from becoming an academic exercise. The failure of contact that I sensed between the Church and the life of society sprang from the end-stopped lines of her word to the world.

My own vague questioning at length found reinforcement in the life and writings of George Tyrrell, the Modernist theologian. He would not have been regarded as the best example of priestly life by most of my teachers at the time. When I talked about him to them they turned the discussion to the subject of Modernism in the Church. It was not any '-ism' that I was concerned with so much as the experience of a man wrestling for the truth. From a conventional point of view his course had been a disaster, but his integrity was untouched. He never ceased to question for Christ's sake the Church that bore Christ's name. Commit himself wholly to it he would, but he would also remain critical of himself and the institution. Years later I was to find the same steadfast brave devotion in Daniel Berrigan's words and example: 'I must draw from alienation the spiritual resources needed to persevere in my search for manhood, conscience, the will of Christ.'

The relation of my questioning to Judaism was soon to become a matter of importance to me. Like most students of that time I was not dismayed that the quest of the historical Jesus had yielded no striking results. The splendour of Christ was untouched and Christendom's image of Him seemed as yet sufficient. With no more than a faint curiosity at first I found myself thinking about the Jews as the people of Jesus. At no time during my theological training had attention been drawn to anything Jewish outside the range of Old Testament studies. A Christian, it seemed, had no need to pursue acquaintance with them. Even so I found myself wanting to see this Jesus through Jewish eyes, to hear his words through Jewish ears, to meet him among his own people. What did they think of him and his work today? I could not but be perplexed by the way Christians appeared from the earliest times to have appropriated to themselves the Jewish scriptures and Jewish teachers while showing little but contempt for Jews.

I discovered that it was not easy to do what I wanted. In the face of the impressive Christology of generations of Christian scholars it seemed almost perverse to ask for anything more. The record suggested that his own people, finding His teaching objectionable and His presence a threat, had rejected Jesus and connived at His execution. Thereafter in a series of clashes of opinion Jews and Christians had drawn apart and developed their different religious faiths. The fracture between the two had become complete. Stubborn Jewry's continuance as a faith was perhaps little more than historical freakishness. The Christian Church, on the other

hand, had grown from a tiny sect into a world-wide society proclaiming the Lord Jesus Christ, the fulfilment of Old Testament
hopes, the Lord of all life. The Gospels presented the Christ of this
Christian faith, the Christ whose true nature theology would at a
later date unfold in explicit terms. This faith men like myself were
trained and ordained to preach. Ordination did not preclude continuing study of the Scriptures and doctrine based on them, rather
it called for it, but the relation of Jesus to Jewry could be said to
have been settled long ago; it was of no more than minor historical
interest today. Historical study could in any case yield only tentative statements, and congregations expected to hear certainties.

I must not suggest that the question of the Jews and their relationship to Christians was of supreme importance to me at that
time. There were more pressing matters claiming the attention of
a man beginning his work as a priest. But the news of the day in
the 1930s made it clear that Jews and Jewishness were still matters
of conflict, still bringing the passions of men into play. Anti-
semitism, not as an academic question but as a brutal reality in the
life of contemporary Europe, had to be faced. There were bestial
and hateful attacks on the Jews, not on the fringes of civilized life
but in the schools, universities, law-courts and streets. A few
voices were raised to condemn these acts, but the churches were
strangely silent. No common appeal was made in their name to
withstand this evil behaviour. Christian history did not account
for the hatred of Jews which existed in the modern world, yet that
hatred continued to grow. So that history, which had avoided this
difficult issue for so long, had strayed tragically far from the truth.

In a study entitled *The Whig Interpretation of History*, ~~Paul Vel-~~ HERBERT
~~lacot~~ spoke of the abridgments which are made in presenting history: 'It is perhaps a tragedy', he wrote, 'that the important work
of abridging history is so often left to the writers of text-books
and professional manufacturers of commercial literature. . . . It
would seem that abridgments are often falsified by the assumption
that the essentials of the story can be told, leaving out the com-
plications. . . . There is a danger in all abridgments that acquire
certainty by reason of what they omit, and so answer all questions
more clearly than historical research is ever able to do.' It was the

abridgments of history, whether by Christians, Hegelians, nation-alists or anti-semites which provided the scenario; in the heart of Europe evil purposes drew their strength from appeals to history. We use words like tragedy and danger to convey the idea of disaster; what was happening in the streets of German was the raw suffering of human beings.

As I followed the news of events in Germany and became in a small way involved in the plight of refugees, the overall question of the relation of Christianity to Judaism took on a new import-ance. Did the kind of paralysis which overtook the Church when it was faced by the Jewish question reflect a more ancient and deepseated trouble? Was it possible that the accounts, set down after the Church had arrived at its commanding position, had treated the events of some far-off stages of its journey in cavalier fashion? Reading facts into history to justify present achievements or plans is always tempting. The successful often have an unchal-lenged field in which they can put to good use their abilities to do this. Later on in this book I shall look a little more closely at what Christian history could do. For the moment I want only to indicate personal misgivings.

These were soon reinforced from another angle. My immediate concern was with a Jewish Jesus. There were lives of Jesus in abundance, all reflecting the faces of those who looked into the well. These were the faces of Gentile believers or critics. What I looked for was the face of a Jew. The search took me to Klausner's *Jesus of Nazareth*, to Montefiore's *Synoptic Gospels* and thence to other Jewish writing. It was a modest enough beginning, but one that prompted more questions. Like one who visits a foreign land, I noted not only novel sights but the absence of things I had hitherto taken for granted. How did Jesus look when the frame-work of Christendom's presentation of him fell away?

Of course it never did. I could no more put aside my Christian suppositions and preconceptions of the New Testament scene and the figures involved in it than I could take myself outside English history. Indeed I realized for the first time that those curious old histories of Britain which began with ancestors derived from clas-sical mythology and the Bible were not without point. They made sense because the derivations from those sources were part of the mind or outlook of the historian's own people. Moses and Elijah and Jesus too were closely identified with Englishmen and Christians, but the kinship was there in something more powerful than blood. These heroes, though grotesquely misconceived, were no strangers and foreigners but fellow-citizens of ours. We were heirs by adoption to the promises made to them; they were adopted into our life.

It was nonetheless the recognition of this adoptive process rather than any sudden perception of a wholly Jewish Jesus that proved to be most important to me. I came to it slowly and with misgivings. It both promised and demanded so much. How far could the modifications of a traditional way of thinking about Jesus Christ be carried without losing hold of what one had judged to be Christian? I gained the firmer outlines of a Jewish Jesus at the expense of a series of realizations of what had gone to the presentation of the Christian Christ. It is a process which most Christians experience today, with varying degrees of perplexity and exhilaration. The outcome, as the authors of the *Myth of God Incarnate* have been at pains to point out, is that from the beginning in New Testament sources it is a 'preached Christ' whom we meet. There is no one fixed figure, but a number of human attempts to put into words what this Jesus had meant and did mean to men drawn into a knowledge of his life and death. His disciples were not inventing a Saviour-Lord but discovering Him through their acquaintance with Him. Because they were His, they had now to make Him their own. The very diversity as well as the obvious limitations of their efforts to do so are the best illustrations that we could hope to have of the impact of His life upon men, and of a Gospel that would continue to bring its impact to men of successive generations. He is exposed to all kinds of mistaken efforts; He will suffer as much at the hands of friends as of foes. Of both, He must sadly observe at times that they know not what they do and extend His forgiveness to them. From both, He will look for repentance and a change of mind; not least from the theologians, whose intentions were good but whose work was frequently a process of mummification.

My study of Jewish reflections upon the life and work of Jesus showed a number of aspects for which words like tradition, appropriation, translation and interpretation had to be used. A Christian tradition had been brought into being made up from various sources. Christians appropriated Jewish scriptures and their great themes. There had had been stages of verbal translation to bring them into use in different times and tongues, and Christian interpretation never ceased to transpose these things into new idiomatic forms. At every stage in the process the relations of men with the 'truth in Christ' were at risk of crass mishandling or pious falsification.

Tradition offered the most obvious source of danger. The problems arising from the way men handled written or unwritten forms of it were sharply defined in the Gospels. Paul wrestled with their bearing upon men's faith in Christ. He spoke of handing on things which he himself had received, but he cannot have been unaware of the changes wrought in men's minds by the way it was done. Pilate grimly observed that 'thine own nation and the chief priests have delivered thee unto me' (John 18.35), which may well indicate how the writer of the Gospel according to St John saw the Jewish dealings with Jesus. Tradition might mean faithful adherence or sheer betrayal, might be the living relation between generations or the dead stifling hand of the past.

Translation was equally problematic. Even the simplest rendering of a passage from one language to another is notoriously a difficult matter. Misconstructions, diminutions, insensibility and a great number of other factors conspire to deflect or defeat honest purpose in such attempts. But there were gains to be made as well as losses to be endured. New understanding could be reached through the effort to leap over the walls of linguistic particularity.

As for appropriation, we can compare the handling of the work of Shakespeare. His plays did not mean to a Frenchman what they meant to either an Englishman or a German. There were deep-seated cultural barriers to be traversed, and the appropriative act hacked and hewed them into shapes unrecognizable to their erstwhile possessors. Thus also our knowledge of what particular meaning a translation of the Bible had had, whether it was the

Authorized version in England or Luther's Bible in Germany, suggests how much alteration could follow. The appropriation would lose sight of the things which had stamped it as the work of a different cultural life.

Did it matter if in these various processes of commending the Christ to a Gentile world a good deal of what was intrinsically Jewish had been lost or mauled or mistaken? If polemics have entered into these efforts, have they added their own distortions to the work? Was it necessary for a vital connection with Jewish sources to be retained? Could the 'preached Christ' be too closely presented in terms of the outlook, beliefs and even political purposes of those who essayed to do it? Barth has sharply commented, speaking of a passage in Genesis that 'it is crystal clear that after their originators found the concept in our passage, their interpretations were one and all fabricated out of thin air according to the different anthropologies of their authors'. It was the interaction of a wide range of thought and purposes which so heavily influenced the minds of those involved. All art, as Eric Gill was accustomed to say, is propaganda. In a century that has known an unparalleled extension of the uses and forms of propaganda for political and commercial purposes, it could not escape notice that Christian art had done much in the formative years of Christendom to shape the image of Christ. After the acceptance of Christianity as the official religion of the Roman Empire, He had been portrayed as the Pantocrator, from whom imperial authority devolved. The icons of Emperor and Christ were virtually indistinguishable; such clothing of Christ in purple was acceptable to one age and an offence to another. It had been done before and would be done many times again. And, how could Christ's own clothes be put upon Him?

Today we need a more deliberate attempt on the part of the Christian Church as a whole, from its scholars to its parochial members, not only to try to perceive the Jewishness of Jesus with more respectful eyes but to bring that same newfound respect to bear upon Judaism as a faith. If Christians are to gain a surer hold on their faith in God through Jesus Christ they cannot and must not be arrogantly contemptuous of ancient or modern Judaism, as has been the case. The two faiths have gone their different ways, but there is good reason to believe that today each might contribute a great deal of help to the other at a time when mankind needs new vision and the revival of spiritual concern.

The groundwork for such a relationship must lie in a revision of the conventional view, so largely taken for granted among Christians, that the Judaism of the first century was a spiritless formal religion, rigidly legalistic, against which Jesus strove and in conflict with which he spoke with decisive authority. Such a view oversimplifies the mystery of His ministry and its rejection and makes His opponents out to be little more than stage villains, and does not illustrate the realities of spiritual conflict. Behind the desperate choices which Jesus and Paul and Stephen and others made lay the whole bitter history of Israel since the Exile, a seemingly unrelieved bloodstained period of torment during which the faith of the Jews was subjected to fearful testing. Crude and violent reactions there may have been, but it was anything but a time in which mere formal religion could survive. And this time not only witnessed Judaism's survival but prepared the way for Christ. George Foot Moore says of those crucial years that the notion that 'Ezra's lawbook turned Judaism into an arid ritualism and legalism is refuted by the whole literature of the following time'.

Nor can we suppose that a Pharisaism which produced a Paul was devoid of spiritual vitality. G. F. Moore goes on to say: 'In a religion which had inherited, as Judaism did, sacred scriptures of various kinds which were all believed to embody divine revelation (Torah), in which God had made known his own character and his will for the whole conduct of life, there is no incompatibility between the most minute attention to rites and observances, or to the rules of civil and criminal law, and the cultivation of the worthiest conceptions of God and the highest principles of morality. . . . On the contrary, the seriously religious man could not be indifferent to any part of the revealed law of God. The same rabbis who extended the law of tithing to garden herbs paraphrased the principle Thou shalt love thy neighbour as thyself, as Let thy neighbour's property be as dear to thee as thine own, and thy neighbour's honour as thine own. . . . They made love of God the one supremely worthy motive of obedience to his law.'

I have quoted Moore's judgment at length because it is still too common to hear sermons addressed to Christians in which loving God and one's neighbour are contrasted with the teaching of Judaism, making nonsense of Jesus's upholding of Torah and of the whole setting of the Sermon on the Mount. It is this recurring denigration of first-century Judaism which is hurtful to true understanding. Between the scholarly estimate of rabbinic Judaism and the content of much Christian preaching there is a gap into which both conscious and unconscious hostility to the Jews has been able to thrust itself.

It is not easy to replace the prejudices and hatreds so deeply embedded in the long history of the relations of these two faiths with compassion and understanding. Only by resolute and determined effort can a new relationship be brought into being. At this point the question is Do we as Christians want this to come about? Are we convinced that this is a major task touching the life and the work of the Christian Church at so many points, its history, its doctrine, its missionary task, its relation with the secular world, that the future will be chaotic unless it is undertaken? Desperate need may drive us towards it but do we see what is at stake?

Christianity took over many magnificent Jewish descriptions of the fulfilment of God's purposes in the creation of the world; its hymns have repeated the glad expectation that the whole world will be filled with the Glory of God as the waters cover the sea. The ancestry of those hopes has not been remembered, any more than Paul's steady assertion that all Israel shall be saved. Within Jewry there has been an equivalent loss of the universality of hope. Today when the nations lurch in uncertain fashion towards the one world that their many achievements make possible, we must turn to the basic suggestion of Israel's faith with new force. It is the faith of a people for ever marching, a people of tents rather than a Temple, a people learning to read God's law in their hearts, a people committed to giving the stranger welcome, facing a new world with a deep trust in God. Our task today is the recovery of what is essentially a Jewish concept of man's destiny.

In one generation, in my own life, the map of the world has been redrawn. Communication between the world's peoples has become instantaneous. The world's food, resources, health, education, even survival, have become facets of one common task. Such changes have put to the Christian Church and to Jewry the question, How now do you see your work? Twentieth century man would put it in different words; for a new man is emerging in black, brown and yellow skin as well as in white, the serfs of old regimes are standing up as men, the sexes are facing each other in wholly new ways. What is needed is a discernment of the image of God, of the fulness of manhood which resided in Jesus Christ, embodied in action which is of common concern for all mankind. It lays on men of all faiths and men of no recognized faith one task: the laying of the foundations of world community, an exercise of the spirit far greater than any yet undertaken by man. In the face of this demand men might quail, but there is a proud-humble truth in Leo Baeck's words in *The Essence of Judaism*: 'So long as Judaism exists, nobody will be able to say that the soul of man has surrendered.'

Our question then is not that of Judaism set apart from the world's problems of common existence but of Judaism which represents them all in the oldest primeval fashion. Christians have at all times made the Jews the image of their own self-estrangement. Modern Europe, still half Christian, inherited and redoubled the hatred as it grew more conscious of cracks running through the social and personal fabric of its existence. The Jew is always the brother rejected, the brother cast into the pit or sold as a slave. The Jew is the man or woman deprived of the dignity of a human being, the despised and rejected, the wretched of the earth. Evil's mockery was at its height when men were goaded to burn and to murder Jews 'after the flesh', when they failed to see Man in the fellowmen they destroyed. The Holocaust happened because men had come to such depths of self-loathing that only destruction of Man could offer relief.

The Jewish question, therefore, cannot die. It is the question of mankind's self-knowledge, of his calling and task on the earth. For too long men reared in the dualist tradition of Europe have built up a culture and the power that made a bid to envlop the world. The result has been confusion. An age-old question presses on the consciousness of mankind, a question compounded of others formulated by the Jews long ago. What is man and what does God require of him? The human response made to the Divine demands, as Israel understood them, has been a melancholy chronicle of mutiny, folly, evil devisings and fears, though enlightened by some snatches of beauty and goodness and a turning again in tears. There have been times in Israel's own history when the light has been utterly darkened, when the best seemed to lose their way in mystical systems and speculation. But the way was not wholly lost. The turning again has not been abandoned. Stubborn Jewry still holds to its faith before the world to remind mankind that its appointment is with a living God.

There are things that can only be seen in darkened skies, questions only heard in the silence of utter dismay. Such a time is ours. We are poised at a moment in history when the madness of mere seconds could unloose upon the world a frenzied self-destruction such as no generation before could have conceived. This is the moment in which the questions put to the Jews may, if heard and answered with fear and trembling yet with trust and hope, be the way of man's salvation. To whom else shall we go? Jew and Christian alike, Jew and non-Jew, may find in Him who they have all in their various ways rejected, despised, spat upon and mocked, their one hope of life for mankind. The furnaces of Auschwitz in which Jewish victims perished may be the fires in which the heart of mankind must be purged anew.

3. Eloquent Dust

'I will show you fear in a handful of dust.'
                                    T. S. Eliot, *The Waste Land*
'I have lately had a sudden conception of the true nobility of men and
women.'

                                    Wallace Stevens, *Letters*

In 1977 many thousands of people visited an exhibition held in
London of work of art and domestic objects recovered from Pompeii, the city which in August, A.D. 79, was suddenly buried
beneath suffocating ash thrown up from Vesuvius in eruption.
There had been, it appears, a severe earthquake some seventeen
years earlier which badly damaged the city but did not seriously
interrupt its prosperous life. The connection between the two
events would not have been readily apparent to the people of the
time.

Today we know a little more about the movements of the earth's
crust and their relation to the pent-up fires within. This knowledge
was not theirs, those people who went about their business as
usual on that summer day, very much as others did on a June day
in 1914 when a sudden shot in a Balkan town disturbed the air.

The beauty of the things recovered from Pompeii, the signs of
luxury and culture, the sense of pathos aroused by the relics of the
chained dog and crouching woman, stirred strange reflections in
the minds of many who went to see them. They found a touch of
irony in the exhibition as a whole. We are less inclined than our
grandparents would have been to moralize upon the scene, less
likely to see the hand of God in such a disaster, more ready to
accept it as an item of news that with dramatic suddenness a

thriving city, an opulent culture, should be blotted out. Great insurers against accidents or even acts of God as we have now become, we are aware always that we live in a dangerous world. Its powers, its wealth, its energies, may run out on us or overwhelm us. Brute fact or act of God, it murmurs to us a memento mori, even while it entertains or gratifies desire.

It is not, however, with Roman archaeology that we are now concerned, but with the bearing of doomladen dust upon our own affairs today, upon the state and future of European society, upon the witness of the Christian Church throughout the world, and all this in relation to what may be called the mystery of Israel.

Let us make dust the starting point of our reflection. The ashes that I have in mind are different from those which must have hung about in Pompeian air for many days after the eruption of Vesuvius. The ashes I speak of are not confined to a single city of the past but lie scattered across the face of Europe now, and are, relatively speaking, scarcely cold. They are due not to a natural disaster but to the most unnatural deeds of men. They lie invisibly upon the soil of Europe as the result of the deliberate acts of the men who burnt the bodies of many millions of men, women and children. We know now how carefully the operation was planned, who carried it out, what the statistics were. 'Into this pond', said Jacob Bronowski, standing some years after the event in Auschwitz, 'were flushed the ashes of some four million people. And that was not done by gas. It was done by arrogance. It was done by dogma. It was done by ignorance. When people believe that they have absolute knowledge, with no test in reality, this is how they behave.'

These things were not done in a corner, though many people professed to be ignorant of them then, and there are those today who write questioning whether they actually occurred. 'At Auschwitz,' says M. Darquier de Pellepoix, once Commissioner for Jewish Affairs to the Vichy Government, in a newspaper report published in 1978, 'only lice were gassed. The photographs of corpses there were faked.' The evidence remains unshaken. There are survivors to tell what happened in the camps, there are the diaries of the victims, there are the testimonies of those who carried

out their orders and the documents of those who had the oversight
of what was designed to be the Final Operation. Of Jews now
living there can be few who have not had relatives and friends who
perished in the extermination camps.

We who now live breathe air dust-laden by the Holocaust. All
our yearnings for an ampler ether and diviner air are so many
escapist dreams unless we recognize this and connect it with things
that touch every aspect of the world's human life. The anti-semitism that finally erupted in the fearful acts at Auschwitz is inseparable from the long history of persecution that played its sinister
part in the life of Christian Europe. To examine the record of that
pitiless inhumanity is to place our society and its values in question.
It calls for an account from Christianity itself which will be painful
to render, and which might keep ancient animosities alive. Yet if
our first business is to try to understand how men have come to
behave as they have to each other, there is good reason for the
attempt.

Pious minds hold that God mercifully remembers that we are
but dust. Much poetry has been written on this theme. We are
persuaded that good deeds blossom from and in the nobler dust of
men and women who have lived generous lives. But if the dust of
Auschwitz is to fertilize a finer flowering of the human spirit, we
must acknowledge the cost of it. We may not stand upon the earth
or breathe the air to good effect unless we know how it was come
by.

Soil reflects soul. The ravaged earth of old mining areas, the
dust-bowls created by reckless cropping, the squalid litter left by
departing crowds, the desolation of decaying inner-city areas, all
testify to the impoverishment of the spirit. This dust-strewn
Europe has its own story to tell of evil things at work. In examining it 'we are probing the ground on which our civilisation
stands'. The winds have ceased to carry the stench of burning
flesh, the ash has settled down, Europe has resumed its busy
industrious life as if the dead had never been. The German Government has paid large sums in reparation and churchmen have
met to face some of the questions which the Holocaust raised.

What has this eruption meant or done for us? What does it presage for our children's children?

Before we attempt any answers we must look at the causes of calamity in the long history of the Western World and in the immediate background of nineteenth and twentieth century society. I begin with something as light as air though it may grow dark with the dust of incinerated bodies; the way in which Jews have been described since the writers of the Gospels first talked about 'the Jews'. As Franz Kafka wrote: 'Words prepare the way for deeds to come. Your words of abuse today may turn into a universally valid principle of denigration, for words are magical formulae . . . words are evil's strongest buttress. They are the most reliable preservatives of every passion and every stupidity.'

Sometimes our greater writers have been guilty. G. K. Chesterton provides many examples: 'It is often noted that the intelligent Israelite can rise to positions of power and trust outside Israel. . . . It is generally bad, I think, for their adopted country.' Again: 'When the Jew in France or in England says he is a good patriot he only means that he is a good citizen, and he would put it more truly if he said he was a good exile. . . . These Jews would not have died with any Christian nation.' These malevolent accusations were made by one who made much of his profession of Christian faith.

We are dealing with a long tradition of prejudice which has tended to use the word Jew as a synonym for an agent of the Devil. The image of the Jew as a parasite, exploiting the labours of others and mercilessly rapacious in his treatment of others made it easy for Gentile authorities to exclude them from incorporation into the life of the community. It was not difficult then to charge them with alien intentions. Catholic practice until quite recent times continued to refer to 'perfidious Jews'. With little charity the Book of Common Prayer of the Church of England in its Good Friday collect lumped together Turks, Infidels and Jews. Thus men spoke of the people of Jesus, His mother and His earliest disciples.

For the greater part of the nineteen centuries during which estranged Christians and Jews have faced each other from within their respective religious traditions, it was to the Christian Church that the Jews owed their most cruel and ignominious treatment. Once in power as the official religious authority of the Empire, it spared no effort to vilify and maltreat the Jews. Great Fathers of the Church, including the golden-tongued John Chrysostom, were accustomed to denounce them as rebels against God and guilty of every infamous practice known to man. Since 'God hates and always has hated them' it was laudable on the part of Christians to hate them too. Their synagogues were nests of idolatry and more harmful than the circuses of heathens. Hilary, Ambrose and Epiphanius were ever ready to denounce them. Both the Councils of the Church and the civil authorities of Rome and Byzantium proceeded to penalize Jews, excluding them as far as possible from the normal life of society, wringing extra taxation from them, and from time to time harrying them with forcible mass-baptisms. Condemned at length to be publicly marked with a yellow spot on their dress, Jews became pariahs to be ridiculed and abused as a matter of course.

The treatment was never uniform. Byzantine Jewry did not occupy a special social category, as did the Jews of the West: its members were not excluded from or restricted to special occupations. They became skilled workers in industries such as the manufacture of silk, they owned land and became farmers. They were nevertheless at the mercy of the changes of ecclesiastical policy of the Emperors who, like Basil I, might decide to intensify the accepted duty of bringing Jews to conversion by persuasion and persecution. The ambiguous situation of the Byzantine Jews appeared most plainly when the publication of legal rulings requiring men to respect Jews and their synagogues and festivals coincided with open persecution. In contemporary Rome, though the Jewish population had dwindled in numbers, there emerged a number of rich, powerful families and numerous scholars. In the life of Islamic Spain Jews occupied places of great distinction. A family of converted Jews in Rome was to number Popes among its members.

Yet the state of the Jews was precarious when they could be held responsible for every misfortune that overtook humanity. In any ignorant or superstitious age every gust of passionate despair, every insane craving could find a convenient object of hatred in the Jews. The preaching of the Crusades led to massacres of the Jews. Plagues and famines were ascribed to their infamous practices, and were made the occasions of pitiless murder. Fantasy, anxiety, deprivation and social myth were interwoven with shrewd political policy and economic conditions to give rise to and to release the frenzied violence which issued in pogroms against the Jews. Disasters like the Black Death, which shattered the normal defences and patterns of social life and left men exposed to despair, inevitably kindled fresh hatred of the Jews.

The pitiless treatment of the Jews in Spain by successive Christian kings has been documented. Hatred of Jews became a popular article of faith, and conversion itself was no guarantee against subsequent burning. The Reformation made little difference to Christian attitudes towards the Jews. No foulness of language was too improper to be used about them, no cruelty too repulsive to be enjoyed in their destruction. Persecution drove them as fugitives from place to place. Nowhere were they safe from barbarous inhuman treatment.

James Parkes concluded his study of the roots of anti-semitism, *Conflict of Church and Synagogue*, with grave words that should be heard by all Christians today. 'Scholars may know today of the beauty and profundity of the Jewish conception of life. They may know that "some Jews" were responsible for the death of Jesus. But the Christian public as a whole, the great and overwhelming majority of the hundreds of millions of nominal Christians in the world, still believe that "the Jews" killed Jesus, that they are a people rejected by their God, that all the beauty of their Bible belongs to the Christian Churches and not to those by whom it was written; and if on this ground, so carefully prepared, modern anti-semites have reared a structure of racial and economic propaganda, the final responsibility still rests with those who prepared the soil, created the deformation of the people and so made these ineptitudes credible.'

They helped to do more. Hatred of Jews among Christians kept alive and nourished two things which went far to weaken and even destroy the true nature of Christian faith. On the one hand it

played upon primitive fears and made fear itself an active principle
of religious outlook and practice. On the other it gave an opportunity for the expression of a hatred of Christianity itself, disguised
as a form of passionate adherence.

'Why are you so fearful?' The question that Jesus is said to have
put to the frightened disciples when He stilled the storm has a
bearing on all Christian experience and history. Christians
embraced a faith that excluded fear, because fear destroys the
relationship of trust between man and God and between man and
man which it is this Gospel's business to affirm. The new Adam
in Christ is free from the fear that caused Adam in Eden to hide
himself, to hide himself not only from God but from his own
flesh. No one supposes that the casting out of this demon of fear
could be lightly achieved or that Christians will not be tempted
again and again to fall victim to it. But what we encounter in so
much of Christian history is the active prompting of fear accepted
as a determinative factor in behaviour. Men are led to shun life in
the world, to shun women, to shun art and thought, because they
are fearful of being seduced. Persecution is quickly invoked to give
teeth to those fears.

It would be wrong to suggest that those fears which came to
play so large and so terrible a part in the life of the Church were
wholly the outcome of the cleavage of Christians and Jews. What
can be said is that with the beginnings of the persecution of those
who held different views and religious beliefs, in the first instance
in the persecution of the Jews, the Christian Church embarked
upon a course which steadily weakened its spiritual authority. It
deprived itself of the authority of love and made way for the time
when secular powers could outdo it in strength and expose its
weakness to a world where brutality reigned. Nor was the field
limited to that of religious beliefs. Persecution created habits of
mind that led men to suspect and oppose all movements of changing thought. In due time the sciences escaped from these attempts
to keep them under control; as a result of this, religion was thought
to be a thing of the past. The Church itself lost all-important time
in learning to relate as a teacher to men in their new-made worlds.

Persecution simply postponed the day when the Church had to face the facts that it had for so long ignored.

As they moved towards life in the modern world Christians bettered their persecution of the Jews; they set about wars of religion with cynical savagery or buttressed political autocracy with compliant religion. The Church entered the modern epoch so tied to the social and political structures of the old order that it found great difficulty in conceiving a ministry to the new one. This attitude was not confined to the Christian Church. Lively minded Jews also found themselves looking upon the Jewish faith, to use George Eliot's words, as 'a sort of eccentric fossilised form' which a cultured man of the world could only deplore or despise. At a time when mankind most needed all the help which religious faith could afford it, both Christianity and Judaism stood in need of profound renewal. Both were to be faced by problems arising from their relations with the State. Both were affected by the historical and philosophical critiques brought to bear upon them from the time of the Enlightenment onwards and by the revolution in scientific thought which gathered strength as the nineteenth century went on. The case of the churches went by default because men continued to try to defend old dispositions of attitude towards the Bible, the Church, the Jews and the world. Too much precious time and energy was lost in struggles amongst the churches and in failure to recognize that a recovery of strength depended upon a new grasp of the Biblical foundations of faith of which Jews and Christians were heirs together. So much of the weakness of the position of the Church in the modern world must be traced in the last resort to its conflict with Jewry.

For the time being, however, it seemed that the Jews alone were under attack and that Christians might at least be able to pass by on the other side. Accustomed to shunning the Jews, the churches of Europe did not see quickly enough the character of the anti-semitic movements springing to life. They therefore failed to read the true signs of the times. The term 'anti-semitism', used with approval, appeared first in 1873 in a German pamphlet devoted to campaigning against Jewish culture and race on the part of the protagonists of a pure Aryan civilization. But the movement to make war on the Jews as part of nationalist propaganda had already gained strength. For the party founded by Adolph Stocker in 1878, for example, it offered the chance to brand the 'Jewish betrayers' of Christian middle-class culture and the authority of the German state. In France where anti-semitism was soon to erupt in the Dreyfus case it was common to speak of Jews and Freemasons as engaged in a sinister plot to wreck Church and State.

So marked was the irrational character of this anti-semitic wave, so ludicrously inconsistent with the facts, that some writers were moved to try to explain it in psycho-pathological terms. It was argued that, just as some men were upset by snakes or cats, non-Jewish people had inherited a phobia that sensed and feared the very presence of the demonic Jew. Others soon developed the theory that deepseated aggressive tendencies in men sought some opportunity to find release, diverting the threatened social explosion into an attack upon an identifiable alien minority. We must needs hate, the argument ran, and Jews were the most convenient targets for such hatred. All loyal and patriotic citizens could be rallied to condemn subversive plotters against the State. Poor workers could be enlisted to movements attacking rich capitalistic Jews. Described by Bebel as the socialism of blockheads,[1] anti-semitism could as easily have been called the anti-socialism of blockheads.

German Jews meanwhile were chiefly distinguished by their efforts to assimilate German politics and culture, and if need be, German religion, as completely as possible. Great numbers of Jews successfully identified themselves with the political and intellectual conditions of Imperial Germany. Few men contributed more effectively to the successful working of Bismarck's policy than Gerson Bleichroder, his Jewish banker and financial adviser. From the days of the philosopher Moses Mendelssohn onwards, Jews had contributed to German intellectual and artistic life. In technology and commercial enterprise they were equally to the fore. Albert Ballin, friend of the Kaiser and chairman of the Hamburg-Amerika line, was but one distinguished example. Such Jews were often marked

1. In L. Dawidowicz, *The War against the Jews*, p.71.

by an anxiety to set as great a line of demarcation as possible between themselves and the hordes of Eastern European Jews who threatened, in Treitschke's imagination at least, to pour out from the inexhaustible Polish cradle 'a troop of ambitious, trouser-selling youths, whose children and children's children will some day dominate Germany's stock exchanges and newspapers'.[1]

'Why do men hate Jews?' Solomon Ibn Varga, himself a fugitive from persecution, had asked the question in the sixteenth century,[2] compelled as all thoughtful men must have been to look deeper than the immediate political or social scene for an explanation of it. Was there an element in European society which in times of stress would give way to self-hating, self-destructive frenzies? For the most part generations of Christian Europeans saw little reason to fear the Jews or to reflect upon the mystery of Israel either in its scriptural form or in Jewry's continuing presence. Theologically they had accepted the idea that they themselves now constituted the Israel of God, that anything of value in Judaism prior to the coming of Christ had been absorbed by the Christian Church, that whatever had developed in Judaism since that time was of no importance whatever. The question was closed. The Jews were irrelevant to the spiritual scene. This was taken for granted and not even the Holocaust could disturb the conviction. George Steiner mentions with incredulity the fact that T. S. Eliot's *Notes towards the Definition of Culture* could ignore that event. 'How was it possible,' he asked, 'to detail and plead for a Christian order when the Holocaust had put in question the very nature of Christianity and of its role in European history?' (*In Bluebeard's Castle*). For Steiner it seemed obvious that because of its ambiguous implication in the Holocaust, Christianity could scarcely serve as the most reliable focus for a redefinition of culture.

The point had not been entirely missed. Alfred Weber's sad book *Farewell to European History* (1945) examined Europe's culture cradled by the Christian Church, undermined by schism, and rent apart by forces of its own creation that proved too strong for its

1. See P. Gay, *Freud, Jews and other Germans*, pp. 126 and 184.
2. See A. Cohen, *The Natural and the Supernatural Jew*, p.12.

spiritual integrity. Weber traced out the paths which brought men to Hitler's feet. But while he referred to anti-semitism as an instance of moral licence, Weber did not think fit to look more closely at the Jewish question or to inquire what bearing if any the long cleavage between the two faiths had had upon the catastrophe in Europe. He stood too near to the scene to be able to evaluate the true nature of such things. Thirty years later we may ask how much we have learned from the wind-dispersed dust.

Among other attempts to account for the resurgence of anti-semitic behaviour in modern times, Freud saw in the hatred of Jews an attack upon Christianity and Judaeo-Christian morality. Despite his profound attachment to German culture, Freud chose in 1926 to call himself a Jew and to dissociate himself from the anti-semitism in Germany and Austria. Somewhat later he made the suggestion that leading Christian anti-semites were often those who came late to Christianity and who came under compulsion. In times of stress these particularly would lay the blame for their troubles upon this 'alien' religion, cast about for a nationalist creed and myths to commend it, and begin to attack the representatives of the faith they rejected. That the Jew has been the conscience of Europe has become a commonplace and in attacking the Jews men have sought to jettison the religious culture which Christians built upon Judaic foundations. If Christianity was to continue at all it must hail a Nordic or Aryan Christ.

It is tempting to look for simpler and more immediate reasons for anti-semitic behaviour. The resentment of Germans at their defeat and at the dictated terms of the Versailles treaty was obvious; the Jews were vicarious targets for anger and wounded pride. But we cannot isolate this eruption of hatred from the longstanding attitudes in Europe, where Jews were cast by Christendom in the role of betrayers and killers of what was most sacred. The Anti-Christ, like the old Vice of Morality plays, had long since been clothed in his Jewish gaberdine. With his fatal inability to 'be like all the nations', the Jew offered a target for all injured parties. Arnold Toynbee points out that the citizens of Alexandria, smarting under high-handed treatment by the conquering Romans, resorted to periodic massacres of Jews. De Gobineau's fantasies helped to create an appetite for a mythology of resentment ready for modern Europe's time of trouble.

Our imagery of eruption holds if we recognize that it is from within the disordered and violent desires of European man that the fires which calcined Jewish bones at Auschwitz were stoked. Undeterred by the warnings of carnage presented by World War I, Europe acquiesced irresolutely in the conjuring into action of programmes of violent reconstruction of human life. The attack upon Jews, which in the nineteenth century represented barometer fashion the strains or pressures affecting men's lives and the nations to which they belonged, became with the Nazis the smashing of the instrument itself. The Holocaust sought to expunge from the life of Europe any witness to a religious component by which its behaviour might be judged. Any voice that might claim to 'set before thee the things that thou has done' could not but be intolerable to the disciples of the new absolutist creed.

Is Europe then to become a dustbowl not of Jews only but of the Judaeo-Christian faith whose representatives failed so signally to raise even voices of protest as the Holocaust was being prepared? 'After such knowledge what forgiveness?', and what in this context does forgiveness mean? Simply to have survived the Nazi regime, for Christians as much as for Jews, is nothing unless both have learned from it truths which are yet more fundamental to human life than the slogans and policies and protestations of purpose to which they assented before. As we muse on the fate of Pompeii we have very good reason to look to our own condition.

Both faiths have in their liturgies acknowledged the message of dust. Ash Wednesday today has hardly the place which Yom Kippur holds for the Jew. All Souls' Day likewise lacks profundity of attention. Good Friday is swallowed up quickly in Easter. A new start must be made today by men of both faiths to learn from the ashes now lying on Europe's soil what God, the One God and Father of both, requires them to learn together. It is not only 'the humanism of the European Jew' that lies in this dust but that of Christian Europe too. One Jewish survivor has written that 'after some delay man will once again develop the requisite inner structures and the greater ability to achieve inner integration that must go with our new conditions of life'. Delay there may be, but both faiths are summoned by a more urgent voice: 'Today, if ye will hear his voice.' Yom Kippur and Ash-Wednesday both call for a more rigorous scrutiny of the stewardship of our lives. We could do worse than begin by asking how the once common life of Gentiles and Jews fell apart.

4. The Parting Of The Ways

'He is the Way.
Follow Him through the Land of Unlikeness;
You will see rare beasts, and have unique adventures.'
                    W. H. Auden, *For the Time Being*

'When the dimensions of faith, hope, love, forgiveness become real
to us, we are given at the same time a freedom, an openness towards
a way of living which is quite new.'
                    John Bowden, *Voices in the Wilderness*

There is a disturbing short passage in the Gospel according to St
Mark, and a more extended version of what may be the same story
in the Gospel according to St Luke, which describes how Jesus
came to His own country or native town, taught in its synagogue,
and aroused not only amazement but also resentment, and hostility. It was a pointer to things to come, to His coming to His own
and His own's rejection of Him which finds explicit expression in
the prologue to the Gospel according to St John. It anticipates the
crucifixion. It foreshadows the great parting of the ways that for
centuries to come would set Christianity and Judaism at enmity
with one another, not because one of these alone represents Him
and is therefore rejected by the other, but because both are His
own and neither has seen Him as He is. Both in their own wilful
fashion have turned away from Him.

We look back at this rejection now from our own cities of
destruction, from the Holocaust and Hiroshima, from the bombed
streets of Jerusalem and Beirut, from our own ravaged personal
lives, no less His own and no less marred by our rejection of Him.

We look at it aware, yet not aware enough, of the burden of human wrongdoing which that estrangement has brought about, at the shadow which it has cast across our world.

It becomes the night sky of the Lord for us as we learn not only to grieve over it but beneath it to turn once again to Israel's God and Father of mankind. The estrangements have come about because we chose our wrongdoings. Our turning towards Him now must include an effort to understand how these were done. It requires of us a patient willingness to look at human history again, to recognize how good resources were turned to serve evil ends, how even the Christian use of the Scriptures, and not least the Pauline Epistles, have, to use Krister Stendahl's words, 'caused developments of satanic dimensions'. Men have built up with plausible devices well-nigh insurmountable barriers of prejudice and pride.

How and when did it begin? The first Christians were Jews. They did not become Christians to break away from Israel's faith or because they were dissatisfied with Judaism. They saw it rather as a fulfilment of that faith. They found no incongruity between their following of the Lord Jesus Christ and their observance of the Torah. 'They, continuing daily with one accord in the temple, and breaking bread from house to house, did eat their meat with gladness and singleness of heart' (Acts 2.46). The brief record preserved in the Acts of the Apostles suggests that they felt themselves committed to and gladly undertook the task of making His Messiahship known to those who had in ignorance rejected Him and brought about His death. They lived from day to day in expectation of His return in glory. They testified to what they had seen and heard of Him in person.

Their enthusiasm attracted favourable, critical and downright hostile attention. They constituted from now on a sect or party within a Judaism which, like a windswept sea, broke into wave after wave of many such movements contesting fiercely with each other for Israel's soul. Regional differences played no small part in these divisions. Distinct yet intermingling were Jews of Judaea, Galilee and Peraea, marked not only by their accents or tongues but by long traditions of local allegiance. More distinctly, the Jews were confronted by the Samaritans, a people of mixed ancestry yet not 'foreigners', who observed the Pentateuchal law, acknowledged the unity of God, honoured Moses as the greatest of the prophets, but maintained a separatist centre of faith and worship over against Jerusalem itself.

Within those broad divisions came others. The countryside bred innumerable Hasidim or holy men whose teaching and mighty works attracted to them bands of followers, presumptuous men on whom the authorities frowned without daring to condemn them. Authority itself was frequently challenged, and was quick to scent the danger. With the Sadducees, the High Priestly families and their kind, resided the dignities of the Temple and its rites; with the Scribes who made the exposition of the Law their profession lay more obvious leadership of the people. The Pharisees as a party embraced a number of schools of thought. The followers of Shammai, who had great authority in first century Judaism, were being challenged by those of Hillel. These groups were engaged in disputes about the relation of the oral to the written tradition, about apocalyptic hopes, about the Messiah, about the resurrection of the dead. The questioning that the Gospels record was everywhere a feature of Israel's religious life, a sign of the fermentation of the spirit of a nation under pressure.

Extremities were no less marked. On the one hand bands of Zealots pressed for militant action to free the land and people from the hated alien rule. On the other, equally ready if need be to defend their cause with arms, were the Essenes, whose expectations and closely disciplined ways of life as communities withdrawn from worldly contacts have come to our knowledge through the Dead Sea Scrolls.

Nor can we separate this explosive turbulent Jewish world from the Judaism of the Dispersion. Hellenistic ideas and influences affecting religion and life were known not only to the numbers of Jews living in the great cities throughout the Roman Empire but had been known for some generations past by Jews living in Judaea. These influences intrigued restless minds and appalled the more conservatively minded. Assimilate or resist was the choice that divided the factions. When Jerusalem was destroyed and the survival of Judaism itself appeared to be at stake it is understandable that an ideological closing of the ranks under Pharisaic leadership should have taken place and that groups not wholly committed to that overriding purpose should have been attacked more fiercely as 'deviationists' by the loyalist faithful.

To add further to the diversity of the scene there were also numbers of Gentiles, Roman officials and their staffs and serious-minded seekers after the truth in all the cities, to whom the Jewish faith as they encountered it in the synagogues appealed so strongly that they became adherents to it. In the cities the cults of the countryside lost their appeal. In the cities too men and women sought a faith that stabilized personal life yet gave scope to 'immortal longings'. It was a world alive to new movements of thought, less antipathetic to a variety of doctrine and creed, less dogmatically controlled than it was to be when the Christian creed became its official religion. Not all Jews welcomed the interest in their faith, fearing contamination. There was suspicion of the use of the Septuagint, the translation of the Scriptures into Greek, so conscious were the Jews of possible corruption by too close a contact with the Gentile world.

Growing up in that swirling tempestuous world and attracting recruits from so many social classes and backgrounds of thought, the first Christian churches could hardly have been unaffected by the diversity. Who indeed was to guide them through these mazes of practice and thought? It is easy to see why some of them talked of following Cephas, Apollos or Paul in the newly-formed church in Corinth. It is unlikely, too, that converts from the Samaritans or Cretans and Arabians failed to present the churches into which they came with their own peculiar problems of assimilation. The existence in the second century of innumerable sects, Cleobians, Dositheans, Menandrianists and the like, points to the reception of the Christian Gospel by men already possessed of a wide variety of religious hopes and habits of mind. No more than Simon Magus did they find it easy to put away such things.

In a short time the followers of 'this Way' were to be found in Antioch and Alexandria, though we have no means of knowing how the Gospel was presented to them and what salient points of its teaching won them to it. Gentile response to it is shown in the Acts of the Apostles (Chapter 10) to have leapt ahead of Jewish expectation. It confronted the Jewish Christians with immediate problems. The practice of centuries was suddenly under question. That the difficulties could be resolved in charity is evident from the story of Cornelius. Peter's account in Acts 11.4–18 of what had taken place at Joppa is said to have been accepted by 'those of the circumcision' in Jerusalem, who not only stopped arguing about it but 'glorified God, saying, Then hath God also to the Gentiles granted repentance unto life'.

But men also have second thoughts. Not all are imaginatively understanding or adventurous or resolute. Old questions kept re-appearing. Some enthusiasts went back on their first steps in the faith. Nonetheless, if the report in Acts 15 of the later meeting in Jerusalem at which Paul defended his work is to be trusted, it suggests that it was still possible to hold together in one body Christians drawn from Jewish and Gentile backgrounds, whatever may have been their relations with the rest of Jewry. But newcomers bring their own presuppositions with them and alter the emphasis which has been established. How soon the Gentile Christians began to outnumber their Jewish brethren in the influential centres we do not know. What we can understand is that their presence was met with a mixture of pride and perplexity. They represented a leap into an unknown state of affairs that tried the courage and wisdom of even the most convinced. Peter is said to have wavered.

The situation was partly resolved but partly made more tendentious by the coming of an outstanding spiritual leader, a man with a mind at once sensitive to the far-reaching questions of doctrine to be faced and resourceful enough to be able to work out the terms in which this disturbing assuring faith was to be presented. Such a man appeared in Saul of Tarsus. What we know of the way in which the problems already raised and dealt with thereafter were handled comes to us largely through Paul's writings, through the details of his work recorded in the Acts of the Apostles. He himself is our principal witness to the issues raised between Gentile and Jewish Christians and between the Jewish authorities and the Christian Church. How soon his writings became authoritative among the various churches, related as they were by no formal organization, must also remain in doubt, since he became a figure of some contention not only for that generation but for those to come. Above all we have to keep in mind the fact that Paul dealt with and thought his way through such matters as they arose, that his work expressed an ongoing deepening perception of what the faith really meant. He did not go back but he never stood still.

This is a matter that has a significant place in the inter-faith dialogue today. Quite apart from the way in which Paul's writings have been used by Christians all down the ages in preaching the Christian faith, we have also to reckon with the way in which they have been regarded by the Jews. For they have been seen as the principal source of the Christian condemnation of the Jews. Paul's words, snatched from their context, have often been used with malignant power. Jewish reaction to this may be mistaken, but Christian theologians have done a great deal to confirm their worst fears.

The grievance is discussed, for example, by Martin Buber in his book *Two Types of Faith*. The author insists upon the importance of both for mankind in the world today and declares that 'they have something to say to each other and help to give one another hardly yet conceived at the present time'. Nevertheless, he found Paulinism a great obstacle to any real understanding between the two faiths. He remarked, and developed the point, that he could not see the God of Jesus and of the Jewish world in the God of Paul. He traced to Paul's teaching a fundamental misunderstanding of the meaning of Torah; that at times it had been regarded as a static rigid objectivized Law, but that it was not in such terms that Judaism or Jesus of Nazareth saw it. In contrast, the Torah for Paul represents frustration, an impasse from which man can be released only by the deliverance effected through Christ; for the Jews, including Jesus, it is the highest point of their relationship with God who has from the beginning called men into a partnership with Him, whose love is daily expressed in all His works. Paul saw no divine compassion, argues Buber, in the dimension of pre-Christian history. All things have been shut up in the aeon

of darkness so that the immediacy of the act of turning to God
had lost all validity. Such depreciation of the creative love of God,
of the image of God in man, in the pastoral love of God for the
nation, was wholly foreign to Jewish thinking. Buber goes on to
suggest that whatever his protestations of concern for Israel, Paul
did contribute to the Christian rejection of Jewry.

A similar note of objection was raised by Leo Baeck and developed over many years. As Friedlander's biography shows, Baeck
moved from outright polemic directed against Paul to recognition
of him as a great Jewish brother but as one who nonetheless 'took
the community of the followers of Jesus out of the context of
Jewish life' (p.12). Paul was Jewish, he argued, in that he treated
his revelation experience as a summons to mission – 'only a Jew
would always be aware that the revelation entailed the mission' –
but in developing the mission he transformed Jewish faith into
something akin to the mystery religions of the Hellenistic world.
That he saw himself indissolubly rooted in Israel's life he made
clear in the eleventh chapter of the Epistle to the Romans, but in
Baeck's view he had already moved away from Israel's faith. 'The
old theocentric faith of Judaism is superseded by a new Christ-
centred faith.'

The truth of this judgment must be considered later. Here it is
better to see it as part of Baeck's long-continuing reflection upon
what he called 'romantic religion' and upon romanticism in political and cultural life. The romantic exalts the moment of revelation, the grace bestowed upon him, the feeling of ecstasy, the
visions of deliverance, the apocalyptic hope, the shift of attention
to sacraments and another world, the resort to myth and miracle,
and all this at the expense of the ethical, the immediate task to be
done, the commandment to be kept, the rational understanding to
be put to work.

To Baeck, Christianity was a romantic religion and very largely
owed that character to Paul, a Jew, albeit one who wanted to
preach a Messiah to a pagan world in romantic terms, terms akin
to if not actually borrowed from the pagan mysteries of salvation.
Paulinism shifted attention from the ongoing experience of man
called to responsible partnership with God to man for whom

responsibility lies elsewhere, from the kingdom in which man has tasks to perform to the hope of a world hereafter. Luther's words: 'What are the Ten Commandments to me? Why should I require the Law or good works for blessedness?' are an example of romantic religion. The great driving force of Paul's faith was not anti-Jewish, but it had an overwhelming sense of pro-Gentile mission which could be used by gentile Christians ready to explicate Christianity in terms which were hostile to the Jewish faith.

Thus, though he himself proudly remained a Jew observing the Law, Paul, in Baeck's judgment, opened the way to the rejection of the Jewishness of the Christian faith, most notably in his treatment of Torah and in his teaching on the Atonement wrought in Christ. It was largely because of the Pauline Epistles that Christians came to regard and speak of the Jewish Law as a kind of bondage, and to see Judaism itself as being almost wholly absorbed in ritual acts, an outward activity that completely ignored the joy and profundity of Jewish devotion to God. The great lyrical delight that found its expression in the Psalms has been lost to sight.

Whatever his intention, Paul widened the gap between Jewish and Christian thinking.[1] 'He opposes the new covenant of Faith to the old covenant of Law, and suggests that the law is something lesser and lower, something temporary, now to be supplanted by faith.' In speaking of Atonement, Baeck further defined what he saw as divisive. 'Atonement is ours; it is our task and our way.' For Paul it became part of the great cosmic drama, and thus left his message open to the Jewish objections that underlay rabbinic fears; for example, that messianism would weaken men's sense of duty to God in the concrete conditions of everyday life.

Thus problems traced to Pauline teaching cannot easily be set aside. Buber has urged in *Two Types of Faith* that it is in Paul's handling of Torah that the principal difficulty lies. While Jesus looked for the fulfilment of Torah, Paul treated it as something whose lack of fulfilment was needed to demonstrate the necessity for grace, and the mystery which Paul invoked and with which he wrestled was that of the aeon delivered over by God to the Powers

1. Baeck, *The Essence of Judaism*, p.264

of Darkness. From the dominion of those Powers, with which no human strength could cope, the elect servants of God were redeemed in an eschatological act by God's love through Christ. It was tantamount to a dismissal of Pharisaic Judaism's conviction of God's daily participation in the life of the world He had made, loved and ruled, and in which his judgement and mercy were always at work. Such Jewish teaching kept alive a trust in the immediacy of God's help and excluded both the absolute demonocracy of Paul's thought and the need for a Mediator. In Paulinism God had virtually been walled round, and access to Him restricted to the one door in Christ. On the characteristic prophetic call of Israel's teachers that men should turn to God with hope and trust in a redeeming love undiminished in all ages, whether of darkness or light, Buber finds Paul 'almost wholly silent'.

When we turn to consider then the time of the parting of the ways it may not be the most helpful thing to have 'his wonderful conversion' in mind as our starting place, if conversion means rejecting an old way of life and taking on oneself a new one. We should do better to concentrate more on the sense of mission, on the extension of the service Paul gave to God, his mission to the Gentile world, rather than upon any breaking of his allegiance to the faith of Israel. It is true that, once he was convinced of the great leap forward to be taken if the news of salvation was to be carried to the Gentile world, Paul used his theological acumen to the full to explain the significance of that news. His writings about it were chiefly addressed to Gentiles, and while he went to great lengths, (to Jewish critics to impermissible lengths), to provide them with a theological justification of their new faith, he did not fail to remind them that they were being graciously included in God's age-long covenant with Israel. There was therefore simply no room for Gentile superiority.

Paul frequently contrasted the two parts of his life, before and after his calling. He is, after the Damascus road revelation, a man who has so utterly found meaning in his life-work that he could hardly fail to give the impression that all that had gone before was mistaken. 'Indeed I count everything as loss because of the surpassing worth of knowing Christ Jesus my Lord' (Phil. 3.8). He

is like a man who has fallen in love. Life begins from the moment
he sees the Beloved. All things are made new. He casts round to
find words that do justice to the life he now knows; he dismisses
what went before. But Paul did not cease to be a practising Jew
nor did he waver in his concern for 'Israel after the flesh'. He could
roundly attack the 'Judaizers' of Galatia because they simply did
not know what they were doing in playing so lightly with the new
Christian freedom, but he was not defaming the ancient faith of
his people. Conversion has been taken to imply that he left Jewishness behind, whereas it is clear that in taking up his apostolic
mission to the Gentiles he saw himself entering upon the fulfilment
of all that Israel's vocation had foreshadowed. It was not a matter
of either/or but of both/and. 'His acceptance of Christ did not
involve the rejection by him of the usages of his people nor a
denial of community with them.' He remained 'the great Jew-
Christian of the earliest age'.[1]

There is a sense in which Paul epitomizes the European achievement. He prefigures that blending of Greek and Roman elements
with the religious genius of the Semitic peoples which was to make
possible the civilization of Europe. He did not discard the religious
tradition of his own people as he laboured to extricate it from its
national and separatist form to become the energizing force of a
universal faith. In deliberately carrying forward into the new era
all that he loved and owed to the Jewish tradition, he divined that
the Old Israel did not cease to retain a significance for mankind
that could not be clearly asserted as yet. The timid fell back upon
the either/or, on the safety of keeping the rules. The rigid
demanded conformity to them. Paul went beyond both. He did
not find it incompatible with his faith in Christ to keep the Law
while welcoming into the Church the Gentiles who did not. He
could stand up with a good conscience against his Jewish opponents
as a Hebrew of Hebrews; he could turn with quite unaffected joy
to Gentiles because they were the first-fruits of the new order
announced in Christ.

As a pioneer must do, Paul took great risks and his explanations

1. W. D. Davies, *Paul and Rabbinic Judaism*, p.323.

were not systematic treatises as Christian theologians later tended to imply. Paul thought his way through as each problem presented itself; he was never simply opportunistic. He did not go back on his conviction that the old Israel would be restored even while he saw himself as the chosen servant of a new order of divine dispensation. What he had to say of that new order he had to expound in such terms as he judged appropriate to it. Like a poet at the height of his power he used what he borrowed very freely to express his vision. Less imaginative men could not but be upset by the freedom and speed with which he took up the new insights and claimed recognition of them. 'This is how one should regard us', he wrote to the church in Corinth,' as servants of Christ and stewards of the mysteries of God.' He insisted that patience was needed to await the still fuller disclosure of God's truth in the Lord's coming. In the meantime he went on with his work.

Much has been made of his use of 'mystery'.[1] It has even been claimed that in using it Paul 'turned his back upon his Jewish inheritance and virtually accepted the Hellenistic outlook' which had made much of the mystery-cults of Attis, Osiris and Dionysus. Yet in almost all aspects of his expressed relation to God through Christ, Paul rejected the individualistic, mythological and deificatory suggestions that belonged to the mystery cults. What stands out is the essentially Jewish I-Thou relation which could be seen in the lives of the prophets. He used the word 'mystery' in a variety of contexts, but always in ways that relate what he speaks of to quite orthodox Jewish hopes. The mystery connotes the depths and the heights of awareness of God, a relationship none the less real for the fact that it breaks through language. This has been most impressively conveyed to generations of English people through its quotation in the service of the Burial of the Dead, and it is used to signify Paul's vision of the event of the Resurrection. The very degree of the objectivity of the word 'mystery' as something which holds things known and unknown together in a bond of faith has been the most satisfactory aspect of its use. It is less well known in the service of Holy Matrimony, where the joining

1. Davies, p.89.

together of husband and wife described in the Epistle to the Ephe-sians as 'a great mystery' is said to signify 'the mystical union betwixt Christ and His Church'. Here again we have firm insist-ence upon the whole Biblical understanding of the part that the 'one flesh' plays in the divine economy. The 'mystery' of iniquity referred to in the Second Epistle to the Thessalonians in terms of the coming of the man of sin has at various times in Christian history served as a focus for its reflections upon evil times and dread things.

To say that Paul used the word 'mystery' in a general rather than in a specifically cultic manner is not to lose sight of the problems he faced in his huge task of presenting the faith in a world rife with speculative teachings so closely associated with it. Because he was writing mainly to Gentiles, he was ready to use terms and concepts that belonged to their world. In his 'all things to all men' remark he acknowledged and defended his practice. He clearly saw the dangers involved in so doing. Two things, how-ever, weighed with him to confirm his choice. The first of these is the unshakeable confidence he had in the Jewish understanding of Creation-Revelation-Redemption embracing the world. He could afford to be freely imaginative or rabbinically ingenious or theologically daring simply because it never occurred to him that the Jewish faith lacked anything that the Gentile world could sup-ply. On the contrary it was out of the fulness of this Jewish relationship with God that his own mission to the Gentiles had sprung. The richness of that faith had overflowed through Jesus to make Gentiles recipients of God's infinite mercies. In the second place, then, he did what any wise teacher would do. He put what he had to give them in forms they could understand. No doubt there were some, perhaps many, who mistook what he said and left to form sects. Human beings can be infinitely ingenious, as he knew, in devising conceits. But it is the very largeness, the breadth and assurance of his grasp of what God was now doing, and doing through him, that gave him both strength and humbled conviction.

Paul does in fact show himself to us like a poet reflecting upon his work. He trembles because the immense significance of the words he is using overwhelms him, he can feel himself simply as instrumental to their utterance, his consciousness of them awes him, for they are not so much his words but words that possess him. He is weak compared with the power they wield. Paul was at all times ready to admit his weakness. Yet it is always from the strength of being made instrumental to God that he works, and a great part of that strength was the Jewish conviction that God had chosen Israel to fulfil His eternal purpose. The Torah had been given to embody the working relationship God had established with this people. Now, in the fulness of time, the appointed conclusion had been made known through Jesus who embodied 'all that God has made known of His nature, character and purpose and of what he would have men to be and do'. In these words George Foot Moore sums up the essence of Torah in *Judaism in the First Centuries of the Christian Era*. They help to make it clear that it was not impossible to hold fast by Torah and to rejoice with an equal devotion in the fact that Christ had come.

Such a belief, coupled with its imperative mission, confronted him with two worlds to be held together. Exhilarated by the response of Gentiles, he must also have been grieved by the rejection of his message by Jews. It is as we approach the heart of his treatment of that mystery of rejection that we come nearest to perceiving the strength of his Jewish faith. The speculative aspects of his work, the tortuous arguments he had employed, the obstinate insistence upon revelation, all these fall into the background when he turns in chapters 9–11 of the Epistle to the Romans to speak of the mystery of Israel. Here indeed is the crux of it all.

The fact of rejection by the Jews had increasingly been made clear. No doubt he reflected as Stephen had done, that it had always been so; but the Promise had held and in what had been shown to him Paul had confirmed its truth. The new Age had begun, and with that he could work assured. But because he was Jewish his heart yearned for his people and he agonized over their fate. Then, with an act of profoundest faith, he turned their rejection of the message of Christ into a mystery of their being rejected by God. That was indeed a going down into Hell, yet, as the Psalmist had known, God was there also and would not suffer His chosen ones to be destroyed. In the most moving passage he put his faith into words. 'For I would not, brethren, that ye should be ignorant of this mystery, lest ye should be wise in your own conceits; that blindness in part is happened unto Israel, until the fulness of the Gentiles be come in. And so all Israel shall be saved; as it is written, "There shall come out of Zion the Deliverer and shall turn away ungodliness from Jacob, for this is the Covenant with them when I shall take away their sins" ' (Rom. 11.25–7).

We can follow his mind as he casts about for illustration. The tearing out and the grafting in of branches of the olive may not be a very good one, but if we read the three chapters as an expression of grief endured in hope and pause on words like 'blindness' and 'until', we cannot believe that Paul ever turned away from his own nation. He made no claims to foresee the future in terms of Jewish-Christian relations. 'It should be noted', Stendahl has said, 'that Paul does not say that when the time of God's kingdom, the consummation, comes Israel will accept Jesus as the Messiah. He says only that the time will come when 'all Israel shall be saved'. 'It is amazing to note that Paul writes this whole section of Romans (10.17–11.36), without using the name of Jesus Christ. The name that meant everything to him he held back for courtesy's sake'. The parting of the ways was not of his making, but he did not fail to declare his conviction that one day the parted would come together once more.

We must look elsewhere for the causes of the parting. We must give full weight to the political conditions that accentuated the hatreds and fears and hardened the attitudes of the leaders of the various sects during those critical years. Insurrection was never far away. Violent reprisals greeted each terrorist act. It was plainly no time for unprejudiced reflection on new, divergent, demanding movements of thought. The fate of the nation was the overriding concern. The remarks attributed in the Gospels to Caiaphas with regard to saving it from destruction no doubt represented considerable sections of influential opinion. 'Jews were', says George Foot Moore, 'both in their own mind and in the eyes of their Gentile surrounding, and before Roman law, not adherents of a peculiar religion, but members of a nation who carried with them from the land of their origin their national religion and their national customs'. For a century past the presence of Roman troops, the imposition of taxes, the merciless suppression of popular movements, had tended to harden nationalistic pride. A Messiah would surely break every such yoke and fulfil the people's long starved desire to recover their ancient glory. A crucified 'Lord' could hardly be other than an affront to such hopes, a kind of sick joke to a people already on edge. Discussion of Torah or Temple in any but quite traditional terms must have smacked of treason. We who know today how deviants are treated in a régime that feels itself threatened can understand how the pleas that were made by the Christian sect were bound to be handled. As the narrative of the Acts of the Apostles makes clear, the Christians could become the focus of a riot at any time.

This then was no time for gaining a peaceful hearing. Crisis came with worsened relations between Romans and Jews when the newly-formed Christian churches were already involved in disputes with the more influential Jewish sects in Judaea and elsewhere. In 50 A.D. it is said that riots between the parties led to their expulsion from Rome. In A.D. 66 fierce fighting broke out in Judaea and four years later came the destruction of Jerusalem itself, amidst fearful carnage. That catastrophe shattered the Jewish state. It must also have destroyed any hope of peaceful relations between the survivors of the Jewish-Christian groups and those of 'Israel after the flesh'. We cannot now know how many of the parent church in Jerusalem did survive, but we do know how one group of Pharisees fared. Under the leadership of Rabbi Johanan Ben Zakkai, these men secured from the Romans leave to migrate to Jamnia, an imperial possession with a considerable Jewish population.

Here they set up a centre of Pharisaic study and practice. It was designed to give Jewry a cohesive pattern of life based on scholarly learning. The work of the teachers at Jamnia was to ensure not simply the survival of the nation but its unification, based upon soberly realistic study and observance of Torah. The longstanding disputes between followers of famous rabbis and questions involving the relation of oral tradition to the Scriptures had all to be settled. It was a work for centuries to come. 'The development which culminated in the codification of the Mishnah of Rabbi Judah the Patriarch about 220 A.D. had its very insistent beginnings in the period of Jamnia.' So influential was it that it has been suggested by Christian scholars that the Gospel according to St Matthew was written as a rejoinder to its work.

The situation for Jewish Christians in Palestine had become grave by this time. At best they could only be regarded by the rabbinical leadership as an awkward anomaly, at worst as a positive hindrance to sensible reconstruction. Antagonism against the 'nazarene sect' grew more acute, so that by A.D.85 the liturgy of the synagogue was provided with savage anathematizing words: 'May the Nazarenes and the heretics be suddenly destroyed and removed from the Book of Life.'[1] The parting of the ways had become policy for Judaism. Rabbinical succession gave an increasing authority to efforts to suppress both heterodox Jewish groups and all mention of the detested Christian sect. The attack upon Gentile Christians was soon to come and to be bitterly repaid in kind.

It is possible that this Jewish policy was influenced further by the spread of Christianity in the Roman world and by the literature it soon produced. Both faiths appealed to Scripture. New interest in the Canon of Jewish Scripture is said to have been stimulated by the appearance of Christian writings appealing to and soon virtually annexing to their own purposes the Old Testament books. Jamnia was concerned with much more than the denunciation of heretics but, despite the continuance of scholarly relationships between rabbis and Christian teachers well into the second century, it built up a wall of rejection against them.

Quite soon the Christian reply took on its own polemical character. The Gospels present with varying degrees of clarity a deliberate opposition to 'Jews' who are delineated as avowed opponents of Jesus from the earliest days of his public life. A new Israel, the Christian community, is set over against that of the Jews. The destruction of Jerusalem lent itself easily to interpretation as a sign of divine judgement given against the wicked. Old Testament

1. W. D. Davies, *The Setting of the Sermon on the Mount*, p.275.

prophecy could be invoked to support these views. 'The Lord, whom ye seek, shall suddenly come to his temple . . . but who may abide the day of his coming, and who shall stand when he appeareth?' (Mal. 31.2.) The Scriptures were searched to provide a full understanding of the works of Jesus. 'All this was done that it might be fulfilled. . . .' The Evangelists are said to have addressed themselves to showing how certain Jewish tenets, whether they dealt with the Torah or the Messiah or the Spirit or the Age to Come, were all perfectly fulfilled in Jesus. His coming had constituted a crisis for Jewry, one of grace for those who believed on Him, who beheld His glory, one of judgment condemning those who did not.

Both polemic against rabbinical Judaism and their own evangelistic task in the Roman world led Christians to assert the new Law in Jesus against the authority of the old. In time any effort to understand or to be civil to Jews gave place to contemptuous dismissal. By the middle of the second century Justin Martyr's *Dialogue with Trypho the Jew* makes claim to a universality that is denied to the Jewish faith. Christianity is beginning to be seen as a worldwide faith. The Jew is already becoming an anomaly.

By the fourth century the parting of ways was all but complete. After Constantine's conversion, Christians were privileged citizens of the Empire, Jewish Christians had dwindled into insignificance and rabbinical Judaism had closed its ranks and defined its life and outlook for centuries to come. Both intellectual and political necessities demanded that the Christian Church set about defining its theological and institutional character. 'With Nicaea', it has been said, 'Christianity leaves the fold of Judaism.' Using concepts, institutions and imagery derived from the contemporary social and intellectual world, the Church faced its great missionary task. Pictures and statues portraying the figures of Christ, his mother and the saints were evidence of the break with the past. That Christ now appeared in imperial style, crowned, sceptred, robed and enthroned, made clear what relations were to obtain in the future. Christianity now had a political aspect inextricably bound up with its theological definition. For some time the Jews were able to thrive, but they lived henceforth in the shadow of the Cross, preserved, it was said, to be converted, in practice to be spurned and hated.

So the two faiths went their separate ways. The legacy of Paul's reflections upon God's dealings with His people was pressed into the service of many versions of highly individualized religious faith till its bearing upon the relations of Jews and Gentiles was lost to sight. There was little need in any case to consider the situation as it had been. In Byzantium, Italy, Egypt, Spain and France the Jews secured wealth, gained influential positions, made their contributions to learning and developed their own immensely erudite schools. It was both perplexing and stimulating to Christian scholars to meet the work of such men as the great Rashi, Rabbi Solomon ben Isaac of Troyes, who in the eleventh century made his contributions to Biblical study.

Meanwhile the Jewish Scriptures, and especially the Psalms, continued to vitalize Christian spirituality. The debt appeared well-nigh inexhaustible but the Christian Church seemed incapable of acknowledging it in a charitable fashion. It had in any case become a persecuting church, and, since that appetite grows by what it feeds on, it found the Jews easy victims for its indulgence. The fears indicated by the desire to persecute were not to be faced. Men lost sight of the truth that the Church had once been made up of Jews and Gentiles who loved each other and worshipped their Father in brotherly love. They still continued to read of the breaking down of the wall of partition, of the unity that had been established in Him, but they did not connect this with the Jews they excluded from their world. They did not ask whether they might one day have to reconsider these things, inquire what had gone wrong, what penitence would be called for, what long deferred acts of reparation ought to be made.

We however have to go on asking it 'lest we be wise in our own conceits' and think that we should not be required to look at them once again. It is not easy to admit that the Church, to which men have owed so much, which has played so great a part in human history until now, chose to act vilely in its treatment of the Jews. It cannot be any easier for Israel, so long bitterly wronged and cruelly abused, to recognize that it too had a part in the putting asunder of what for a brief period held together as a symbol of that which Israel's God had purposed for his world. We cannot undo the past but we can learn from it. The night sky is quite rightly an invitation to sorrow, a time to put off the finery that the world is accustomed to use, a time to look once again at what was both wittingly and unwittingly done.

The putting asunder of Jew and Gentile has stamped Christian history with fateful consequences of which the Holocaust is but one. The mystery of Israel has not grown any the less demanding of our attention since Paul pleaded in vain for recognition of it. The other road is still there. It was a Jewish Jesus who called upon men to tread it.

5. The Jewish Jesus

'So I saw him and sought him; I had him and wanted him. It seems to me that this is and should be an experience common to us all.'
Julian of Norwich, *Revelations of Divine Love*

'If Messiah should come "today", the remnant will be ready to receive him.'
Franz Rosenzweig, *The Star of Redemption*

In so far as we think seriously about Jesus, no man's presentation of him, not even that which we ourselves have cherished hitherto, can satisfy for very long. The Jesus we seek is always striding on ahead of us. The Gospels themselves are insufficient. They point to things unsaid, to things which they encourage us to expect, to things which lie beyond yet have bearing upon our inmost life and the world we live in. But their insufficiency is entirely right. They are signposts and not destinations. They demand that greatest of God's gifts – imagination – if they are to bring us any distance along the road of which he is both the way and the goal.

The purpose of this chapter may be stated briefly. Any move towards greater understanding between Christianity and Judaism must find common ground from which they may both regard Jesus or ground from which he is seen by both faiths with respect. There must be an end to that ancient and foolish 'annexation' of Jesus, whereby he is treated as if he belonged to the Christian Church. Suspicion of him on the part of Jews must also be overcome. For some time at least at the beginning of Christian history such common ground did exist. 'To them which are called, both Jews and Greeks', wrote Paul, Christ was 'the power of God and the wisdom of God'. These words power and wisdom excite a great deal of scholarly comment. They are loaded words. Yet if they do suggest that already the Jesus Christ of whom they are spoken is being seen in an unusual light (and as some would think a dangerously distorting light), this Christ was also the Jesus whom men had put to death, whom His friends believed to be raised from the dead.

That common ground was soon lost, swallowed up by rival religious feuds. How many were able to avail themselves of it we cannot now know. For centuries to come there was to be virtually none at all. Must it go on being so always or do we believe that under the good hand of God it is possible to find new ground on which the two faiths may stand together to hear His words? Can the interest in Jesus shown by so many Jews today be met by a readiness on the part of Christians to look again at what they themselves would wish to say of him? Do Christians really believe that what has been said so far is all that needs to be said and that it has been said in the only possible way, that it must do duty for all time? Is it conceivable that what was said in good faith years ago may today be a stumbling block, a barrier of words, to hinder men – and not Jews alone – from hearing and seeing him for themselves? May it be that Jews can help Christians today to look once again at Jesus himself and see him with new eyes?

In view of the long, bitter past, questions like these can look like an attack on positions sacrosanct to those who manned them. So great a divide, created over the years, will not be easily crossed. The warnings are many. 'The real issue in recent study,' wrote Hyamm Maccoby, 'is whether traditional Christian theological views of the life of Jesus – that he created a new religious outlook; that he thereby incurred the enmity of the Jewish religious establishment, the Pharisees; that his death was a voluntary sacrifice, not the failure of his hopes – can be maintained in the face of the Jewish interpretation of Jesus's life'. That statement may not do justice to what is really involved in the search for a new understanding of Jesus and it may fall far short of the sceptical probing that Christians themselves feel constrained to pursue in their handling of the records of Jesus, but it alerts us to dangers ahead. As

Jesus himself is said to have warned men, tradition is less important than learning to love God and His children, but tradition weighs heavily with us all. Our accustomed ways of thinking go far to determine what we shall think in future.

In thinking of Jesus we must struggle with those things that threaten to break through language and escape, and we are tempted to take short cuts or to improvise roads of our own. We quote from Biblical texts and use them as if they were precise theological statements, forgetting that those who wrote them were in a similar position. Working back from our own beliefs we simplify what was all-important but often obscure and confused to those who set down their halting brave words.

That we 'would see Jesus' is therefore an intention that today may quite properly require us to make somewhat lengthy detours from the path we had supposed led to him. To see Jesus the Jew we have to look longer and closer at the Judaea in which he lived, at the world of ideas and actual things amongst which he moved, at the currency of beliefs and hopes that passed between men at the time. We have to try to get into the minds of men who thought and did those things that are recorded of them.

Today we are also more aware of what is involved in 'seeing' Jesus, that is, of what religious experience can be like, how varied and how complex the weaving together of fears, hopes and beliefs can be, how quickly men in times of excitement are ready, as Paul and Barnabas found at Lystra, to deify ordinary mortals when they live in a world that expects the gods to come down and move amongst men. We have to weigh up with cautious and critical acumen that strangely innocent amalgam of bewilderment and conviction that constitutes radical religious experience. Our psychological knowledge has opened up enough knowledge of the interior of the mind to make us hesitate to be too dogmatic about the vast continent to be crossed if we would come to the Galilean Jesus. Above all we have to ask ourselves how much we really desire to break down the wall of partition that has set Jews and Gentiles apart.

Are we ready to go on seeking to do this despite what the years have done?

Two things confront us. The Jesus we meet in the Gospels is already, though perceived in various ways, the Christ, whatever that word may have meant. Even so behind that christological prelude and all the christology that the Church has ever produced stands the Jewish Jesus. Perhaps He has been made to stand too far behind it, His Jewishness lost to sight. Secondly, to use J. L. Houlden's words in an essay on the place of Jesus, 'Doctrinally speaking Christology is, in the New Testament, despite all appearances, wholly secondary. It is a disguised way of speaking about God.' This is a complication. We have left Judaea for the heavenly places; this was heaven and earth in little space. Could we really expect, unless we assume a fundamentalist inerrancy for the Gospel writers, that they would manage with their words to encompass so vast an arc of vision? They were bound to prove that all language no less than our righteousness is, in respect of God, but filthy rags.

Nonetheless they set down what they believed. If the drama they thus recorded meant using stage sets called variously Galilee, Samaria, Jerusalem, and figures named Pharisees, publicans, Romans and the like, they did it to represent what had happened on Jewish soil. Their beliefs about God may have been in the process of change but behind them loomed not the God of a party or sect but the God of Abraham, Isaac and Jacob, the God of the fathers who had looked for this day when He would in next-to-unutterable fashion glorify Jesus. The drama in any case speaks for itself. The Gospels, though lacking a portrait as such, never cease to compel an awareness of Jesus the Jew.

'But whom do ye say that I am?' (Mark 8.29a). The question that Jesus is said to have put to a handful of friends has been heard round the world. How that question is answered today throws light on how the christologies of the New Testament came into being, how the experiental gives place to the credal, how each generation endeavours to see in its own way what Jesus revealed of His relationship with God.

We may also learn a good deal about men's search for the imagery with which to express their own religious experience, and of their confusion at the lack of adequate images. Man may find little meaning today in the titles Messiah or Lord but his desire to see and portray or have portrayed for him the figure of Jesus is as avid as ever.

Be that as it may our purpose compels us to start with a number of questions that arise from our own situation, from life in a post-Auschwitz world and from our desire to keep that event in mind. It invites us to think what Jewishness means and why it has become, with Christian connivance, such a source of hatred and cruelty. The train-loads of Jews on their way to the death-camps passed through countrysides dotted with Christian spires. There were churches not very distant from the camps where Jews were gassed and burned. Those spires were symbols of a faith whose adherents were largely insensitive to the fact that that faith had sprung from the impact of the life of one Jew upon the world, and still more insensitive to any sense of relationship to Jews who had grown up in their cities and towns.

Auschwitz was an attempt to erase the Jew from the human scene. Have we yet understood the significance of that intention? Have we really assessed its bearing upon the fate of the Christian Church in the world, upon the future of human society itself? Despite the Holocaust there are millions of Jews in the world and there are also people who clamour for the completion of Hitler's unfinished work. Of the rest we may ask if they simply hope that the 'Jewish question' will die down like a fire going out or whether they have begun to see a new light that points towards much-needed changes in the way in which human life as a whole is regarded.

The Christian Church is not indifferent to or unaffected by such profound changes. Some of this concern has already prompted considerable rethinking of the doctrinal statements of the Christian faith. There is widespread feeling that the way in which the belief of the Christian Church was once formulated and conveyed to men is unhelpful now. The thought-forms of a world that has passed away and its orthodox formulations hinder rather than help the presentation of Christian teaching in our time. Has the moment not come to look at the rock from which we were digged and see for ourselves who and what he is?

And do not those traditional formulations, using thought-forms congenial to early times to commend the faith in so doing deform it, enclosing it, constricting it or hiding its original nature? Worse still, the forms themselves were accompanied by authoritative rule that placed them beyond revision. This attitude led not only to outright persecution of those who appeared dissatisfied with them but also to the rejection of the very idea of change. In a world like that of the crumbling Roman Empire where change was the most obvious feature of day-to-day life it was true that men wearied by the changes and chances of fleeting life yearned for dependable foundations, but a church could not hope to reach men at the neuralgic points of their lives unless it had understood what the new world they lived in was really like.

It is in the context of this thinking that the question of Jewishness now arises. By learning to see afresh the Jewish Jesus the Christian Church might see how the overhauling of its whole mission and the restatement of its faith might be undertaken. Is it not possible further that great strengthening of faith and enlargement of vision might follow from such an effort?

This may be desirable, but how can it be effected? The Gospels were not written to present their readers with a detailed picture of a first-century Jew. They represented the impact of this man's life and death upon a number of people, of whom the majority in the earliest days were Jews; they were not concerned with that but with the relationship with God that been opened to them through him. They were filled with an overwhelming sense of new life begun and lived in the fellowship initiated by him and charged with spiritual power derived through him. They were ready and anxious to extend that joyous experience to others. It was a great break-through in the relationship between God and man. The immediately convincing manifestation was to be the vigorous life of the communities that sprang up 'in his name'. Hard upon these would come the question of what 'in his name' meant. Very frequently in their preaching or on trial the earliest followers of Jesus were required to give an answer. The Gospels could be said to be formal attempts to give that answer. They answer the question of what He meant to their writers and to the small groups of Christians with whom they were in touch.

Further, religious thinking is not ordinarily susceptible to rapid change; on the whole it is conservative. Only under certain conditions of intense excitement in which illumination or revelation or in some instances 'possession' occurs does it undergo radical change, take on new forms, and compel its followers to adopt new ways of living and expressing their faith. What we see in the Gospels is the occurrence of a quite extraordinarily rapid process of change. The four evangelists are unique witnesses to it. From the death of Jesus, the account of which probably furnished some of the earliest written documentation to the Gospel according to St Mark, from St Mark to the Gospel according to St John, no matter whether we shorten or lengthen these periods by a decade or two, there takes place an astonishing event for which it would be difficult to find a parallel elsewhere. What we watch in the course of this writing of the Gospels, which actually introduce us to a process already well under way, is the shaping of a new world-faith. Some centuries would pass before the credal formulation was complete, but in essence the movement has taken place by the time that St John's Gospel came to be written.

It can be described as unparalleled because it took place not against a background of no faith or of primitive religious cults but in the very heart of an ancient mature religion of great vitality which at this critical moment in its history rejected the man round whom the new movement gathered. The paradox is quite awesome. The new movement is utterly Jewish, its leader a Jew, its scriptures the writings of Jews, but already the Gospels are speaking of 'Jews' as its declared opponents, as those who procured Christ's death. While the movement must have numbered amongst its ranks Jews who found no problem in following the new way, the authorities were already condemning it.

If we speak then of a 'Jewish Jesus' do we see Him as a nonconformist or dissident Jew or as one representing the quintessence of Jewish faith? A great many times in Jewish history the true line of faithful adherence to Israel's God lay through a single tribe, a small company of devoted men or even a lonely prophet, all ranged in opposition to the official leadership of the day. Is Jesus to be seen as a misguided heretic or as a man the intensity of whose relation

with God blew a hole in the fabric of Jewish religion of the day
and swept a number of obscure Jews into a realization of faith in
God, a realization of such vital force that they felt free to appeal
to all the world to come to it? Only the latter view can account
for what happened and for the difficulties which the Gospels themselves record. One feature of these is the fact that the followers of
this way did not regard themselves as a breakaway body but
continued to worship God as their fathers had done in the new
power they had gained 'through Jesus' their master. The synoptic
Gospels do not suggest that Jesus's religious practice or teaching,
notwithstanding the freedom and the authoritative manner he
appears to have shown, broke away from the Torah. St Matthew
indeed seems anxious to stress by all possible means the closest
identification of Jesus with Torah itself. No accusation was levelled
against him on grounds of breaking the Law when he was examined before the Chief Priests. He lived and died as a Jew.

It was not with his Jewishness however that the Evangelists
were mainly concerned. Even St Matthew, whose reference to the
'Jews' as a hostile body is restricted to a single passage, implies a
Christian community set over against the Synagogue, itself the
heir of the promises made to the fathers and called out by God to
be a peculiar people. Proclaiming Jesus as the personal fulfilment
of Torah, St Matthew may have been consciously challenging the
rabbinic Judaism of Jamnia. For the rest of the Gospels the emphasis was largely dictated by what has been called the leap of the
Church from its narrow Judaean birthplace into the wider Egyptian, Graeco-Roman and Syriac worlds. It found Jews in all parts
but it was not of Jewishness as such that the writers of the new
Christian scriptures were anxious to speak. The extent to which
they were influenced by Philo and by mystical writings then current in various places must remain a conjectural matter. What they
did set down was focussed almost entirely upon the person of Jesus
himself.

This means that we must be prepared to accept a good deal of
the background of the Gospels as the material needed to locate the
crisis of Jesus's coming among friends and foes. The most obvious
of these is the group of Pharisees. They appear in the Gospel story

as the hostile critics of Jesus and the objects of angry denunciation on his part. As a consequence Pharisaism was to become in Christian tradition a synonym for hypocrisy. To Jews this at once appears objectionable on several accounts. Leo Baeck observed: 'The passages in the Gospels that refer to the Pharisees have no historical significance.' It would be hard to believe from the Gospels that Pharisaism of that time had experienced the leadership of such men as Hillel who had arrived from Babylonia and studied at the feet of the leading Jerusalem Pharisees about 40 B.C. 'In his work,' writes Nahum Glatzer in *Hillel the Elder*, 'we witness the emergence of classical Judaism.' Hillel is known to have resisted the individualism of sectarian groups, called for sound learning as part of the worship of God and insisted upon humility as the true foundation of living.

Such opinions might well be thought to be simply partisan efforts to rebut the traditional denigration of Pharisaism but it is with the historical aspect that we are concerned. The more closely Israel's history has been studied, the more the verdict of the Gospels appears to be unsupported. In George Foot Moore's study of classical Judaism he points out that while men making more show of virtue than they really possess are not peculiar to any one age or creed and therefore certainly did exist in Jewry, the idea that 'the Pharisees as a whole were conscious and calculating hypocrites whose ostentatious piety was a cloak for deliberate villainy is unimaginable in view of the subsequent history of Judaism'. That Judaism survived at all was largely their work. 'They successfully charted a future for Rabbinic Judaism, centred in the synagogue and its liturgy of prayers, and in an ever-deepening and broadening immersion in Scripture.'

How far does this unhistoricity extend? How much does it affect the presentation of Jesus? Jewish scholars have not been reluctant in recent years to pay tribute to Jesus as a great teacher. In *Jesus the Jew* Geza Vermes describes him as 'second to none in profundity of insight and grandeur of character' and adds that 'he is in particular an unsurpassed master of the art of laying bare the inmost core of spiritual truth and of bringing every issue back to the essence of religion, the existential relationship of man and man and man and God'. Judgment of much the same kind was made by Klausner who spoke of 'the sublimity, distinctiveness and originality in form unparalleled in any other Hebrew ethical code' of the teaching of Jesus. What we look for however is comment that more consciously takes confrontation of historically long-divided faiths as its starting-point. Such a view may be found in Samuel Sandmel's book *We Jews and Jesus*.

Sandmel therefore begins by emphasizing that American life has provided the most favourable conditions ever enjoyed by the Jews of the Diaspora and that he and those for whom he was writing had therefore been spared some of the more obviously embittering experiences that in the past had prejudiced discussion. The conditions brought their own kind of temptations. What he sought to provide was an understanding by Jews of the Christianity of the American people among whom they lived while retaining the separateness of their Jewish faith. It was an attempt to use an opportunity provided by the New World to redress some of the barbarities of the Old and then to look further at what is involved in this religious distinction.

How much can we know of Jesus? To this cautious scholar the question is hard to deal with. In his lectures on the First Century in Judaism and Christianity, Sandmel sought to make clear that 'precise history and over-precise theology, quite apart from the important issue of bias, begin to appear to me as delusions because the amount we know is overbalanced by the greater amount that we do not know'. Christian scholars have always known that but Christian preachers have often been less restrained. Since the Gospels themselves were partisan it has never been easy to handle them with objective intent.

Greater precision in historical knowledge did not render any less difficult the task of understanding what moved men of Jewish and Christian faith in the first century of this Christian era. What the devotee sees and draws out of his beliefs remains obscure to those unimpressed by its tenets. To Sandmel the figure of Jesus remained enigmatic as ever before. He went on to declare his opinion that 'Jews and Christians are farther apart today on the question of Jesus than they have been in the past hundred years, and this despite other ways in which Judaism and Christianity have drawn closer to each other than ever before'. The growing historical knowledge had added to rather than lessened the theological burden to be faced. It suggested that what was most needed was new theological insight to begin to unravel the knots and entanglements of the centuries past. Sandmel therefore summed up his study of Jesus saying: 'We have not believed that Jesus was the Messiah, we have not been willing to call him Lord, we have not believed that the Logos became incarnate as Jesus, we have not believed that Jesus was, or is, the very Godness of God.' For good measure we might add that elsewhere he wrote, 'it is a hopeless task to disentangle history from non-history in the narratives of the Tanak, or of the extra–Biblical literature, or of the New Testament. We cannot be precise about Jesus. We can know what the Gospels say, but we cannot know Jesus.'

This seems unlikely ground for any attempt at dialogue but it compels us to realize that much of our difficulty lies not in confrontation with others but with ourselves, in the fear of unresolved opposites in our own make-up. This is the challenge that the Church must now face, for it may be compelled to rethink its understanding of Jesus in relation to Israel's calling and to see the debt its own mission owes to the Jewish faith to an extent never previously admitted. A premature universalism may have to give way to forms of pluralism in social and religious matters. Such a Church would not be an easier one to belong to, but, less obtrusively an institution, more consciously a fellowship. Such a church might be better equipped to continue the challenging witness to God in the world that the Bible regarded as essential to Israel's calling.

The first steps towards a practical concern for the Jewishness investing the figure of Jesus would lie in the question What was Jesus? rather than Who was Jesus? The Gospels have already directed attention to the latter question and much Christian christological study has been devoted to examining the answers suggested by titles ascribed to Jesus. The Christ, Messiah, Son of God, Son of Man and Lord have all been turned to account. The theological structures erected upon them have been impressively put together and in the light of the subsequent growth of the Church's christology would appear to be justly conceived. But what faces us now is not that kind of question or answer. We are being asked to look further back to Jesus's working life.

The first thing that stands out is the preaching of the coming of the Kingdom of God, a matter of such importance that I would wish to consider it in a separate chapter. That it was largely displaced by questions regarding Jesus is made clear in the writings of the Evangelists and St Paul. Within a few years the minds of His followers were, according to these, more deeply concerned with His Messianic character. 'God has made this Jesus, whom you crucified, both Lord and Messiah.' The preaching of Peter, Paul, Philip and Apollos is cited to confirm it. The passion and resurrection stories were swiftly woven into the fabric of messianic imagery. The Johannine Jesus is said to declare in straightforward terms, 'I that speak unto thee am He'. His Jewish hearers are described as divided in opinion about His messiahship but the Samaritans affirm stoutly that 'we have heard Him ourselves and know that this is indeed the Christ, the Saviour of the world'.

Preaching has played so great a part in Christian history and the 'preached Christ' become so impressive a factor in its religious experience that it may appear foolish to question its ability to represent what we are really concerned with, the religion of Jesus. The writings we have are themselves a compound of preaching and liturgical practice, immensely important as evidence as to how Christians tried to express their understanding of Jesus but telling us even more of the difficulties that beset such efforts. The Word was made flesh and they had beheld His Glory. In the flesh they had handled the Word of Life. What they did in preaching and writing was to try to put that into words and the long process that includes the huge story of Christian preaching and the Creeds and the Tome of Leo, St Augustine, St Thomas Aquinas, Martin Luther, Karl Barth and thousands of others was begun. Admittedly what mattered at any time was the way that the Word found its way through men's words and took flesh in men's lives and of this there is much to thank God for. But the Holocaust as an event in Christian history suggests also that men's words obstructed that

Living Word that essayed to dwell among men and the roots of such an appalling obstruction go back to the earliest days when men fitted Him into roles or expounded their discernment of Him in terms of current hopes. It could not have been otherwise but we must at least to become aware of its having been done and of what followed as its result.

Men are quick to use labels and titles to 'fix' situations and to impose their own favoured patterns on what a great teacher says and does. The use of the title Messiah was a case in point. It aroused such variety of feelings and hopes that Jesus may well have been reluctant to use it or allow it to be used in speaking of his mission. Messianism was too violent a tide to give a true character or direction to his work. We know, for example, that the Dead Sea Scrolls communities thought in terms of no less than three messianic figures, royal and priestly and prophetic. Elsewhere political and apocalyptic hopes had thrown up their various patterns of this rod out of Jesse's stem.

Neither in Galilee nor Judaea could the political situation be other than explosive. In the two centuries that followed Pompey's capture of Jerusalem in 63 B.C. both areas were hotbeds of violent messianic movements and of guerilla warfare whose ferocity was intensified by the brutalities of the Romans and the cruelties of the Herods. Liberation at the hands of a warrior-Messiah continued to kindle the hopes of this turbulent people despite the slaughter that each uprising brought in its train; the final outburst of Bar Kokhba in A.D. 135 inspired such zeal that men like Rabbi Akiba could hail its leader as Messiah. No movement that drew crowds to listen to a leader could be seen by rebels or by rulers to be without political significance. No set of teachings or way of life that impinged upon the lives of both men and women to such an extent could fail to have repercussions. We cannot from evidence in the Gospels and elsewhere do more than conjecture what relations with John the Baptist or with the Zealots the followers of Jesus of Nazareth had, but that Jesus himself was regarded as a political threat is recorded in their words.

The influence of the apocalyptic utopianism of the time is even harder to assess. There can be little doubt that it contributed its own fervour to the tensions of thought and practice of the people among whom Jesus moved. Some of its features found their way into Christian writing. Embittered men found strength and courage in the expectation of the coming of a Messiah who would execute God's wrath upon tyrants and evildoers, roll up the scroll of temporal history and inaugurate the kingdom of righteousness and peace. Opinion might vary as to his nature, to his powers over life and death, to his reign in relation to judgment and the world to come, but the strength of the expectation was in no way diminished by this. 'Messianic legend' writes Gershom Scholem in *Sabbatai Sevi*, 'indulges in uninhibited fantasies about the catastrophic aspects of redemption.... Far from being the result of historical process, redemption arises on the ruins of history, which collapses amid the 'birth pangs' of the messianic age.' The study which Scholem has made of the movement which hailed the Sabbatai Sevi in the seventeenth century helps to make clearer the kind of conditions which must have made their impact on Jesus's work. Embracing Jews rich and poor from the Yemen to Poland, strong enough to survive its Messiah's betrayal of his own cause, this later messianism drew its strength from the religious inspiration supplied by Kabbalism to men whose social, political and economic distress made them hunger for deliverance. It needed only the appearance of a leader with charismatic authority to challenge and sweep aside that of the traditional rabbinical teachers.

Out of such conditions, misconceived in and often considerably hampered by them, emerged the church of the followers of Jesus. If we ask why militaristic, political and utopian movements such as those of the Zealots and Essenes failed to do what these men did we are on the track of the work of the Jewish Jesus. Jewishness means in this context something more fundamental than these various factors, something inclusive of all human effort but unaligned to a particularist cause. It is Hebrew religion, power greater than anything that either priests or scribes knew, waiting to be unlocked by one in whom it was truly alive. To speak to the inmost core of men's souls and to the human nature that yearns to know and be known of God, it needed a voice of one who himself knew God in that way, who could speak of it in the whole way he lived it.

Such a one was Jesus of Nazareth. In Him something more profound than political or apocalyptic messianism took flesh and worked amongst the men of that troubled tempestuous world. The titles, the concepts, the doctrines, all that men later as well as during His life used to speak of Him fell so far short of the reality of His expression of life lived with and to God and man that they initiated the process of limiting what He had done and was. They could not help doing that, but in spite of them we can still ask what must the reality of the meeting with Jesus have been like if, along with all the distortions, misunderstandings and misrepresentations that immediately surrounded it, the life of the Christian Church was implanted on such a soil. It is the marriage of realization and unrealization which is the best witness to what he did. He chose to mine deeper into Israel's knowledge of God, profound as that was, grasped what was there at its heart, and in his own living showed what it was like to men. How can you put that into words? It is in this sense that Jesus fulfilled what the Jewish scriptures had said of God. It is in this sense too that Jewishness is the taproot of Christian living. 'The Christian Church,' T. F. Torrance has said, 'has no independent existence apart from Israel; it is only through and with Israel that we Christians belong to the One People and Church of God.'

The mining process, as I have called it to account for it on the human plane, was carried out in the vein of Hebrew prophecy. Whether we call Jesus a prophet or 'only a prophet' or one greater than any prophet, what matters is that we understand first what prophethood or prophecy meant in the Hebrew sense. It takes us at once to the most fundamental questions of Hebrew religion. Can men know God and His will? Can they live out that will in human life? The answer to these questions, the most important in human history, came through the prophets. They moved towards the realization of the truth that the living Yes to them must mean the life of a man and a people. To say that such men knew God means much more than saying that they had messages to deliver. Hebrew 'knowing' is the total response to the one whom it claims to know. It finds consummation of being in its self-giving to the one who is known. Hence it is often in terms of sexual union such as inspired the Song of Songs that it is expressed, but it transcends that relation too. It came to speak rather of friendship as its supreme description of Abraham and Moses in relation to God. It appears again in the words of Jesus to the disciples in John 15.15, 'I have called you friends' and carries the implication that they are called to participate in the love with which God loves us, the love that is within the Godhead itself. It could be expressed in the Johannine words that 'I and my Father are one' and eventually find scope in Christian Trinitarian doctrine. It is that which indissolubly unites love of neighbour and love of God.

Seen in this way Jewish prophecy cannot be treated as if it were no more than a prelude to the work of the Christ, nor can Torah be thought of as simply an interim guide. It means that after so long a time of misjudgment Christianity must begin to take seriously in its own right the relation of Israel to God. For Christianity cannot truly know Israel's greatest son if it fails to learn from him how he himself understood Israel's calling. We cannot know what being 'more than a prophet' means until we have wholly trodden the way of Israel's prophets. From them we need help to appreciate what was at issue in Jesus's work among his own people and what was so often lacking at critical times in the history of Christendom later.

For this we have good authority in Jesus himself, in that he used their words and works as the ground of his own, and sadly compared the reception given to him with theirs. Israel's dealings with prophets foreshadowed the worst, and the tombs of those slain were witness to what was to come. Nonetheless the prophets did constitute a true point of engagement between God and man, did provide the critical judgment by which Israel's response to God was challenged and purged. The character of Israel's life as a nation had depended, as Jeremiah had insisted, 'since the day that your fathers came forth out of the land of Egypt unto this day' on God's action of sending his prophets to them. When they failed to be true to their mission it fell to Ezekiel to denounce them. When Israel dishonoured both God and his Torah, the later Isaiah came to speak of redemption through the burden of suffering borne by the servant appointed by God. The last note of canonical witness urged men to await the coming of the herald that Malachi spoke of (Mal. 3.1.). 'If they hear not Moses and the prophets, neither will they be persuaded though one rose from the dead' (Luke 16.31).

From such a foundation Jesus did not fail to take up his own work. He did not reject the hope of his friends on the road to Emmaus that he should have proved to be mighty in deed and word but carried them further through his own words 'beginning with Moses and all the prophets' to understand what he had done. It was such a golden string that Jewish Christians took up as their guide when they in their turn were required to expound their faith. To the crowds assembled in Solomon's porch Peter spoke of the saying of Moses concerning the prophet 'whom the Lord your God shall raise up unto you of your brethren like unto me' (Acts 3.22). In Jesus that word had been fulfilled. To the crowd at Pentecost he had declared that this 'Jesus of Nazareth, a man approved of God among you by miracles and wonders and signs, which God did by him, in the midst of you', had been made 'both Lord and Christ' (Acts 2.22). God's covenant had been fulfilled in him whom God had raised from the dead.

I am not suggesting that all Christian devotion to God went wrong when that golden string of Israel's prophetic witness was let slip and other more tempting engagements were made with the culture and powers of the Græco-Roman world. But that much did go wrong must be admitted. 'The predicament of contemporary man is grave', the Holocaust witnesses to something terribly wrong, the life of the Christian Church bears too many of the scars of the triumph of evil to permit us to be complacent. The catalogue of the victories of the prince of this world, in which Auschwitz is but the latest of his crimes is saddeningly long. 'The conversion of Constantine which subjected the Eastern Church to the imperial power; the legitimation of persecution; the raising of the flesh to the rank of the Devil himself as the enemy of man, and the inhuman doctrine of predestination which the great Augustine bequeathed to the Western Church; the great schism between East and West; the dissensions and corruption of medieval Chris-

tendom; the religious wars of the sixteenth and seventeenth centuries; the rejection of Christianity by the French Revolution and
the instant corruption of the ideals of the revolutionaries themselves. . . .' – the list is R.C. Zaehner's and we can all of us add
to it and bring it up to date. Many Jews from far-off days until
now have rejected a Christ presented to them by this Church. Is
it quite so certain that they were wrong to turn away from that
face?

> Was our outrage sore? but the worst we spared,
> To have called these – Christians, – had we dared.

What if so-called Christians, wise in their own conceits and exalting themselves not him, have made themselves into the stumbling-
block that prevented men's feet from coming to him?

Human self-deception is a familiar theme in Jewish scripture.
The prophets took up the charge in every generation that Israel's
monarchy, Israel's priesthood, Israel's Temple and Israel's soil
could all be made agents of false relations with God and man.
When in the course of time men carried the news of Israel's God
into a much wider world they were more than ever exposed to
such temptations tricked out in yet grander garments, and the
Israelite voice in them was silenced.

The subtlest of all such was that they should present the image
of God in their own chosen terms. I believe that Sebastian Moore
is right in saying that 'Christian history has been burdened with
a Messiah such as never existed' and that this 'has prevented the
loving meeting of Christians and Jews in the Man who is Everyman, the Man of Sorrows, our man, the new man.' A mythical
figure was devised to turn men's eyes from Jesus who lived and
died a Jew, the Jesus who had lived the revelation of God the
Father of all and who had chosen to die that all the false images of
God should be overthrown. But Moore continues: 'Christians have
partly undone the crucifixion and made of the Christ a concreti-
zation of messianic prophecy rather than its mysterious fulfilment
through the alchemy of the cross.' Crowned once derisively with
thorns, he was to suffer more insidious mockery when the time

came to bring him before the world not as victim but as the Roman Governor's client!

Truth will nevertheless prevail. The falsification of the Cross cannot hide the truth that rejection itself reveals. In the goodness and the severity of God, Golgotha returns and its name is Auschwitz.

6. The Lord's Song In a Strange Land

'History is only dead when the living discard it.'

A. Cohen, *The Natural and the Supernatural Jew*

'Modern man is reborn when be becomes convinced of his role in history.'

L. L. Whyte, *The Next Development in Man*

A scene for Goya or Gustave Doré: a prison camp crammed with several hundred gaunt, grey-faced, weary men, marked out for death, who stand and listen to a lecture given by one who is at all points like each one of them. Its theme is human history from ancient times until today. The scene is the concentration camp of Theresienstadt in June 1944 [1] The speaker is Leo Baeck.

The minutes of men's lives ebb out as he tells of history's concern for the continuity of life, of life becoming conscious of itself, of its course, its problems, its achievements, its destiny and meaning. The night sky here is very close, the darkness visible, but something wrought through thirty centuries of Jewish life is being confirmed. A task once undertaken in faith on such a night is being faced. The Jew, whether speaker or hearer, reaffirms his recognition of it. That part perhaps needed a surrealist painter to do justice to it; one like Miro of whom it was said that he knew that you can see further by night than by day.

---

1. Theresienstadt was the cynically bleached Black Lie, as Lucy Dawidowicz calls it in her book *The Jewish Presence*, which was provided with sham amenities to deceive Red Cross visitors and to assure the world that Jews were being well treated.

By his servant Moses the watch was set
Though near upon cockcrow we keep it yet.

The lecturer spoke quietly of historians from Herodotus and Thu-
cydides to Ranke and Mommsen, talking of the great Greeks and
Romans first of all. Their achievements had been magnificent. In
them the human mind had soared. They had bequeathed to others
a well-nigh inexhaustible inheritance. Yet from their life and outlook something important had been missing, some basic element
without which all else must finally wither, some reality needed to
renew a nation's life.

Then Baeck turned to speak of his own people's history to that
doomed audience of fellow Jews. He was now seventy-one years
old. Since 1933 he had been the president of the representative
body of Jews in Germany, the rabbi chosen to speak on behalf of
this people marked down for destruction, the man of God whose
integrity and wisdom would be tested day by day as he struggled
on their behalf. He had refused to leave Germany when pressed to
do so. He had chosen to stay with those who needed him. His
lifetime's work was being not so much interrupted as carried to its
maturity by the experience of the concentration camp.

Forty years before, like a stripling David, he had challenged the
great Harnack on the grounds that that erudite man had failed
completely to understand Judaism. In his own book, *The Essence
of Judaism* (1905), he had set before the world his own reading of
the essential character of the Jewish faith. The word 'history'
appeared in its opening sentence. Half a century later in the book
This People Israel, embodying all that he had learned and taught in
the intervening years, he described the special history of Israel and
its bearing upon all human life; special because, as he insisted,
'Israel saw history as the law of a higher will, as the moral law –
it encountered a commanding legislation, entering history out of
the eternal, infinite beyond'. It was a special history too in that it
conjoined creation and revelation in the shared experience of the
generation of this people, not for its own sake only but for that of
the world. It was special because it was the representative history
of mankind, disclosing the underlying meaning of all human his-

tory to which men turn when the threat of meaninglessness pressed heavily upon them.

'True history,' Baeck urged, 'is the history of the spirit, the human spirit which may at times seem powerless but ultimately is yet superior and survives, because even if it has not got the might, it still possesses the power, the power that can never cease.' Baeck spoke of the particularity of the history of the Jewish nation, of their calling derived not from themselves but from the living God, itself the stamp of their unique condition. 'It is almost as if it is a word that the Creator pronounced for one time only.' It was dangerous intoxicating stuff and under a night sky the tragic irony of it was hard to bear.

True history, words spoken of in the present tense, and therefore demanding of each generation a reinterpretation, an unending mental and spiritual struggle, an eternal questioning and beginning again. The life of this people lay in its response to divine initiative, in its obedience to its supernatural calling. It must ever be learning to transform the revelation of yesterday into the vision of the present, for ever experiencing a rebirth. It has been said that Judaism knew no great occasion like the Renaissance in Christendom's cultural history. The truth is that it managed to retain an ability to come to many rebirths. Its true historians were the prophets who summoned successive generations to acknowledge the mystery and the obligations of this people's life. Much wilful wrongdoing, folly and pride had come near to wrecking its course, but always renewal had come. 'Time and again a voice cried out of the mystery. When the people heard it, it knew in days of confusion where clarity was, and in days of darkness where light will shine.'

Baeck knew and avoided the temptation to impose upon history a scheme or convenient pattern. He chose rather to characterize Israel's experience in a number of epochs in which she gained recognition of the oneness of God, the oneness of the life of the people, the oneness of God's kingdom. Now in the time of this present unspeakable agony a fourth epoch was being disclosed, one of hope set over against the many more frail expectations of men. It was hope for the world spelled out in the suffering of one people. Inwardly set to bear witness to the commands of God, to know the polarities of law and grace, of freedom and obligation, its task in the world was to bring all mankind to the knowledge of true human life, a life in process of being created by God. Judaism must teach mankind to look with new eyes on the human story; it could do so only by faithfulness to its own. 'To find the cause of mankind in its own cause is the greatest thing that can happen to a people' (Friedlander, *Leo Baeck*, p.219). Its whole presence and being in the world could be described as 'a sermon to the world' to be preached whether men would hear or not.

It is not difficult to observe the shameless uses of history to gratify the nationalist and imperialist lusts and ambitions of the great European powers. It is harder to detect the more subtle complacent misuses that cause a history to be written with an affection of objectivity but lacking the power of self-scrutiny and humble recognition of the complexities of human affairs. We are reminded 'that all history perpetually requires to be corrected by more history'.

It cannot be easy therefore for Christians to do justice to Baeck's pronouncement of Israel's calling or appointment with history, and thence to hear patiently his attacks upon Christian dogmatism and his claiming of Jesus for the Jewish tradition. History as written by Christians has not looked closely at the Jews nor has it built up a tradition of constant concern for peoples and causes peripheral to its own position. Auschwitz has made it abundantly clear that the writing of history as an exercise in the pursuit of truth is a far more difficult matter than men have yet admitted. Their traditions, their causes, their sympathies, have played a much larger part in their work than they ever suspected. We might ask of all historians at what point do their sympathies fail and why.

Furthermore it is the more difficult to relate, as I shall show later, the writing of 'sacred history' to those forms which are concerned with political or social matters. To introduce God as protagonist in this play is to give to all other actors, their designs and words a theological character. Jewish history stands on this footing. So too did Christendom's history but within it has grown up historical study which has no need for that hypothesis. Can such an approach make contact with views like that of Baeck and see the Jews as a nation set over against all other nations, not because they were wiser or more humane than others, nor by the interplay of political circumstances in a complicated struggle between great powers, but because God's choice was at work to use them to further the salvation of mankind? Hebrew records themselves remind us of Joseph recounting his dreams and provoking enough irritation to ensure his rejection.

Yet historical consciousness did mean for the Jews that relation with God, and our history today must take notice of this relationship. It shaped and sustained the Jewish people. It was something they struggled against as well as for, since it involved them in difficulties that no other people shared. Their own grasp of it was fitful and their sacred writings contained divergent and diverse views of its significance and obligations. What we watch in the records of the fortunes of Israel's monarchy, priesthood, messianism, mystical teachings and apocalyptic hopes, is a prolonged effort to come to self-understanding. There was not, and cannot be, anything automatic about it. Reflection discloses some of its features but cannot do more than point to the learning process. It is more exactly a meta-historical consciousness that it is Israel's task to lay hold of, to distil from historical insight. It was a seemingly impossible task laid on men compelled to be wanderers, on those to whom assimilation or oblivion offered so much, but it has been borne in upon them that it was an inescapable one. 'No racial or ethnic unity,' wrote Arthur Cohen, 'helps us to survive. We are destined to disappear if our existence depends solely upon the slow action of history.' that is, of history as the Gentiles have understood it.

So much is at stake for both Jews and Gentiles, if Auschwitz is not to be repeated, that we must needs make this question of history and historical consciousness the key to our approach to both faiths and to whatever dialogue is to be attempted between them. Understanding of history in relation to faith is crucial here. Baeck rightly sensed that in the post-Auschwitz, post-war world Judaism would be faced by quite new problems which in their turn reflected those of the non-Jewish world. Arab nations possessed of great wealth and newly awakened Islamic purpose, African peoples politically free but more economically dependent than ever, world-powers of the stature of China and Russia, would alter world human relations. The task of informing historical consciousness has grown greater with this confusion of voices. It was but yesterday that European historians still thought in terms of the concert of Europe and the cultural life it had known. To the men of the enlightenment it had seemed obvious that they had only to trace and describe the emergence and triumph of reason in human affairs. That bright day had faded but what of the night?

What emerged, and attempts to write histories of the two World Wars made this painfully clear, was the confession of inadequacy for so profound a task. It was as if the imagination needed to comprehend what had happened in Europe and elsewhere had not existed. A reviewer of Lucy Dawidowicz's book, *The War against the Jews, 1933–1945,* remarked that few historians had as yet grasped the monstrous nature of Hitler's project to eliminate Jewry because they approached it with systems of evaluation and explanation which they had been accustomed to use in relation to other features of their historical study. What the Holocaust did was to suggest that such systems had been inadequate all along. In writing about Kafka, whose personal dilemmas and fantasies looked like micro versions of the political scene, George Steiner made the comment. 'The world of Auschwitz lies outside speech as it lies outside reason. To speak of the unspeakable is to risk the survivance of language as creator and bearer of human rational truth' (*Language and Silence*).

To whom shall we turn at such a juncture? On the far side of this chasm that opened in Europe, Lord Acton wrote on history's behalf; 'Resist your time – take a foothold outside it' but the advice may be less helpful than he would have wished. The writing of history has become the exercise-yard of Marxists, neo-Marxists, Idealists, Utilitarians, Freudians and Jungians, each claiming more insight than others. The re-writing of history has frequently meant expunging the features no longer in favour. We are forced to ask then where the ground of any such foothold is to found, where human conscience can carry the weight of such disclosures of human behaviour as the Holocaust affords. Not the Gentile, nor, to use Arthur Cohen's words, 'the natural Jew' can hope to do this but only the supernatural Jew to whom 'each moment is abundant with the unrealized possibility of God in history'. Because the Holocaust has destroyed for both natural Jew and Gentile alike the possibility of grappling with human life without this renewal of 'history with God' its pursuit may become redemptive, the problem of history may now become of supreme importance.

For the moment however only tentative movements in that direction have been made by either faith. The natural Jew is likely to be heard in Israel proclaiming the 'right' of the Jewish people to take over every scrap of the land which God once gave to them. The supernatural Jew will look further and seek to commit World Jewry to movements of change throughout the world to realize the potential life of mankind. Among Christians the first indications of quite new attention to history can be seen in the work of the World Council of Churches, in Papal encyclicals like *Ecclesiam Suam* and *Populorum Progressio*, and in a number of both Catholic and Protestant theological writings. 'Since the Church lives in history', stated *Populorum Progressio*, 'she ought to examine the signs of the times and interpret them in the light of the Gospel. Sharing the noblest aspirations of men and suffering when she sees them not satisfied, she wishes to help them to attain their full flowering, and that is why she offers men what she possesses as her characteristic attribute, a global vision of man and of the human race'. The next steps have yet to be made. It is not easy to say how pressing a sense of urgency is felt among those who welcomed the words, nor how aware men have become of·the changes which would give flesh and blood to that vision.

No less emphatic has been the rethinking of history's role among Protestant theologians like Pannenberg, Moltmann and Tillich. Each has contributed to a new view of the spiritual disintegration of Europeanized society with its loss of meaning in terms of personal and community life and has directed attention towards the future, towards the boundary which affords a new meeting with God. Each has emphasized in distinctive fashion that more profound understanding of man and his coming-to-be must depend upon a new grasp of the historicity of human life, on new humbled awareness of our being called on to take part in the creative purpose of God. Faith means in such a context a commitment to Christ which enables men to resist the idolatry of present achievements and patterns of human effort and to go forward towards a remaking of human life in response to the Spirit of God.

The same note appeared in *Christian Believing*, a report by the Doctrine Commission of the Church of England published in 1976. Changed methods of historical study linked with new sciences of sociology and social psychology had revolutionized human self-understanding and brought forward a need to rethink the doctrinal and biblical foundations of Christian faith and the structures of though and practice erected upon them. 'The shattering changes in the understanding of reality that have marked the modern world have forced us to face the fact that man is an historical being, that he exists in a continuum of change, and that he cannot therefore take for granted that all ages and cultures shared his own principles and forms of thought' (*Christian Believing*, p.10).

All brave assertions that the acceptance of historical critiques and a greater knowledge of what had gone into the shaping of Christian belief would not destroy faith but would rather contribute to strengthening it had however to be tested at the levels of popular thought. One result of the quickened pace of change in religious studies had been a widening of gaps in the outlook of various groups of Christian believers. More intensive use of the modern media of communication not only amplified controversy but tended to increase the fears of many that the sole outcome would be the undermining and destruction of fundamental Christian beliefs. A suspicion that scholars were only a negative factor in the reshaping of men's thought, a fear that too much of traditional religious practice was being abandoned, tended to bring not confident welcome but resistance to much that was offered. In times of great social stress this confusion leads to those outbreaks of violence that once brought about attacks on the Jews. They may do so again. The approval of change is not easily purchased. The Holocaust represents a fearful rejection of the demands symbolized by the presence of the Wandering Jew.

It is for this reason that the presence of Jewry and the implications of Judaism together with Christendom's sorry record of facing them needs to be made explicit. It is this which is still largely missing from Christian thinking. The Holocaust has not been felt in the marrow bones of contemporary Christian life. One illustration may be given. There is much wisdom and learning in Charles Davis's book *God's Grace in History* (1966). It is an important example of the kind of literature needed for the re-education of men and women prepared to examine their faith and their relations with their fellow men in the world today. Yet, apart from one reference to the Judaeo-Christian element in Western culture, the Jews and Judaism are passed over in silence. How is it possible, we must ask, in speaking of God's relation to human history, to ignore so utterly the experience, the teaching, the very existence and fate of the Jews in the world, the people who symbolize history in themselves? 'Get thee out to a country that I will show thee' is the epitome of Jewish existence.

The omission is the more painful in that Charles Davis is so ready to note wrongdoing in Christian history and to direct attention to 'the partial premature' character of the Church in the Middle Ages and the uncovering today of an absence of Christian faith both in cities and countryside. Did some of that failure stem from lost contact with Israel's conception of faith and the service of God? Furthermore, in the world today, it is recognized that Asia, Africa and the whole extra-European world must contribute to the refashioning of human life in world society, yet the Jews, who have been 'abroad' far longer than other peoples remain unnoticed. How can it be possible to speak of Christianity being 'inserted' into the historical process without reference to the part of the Jews?

It is possible because as Christians we have grown accustomed to doing it, because we have been reluctant to examine closely Christendom's presentation of the Christian faith and to recognize how 'dated' are many of the features so commonly accepted as being there from the beginning. The medieval world-picture has vanished because men have changed their manner of life and the picture no longer fits. What has failed to arrive is a post-Christendom working hypothesis in which a Christian supernatural history makes full use of what modern historical learning affords. We are still in an uneasy phase in which ecclesiastical history is offered instead. In his introduction to the study of modern ecclesiastical history, (*The Pelican Guide to Modern Theology*), John Kent observed that so much writing appeared to be the work of the propagandist, ready if need be 'to varnish a little the story of what the Church had done in the world'. He went on to deepen his objection. 'It is a very unsatisfactory state of affairs (– he was speaking of the history of Christian mission –) if one feels obliged again and again to turn to the secular historian for a more convincing interpretation of the mass of facts which writers like Latourette collect.'

More than half a century ago von Hugel was calling for readiness to give free play to the scientific and historical spirit that it might help to bring the insights of Christian faith once again into a central position in human life. He did not doubt the ability of this spirit to underpin and sustain both personal and social life given the enlargement which such freedom would bring. 'Without such correction,' he wrote, 'religion becomes defensive and resistant to change, unable and unwilling to appreciate the many-sidedness of human life, jealous of the achievements of men that it could not instantly control, blind to the fact that the religious life must somehow be the richest by learning to deal century after century in welcoming, assimilating, renovating, the new experiences which this scientific spirit afforded.' Religion needs to be freed from ecclesiastical history, nourished by the scientific, that it may become the kind of history that can be prayed by men summoned by God to stand on their feet in the world He has made.

Much of the unpreparedness of the Church to deal wisely with the events of the modern world, – including its attitude towards the Jews – can be traced to halfheartedness in respect of history. It is a failure to sing the Lord's song in a strange and admittedly bewildering land. Ecclesiastical history has tried to walk delicately through the morass of the turbulent modern world. It has failed almost wholly to develop the kind of critique that was needed to show this emerging world the significance of its struggles from the eighteenth century onwards. That men felt the need was evi-

dent in the Enlightenment. In France, Germany and England a
new philosophy of history was propounded. Contacts with the
civilizations of China and Persia awakened a curiosity and interest
in the cultural factors contributing to civilization throughout the
world. The 'philosophes' directed attention to ideas of progress
sustained by education. In the face of ecclesiastical displeasure men
such as Voltaire, Helvetius and Holbach worked to shift attention
from the traditional glorification of empires clerical and lay
towards the progress of civilized societies. No less opinionated
than their clerical opponents they denounced them as unscrupulous
enemies of progress and, while concentrating their main attack
upon the Christian Church, did not spare their contempt for the
Jews.

The movement towards a new evaluation of history nevertheless
hung fire for, with few exceptions, the men of the Enlightenment
were not ready to set about historical research or to replace with
new forms the conventional presentation of history. Much of their
work was in essence anti-historical. It was not from the declared
opponents of Judaism and Christianity that the changes were destined to come but from certain exponents of those faiths, who
began to make appeals to history to support declarations of faith.
The Tractarians are among those who showed willingness to re-
examine the history of England and Christendom and to make the
new use of methods of historical interpretation. It was a movement
of thought that was to gain classical exposition in Newman's *Essay
on the Development of Christian Doctrine* and in *Tract 85*, in which
he wrote of the Bible: 'Whatever else is true about it, this is true
– that we may speak of the history, or mode of its composition,
as truly as that of other books; we may speak of its writers having
an object in view, being influenced by circumstances, being anxious, taking pains, purposely omitting or introducing things, leaving things incomplete, or supplying what others had so left.
Though the Bible be inspired – it has all the characteristics as might
attach to a book uninspired – the characteristics of dialect and style,
the distinct effects of times and places, youth and age, of moral
and intellectual character.' Many years would pass before the full
weight of the teaching of the *Essay on Development* would find

general acceptance in the great churches of Europe, but it would not be unjust to read in the *Declaration of the Second Vatican Council* on religious freedom, with its reference to the consciousness of contemporary man as that from which the Church may learn, an acknowledgment of a longstanding debt.

How difficult progress towards a changed view of history in relation to matters of faith and Church life, and likewise how influential, could be seen in the fortunes of numerous now half-forgotten works such as Milman's *History of the Jews* (1830). Milman treated his Old Testament materials with great caution and respect. He did not question their historical authenticity, he had no archaeological 'finds' to discuss, no contradictions to resolve. He simply rewrote the Biblical narratives in a lucidly straightforward way. It is a measure of what had to be faced – and how far we have travelled since – to note that his plain English, describing Abraham as a sheik and the Jews as an oriental tribe, was enough to arouse an outcry and storm of protest from the conventionally religious minded who regarded this way of treating the Scriptures as wickedly subversive.

Milman was innocent of any purpose but that of making the sacred history, as he thought, more intelligible to its readers. He was probably quite unaware of the fact that his knowledge of contemporary European scholarship did modify the way he thought of his subject and did set him apart from less well-informed people. His work was later to be described by Stanley as 'the first decisive inroad of German theology into England, the first palpable indication that the Bible could be studied like another book, that the characters and events of sacred history could be treated at once critically and reverently'. Slight as was its critical freedom, it denoted change. Strauss and Feuerbach were already at work and the orthodox scented danger. Something more revolutionary than either Milman or his critics could have foreseen was beginning to make its way.

More striking at the time was the fact that Milman saw fit to conclude his History with a lengthy chapter on contemporary Judaism and a reflection on Jewish culture. To appreciate the force of the pleas he made it should be recalled that Jews in England were still living under great disabilities, although, scarcely more than 20,000 in number, living mainly in London, their unpopularity, despite the anti-semitism of men like Cobbett, was declining and their abilities gaining more recognition. Nathan Meyer Rothschild, the principal agent in financial transactions between the British and foreign governments, was soon to be elected to represent the City of London in the House of Commons. Then the traditional hostility asserted itself and bills to remove Jewish disabilities and to permit him to take his seat were defeated in the House of Lords in 1848, 1849, 1851, 1853, 1856, 1857, and 1858. In the latter year compromise was arranged and the words 'on the true faith of a Christian' omitted from the oath. Despite the liberalism of Russell and the eloquence of Bentinck and Disraeli, conventional opinion still found its voice in men like Ashley, content to declare that Jews were 'voluntary strangers here, and have no claim to become citizens but by conforming to our moral law which is the Gospel'.

The historian in Milman thought and saw further. He was not afraid to speak clearly about Christianity's record. 'To work any change on the hereditary pride of the Jew, on his inflexible confidence in his inalienable privileges,' he said, 'it must put off the hostile and repulsive aspect which it has too long worn; it must show itself as the faith of reason, of universal peace and goodwill to man, and thus unanswerably prove its descent from the All-wise and All-merciful Father'. Well aware of the fact that throughout Europe, despite the work of Napoleon, Jews still laboured under the most intolerable political and social disabilities, Milman urged that Christians must contribute to the spread of their own faith on the merit of how they behaved towards the Jews. 'The more enlightened the Jew becomes, the less credible will it appear that the Universal Father intended an exclusive religion, confined to one family among the race of men, to be permanent; the more evident that the faith which embraces the whole human race within the sphere of its benevolence is alone adapted to a more advanced and civilized age.' Against this plea there would fall the cold words, 'Do we need to adapt?'

The truth is, and this is but reflection of the lack of historical thinking that marked the Church as an institution, most Christians were out of their depth when it came to dealing with Jews. For the most part they could ignore them and the habit of doing so contributed to a disastrous blindness to the manifold changes of thought and practice gathering strength in the contemporary world. The typical attitude did not escape the sharp eyes of England's most famous Christian Jew. Disraeli's novel *Tancred* (1847) described a young English nobleman, shocked and dismayed by the inanities of the social, political and religious life around him, being persuaded to visit the Holy Land 'to penetrate the great Asian mystery'. There in a number of bizarre adventures he is confronted with the Jewish relationship with God, the continuing conversation between man and his maker. This is the land and the people to whom God still speaks.

Leslie Stephen's description of *Tancred* as 'mere mystification' summed up the average Englishman's reaction to it; the 'mere' betrayed a sense of discomfort at finding himself at a loss in this Jewish world. *Tancred* was not a great novel but it took its place among those lively and often painful books – *The Nemesis of Faith, Loss and Gain, Robert Elsmere* and *The Way of all Flesh* – which pictured some issues then facing the Church. Only Disraeli's book attributed the weaknesses of the Church to its loss of Jewishness and its part in the persecution of Jews. No other author would have dreamed of contending that it was to the Jewish people alone that God had spoken and revealed Himself or that all that was truly spiritual in human life had sprung from this people singled out by God to instruct mankind. No other author would have dared to assert so boldly that all that was best in the Christian faith derived from its Jewish source, that Jesus Himself was the greatest of all Jews. *Tancred* passed over matters of Christian theology, brushed aside dogma, and discussed very lightly how the two faiths might be related. What is of interest still is the fact that this utterly realistic politician, who so frequently showed that he understood Englishmen better than they understood themselves, should testify thus to the reality of the Jewishness of the faith.

The battle for similar understanding was to be very protracted. One other mid-Victorian example may be cited. In the years between 1857 and 1876 Arthur Stanley's lectures on ecclesiastical history appeared, the *History of the Eastern Church*, and the *History of the Jewish Church*. They aroused the same fears and opposition as had confronted Milman thirty years before. Dr Pusey wrote to say that 'the reports which I have heard of your lecture on Abraham were very distressing to me'. Stanley believed that his work on the Jewish Church would be his principal contribution towards the equipment of the Christian Church of his day to engage with the life of the modern world. Like Tancred he felt uneasily that something was missing from the resources of his own Church. Knowing what was furiously debated in religious and philosophical circles on the Continent, he was troubled that so few of his contemporaries seemed to be aware of the debate. Committing his unease to words, he wrote: 'the history of the religious thoughts and feelings of Europe cannot be understood without a full appreciation of the thoughts and feelings of that Semitic race which found their highest expression in the history of the Jewish nation'.

Stanley was not so much being 'soft' towards Judaism as 'hard' towards a Christianity which lacked something essentially Jewish. As far as Judaism was concerned his sympathies were narrow. 'The more we study the Jewish history,' he wrote, 'the more we shall feel that it is but a prelude to a vaster and loftier history, without which it would be itself unmeaning. The voice of the old dispensation is pitched in too loud a key for the ears of one small people. The place of the Jewish nation is too strait for the abode of thoughts which want wider room in which to dwell.' He went on to argue that after Apostolic times Jews had made no more contribution to the spiritual welfare of mankind.

It was politely said. The Chosen People, having executed their task of providing a prelude to a more favoured dispensation, were bowed out. Their task was done. Stanley did not despise or hate the Jews but he saw no reason for paying attention to them as the exponents of a living faith. What worried him was the thought that the Christian Church appeared to have forgotten or mistaken essential features of the prelude itself. He was well aware of the dangers to which any institution like the Church was exposed in times of rapid changes of thought, and especially so when its professional watchmen appeared to be blind to the signs of the times. He had his own limited field of historical writing, namely ecclesiastical history, isolated from the total history of man's life, and in it we read the evidence of much more widespread blindness to the growing gravity of the situation. Jewishness to him meant recognition of the task of having to serve God in all the vicissitudes of a seductive or hostile world not by withdrawal from it but in active engagement with it. Isaiah's watchman troubled his mind's eye. He saw with dismay how easily men who called themselves 'Catholic' were insensitive to whole areas of life. He realized that religion itself could die if it lost its soil in the turbulent world of men's total life. He grieved at the thought that were the Christian Church to come to an end or to devote its attention to no other objects than those which it had hitherto sought, it would do so, with its resources wasted and its hopes unfulfilled.

I have dwelt at this length on two very minor nineteenth century ecclesiastical writers of history to make clear how difficult it was to introduce Christians to an understanding of history such as Baeck later called for among his fellow Jews. The second half of the century saw a remarkable change of outlook and method among historians – many of whom were churchmen. When Creighton became Professor of Ecclesiastical History at Cambridge in 1884 he insisted that the subject be studied in the same way as any other branch of history. 'The Church and the world must be studied together in their mutual relations.' He went on to observe that 'like all intellectual disciplines history has her own laws and only by remaining true to those can she match herself with Life'.

That was well said. The outcome in scholarly history was distinguished. But looking back upon it there appears to have been something lacking in terms of what Baeck has called the history of the spirit. It was not that religion did not receive respectful and appreciative attention. The achievements of Christendom were more soundly appraised than ever before and historical inquiry gained a freedom with regard to religious matters that struck some devout Christians as entirely shocking. Nevertheless the bolder spirits prevailed and went to work with determination in all fields of Biblical, doctrinal and institutional religion. What did not appear was the kind of historical writing that von Hugel looked for and which he hoped, perhaps misguidedly, that men like Troeltsch would write. It would see the Church and its faith immersed wholly in the world and refuse any kind of ecclesiastical abstract purporting to be its history. It would equally-firmly treat its subject in terms of the Spirit, in terms of a faith in God which made it more and not less critical of the religious aspect of human life. One word characterizes its quality; watchfulness. It offers no theory of how God speaks or acts in history but it looks at the subject-matter of history convinced that He does so, and that it is our business to observe the results. It is that attitude which made this so-Catholic mind akin to that of the 'supernatural Jew'. Its business was to be wholly alert to the things which God did and men did in reply to Him. It was this spirit that was lacking in Christian Europe when the Holocaust came about. Ecclesiastical history was still too strongly entrenched.

I have mentioned earlier the Papal encyclicals and the agenda of the Second Vatican Council as expressions of a desire to reorientate the attitude of the Church to the world. Among the many difficult questions which pressed for treatment the case of the Jews was one of especial difficulty. Viewed in retrospect it involved the Concordats entered into by the Church with Mussolini and Hitler and the treatment of Jews by the Fascist and Nazi authorities. In terms of the contemporary political scene it raised difficulties with regard to Arab-Israeli relations. Pope John had expressed a new sense of concern for relations with Jews and there were many distinguished Christians who were anxious to make reparation for the anti-semitic hatred that had marred the public and private utterances of Christians for so long. There were hopes that true penitence could be expressed.

Such hopes were soon frustrated. A statement was drawn up with this purpose, but opposition came at once from those who objected on political grounds and those who, like Cardinal Ruffini, declared dislike for what was described as 'a panegyric of Judaism'. A further attempt to recommend that there should be a reciprocal esteem and knowledge between Catholics and Jews, and that the persecution of Jews in recent times should be condemned as well as deplored ran into difficulties at once. The final statement could in fact be said to represent one more triumph for ecclesiastical history in that it did little to provide an unequivocal rejection of the ancient charge of deicide made against the Jews, and still less to condemn the anti-semitic persecution that had sent millions to a horrible death. It contented itself with deploring what had happened; not even this resolution was passed without opposition.

Something more than the outlook of ecclesiastical history is called for if the Christian and Jewish faiths are to do their work for God in the world today. Of the Jew it has been said that his task is to stay with God, of the Christian that he must go out into the world to witness to and work for God's Kingdom there. Members of both faiths need to clarify their objectives and hold fast to them by sense of history which they use in interpreting their own lives and service of God in the world. All history today must be seen from the angle of world history but the difficulties to be faced in undertaking to treat it in that way are immense. We may look back to the kind of world history projected by H.G. Wells and his blue-prints of *Things to Come* as paper charred into dust by the Holocaust and its demonic context. We cannot however lose sight of the fact that the Holocaust's lesson is that without a quite different historical vision men will not behave in a radically different way. The task committed to Christians and Jews is one in which both help towards the shaping of world-history written as it were in the presence of God, a *Civitas Dei* for mankind today.

What this task entailed was outlined by John Macmurray whose book *The Clue to History* (1938) set out its terms and whose *Search for Reality in Religion* (1965) described the approach to it in autobiographical fashion. He began by asking how Christianity had acquired its idealistic and therefore unreal character, losing its essential Hebrew nature and becoming in our own day the object of Marxist attack. The question directed attention to the Hebrew understanding of history, recorded in the Old Testament writings, as the action of God in the world, summoning Israel to co-operate in doing His will. To fulfil that divine intention Jesus himself undertook his work, seeing himself as one sent to do this and enlisting others in a like commission.

The understanding of the co-operation of God and man had been arrived at and maintained in the life of Israel in the course of continual struggle. It was in the totality of the everyday working life of this people that the truths of God, set out in the Torah as obligations laid on them, were established or rejected. The religion had its priesthood and cultic rites to be scrupulously observed but it had also its prophets to lay bare the basically ethical requirements of the service of Israel's God. Righteousness alone exalted a nation. The business of law and prophets was to make clear what the God of Righteousness required of His people. The historians' task was to trace out the line of Israel's fortunes as she kept, wavered or wickedly departed from those specific demands. Progressively the insights into their moral and spiritual significance deepened, bringing men face to face with the problem of suffering involved in the service of God.

What was at stake then was the attempt to order the life of a nation continuously in obedience to God's revealed Word. It was no idle claim that no other nation knew or had known such an attempt. The ambitions of kings or priests subject to dynastic feuds or religious syncretism swayed and determined the behaviour of other peoples. Israel was constantly threatened by temptations to be like them, to adopt their gods and to let the internal life of her people take on the characteristics – violence, deceit, fraud, lechery and cruel oppression of the weak and poor – of her neighbour states. It fell to the prophets throughout the years to denounce such fallings-away and to insist that all Israel's institutions – the monarchy, the priesthood, the Temple itself – should be constantly re-aligned to the requirements of God. It was they who recognized and drove home the point that the health of this nation turned on the choice between true and false religion. True religion, true service of God, lay in the upholding of the life of the community in just and merciful treatment of man and beast.

The Hebrew people learned the nature of history as the history of the Spirit in the course of the struggle to maintain that commitment to obedience to God in terms of the life of genuine community. Defaults, disasters, defeats did not wholly deflect them from it. Engaged in the task of giving bodily expression to the requirements of the Spirit – justice, love, truth and mercy – they also saw that they must continue till the purpose of God who demanded it should be seen and honoured not only within their own nation's life but throughout the world. They themselves were a people taken up into partnership with God for the express purpose of bringing about universal acceptance of the service of God. In that instrumentality lay the destiny and glory of this people. 'In thee and in thy seed shall all the nations of the earth be blessed.'

This view of history is of necessity forward-looking. It expects to see the approaching consummation of God's purpose. It reads the signs of the times as evidence of God's hand at work. In this the Hebrew conception of history sharply differentiates itself from that of the ancient world. The end is not yet until all things acknowledge the will of Israel's God. In the meanwhile, within Israel itself, the struggle to keep the course clear goes on. It was into such an understanding of history and religion that Jesus of Nazareth came, claiming his work as the fulfilment of Law and Prophets.

The essential Hebrew message as to the meaning of history was not changed by His coming but carried to its universal dimension. In the face of the seemingly all-powerful Roman Empire, the predominance of Graeco-Roman culture, and a corrupt self-destructive régime in Judaea, Jesus brought into being the nucleus of the world-wide community that was to be. How baffling yet how compulsive His work was is clear in the Gospel record. Being utterly faithful to Israel's calling could at this point be openness towards mankind. The Samaritan, the Roman, the outcast, the despised, were there to be met as brothers. Jesus called his disciples 'friends' not servants because they were meant to understand his work and to embody it in their own flesh. They were to address themselves fearlessly to the whole world without letting go of a particle of God's truth revealed to the Hebrew people.

The Christian Church was rooted in the experience men had of God's purpose being achieved in their midst, in their being with Jesus in such a communion and fellowship that his death on the Cross could not destroy it. The Church went forward with that understanding of history to hold to and to work out. With it the members were equipped to face and withstand the hostility of all organized worldly powers intent upon withstanding the purpose of God. Indeed they were warned that it would be so and assured that only the fellowship built on the rock of His unconditional love would endure. God would not fail them in the hour of their trial.

That sense of history was lost as the Jewish element in the Christian community sank into insignificance. Accepting the status of official religion in the Roman Empire it exchanged its fellowship life for the organized structures of a religion. Very soon it expressed its despair of the world by turning to a two-standard version of Christian life, elevating the life of withdrawal from worldly affairs to be the supremely virtuous way. It transferred men's attention and hopes towards another world in the heavens and drained human history of all significance save that of securing a passport to life hereafter. With that dualist outlook the Church strove and failed to control human life. The world thus despised took revenge and steadily degraded the Church, using it when it thought fit to do so, ignoring it when it pleased. Having largely lost its Hebrew conviction of history, the Church was powerless to arrest that process. There can be no turning towards the true life of the People of God until such historical consciousness is restored. God's purpose will not be defeated. His Kingdom will come. His agents, as prophets long ago warned, will be, in default of those who still call on His name but in truth know Him not, the heathen like 'Cyrus my anointed', the nations who bring forth the fruits and not simply the words of right living.

The Holocaust is an event in this historical battle, a battle for the understanding of history itself in those Jewish terms which Moses, Elijah and Jesus himself understood it. It was an assault on the Jewish people that was meant to be final, an attempt to root out of the system of human life a people who kept alive witness to a conception of life that defied all power but God's, all relations but those of mercy and love, all intentions but those of truth. The sin of our time was that at such a moment the Christian Church was too inert, too compromized by its involvements with the powers of the world, to see and take its true part in that struggle for witness to God. What faces us now is the need to repent of such hideous blindness, to seek ways of setting about new life, to learn what these times present to us as our task. A true sense of religious history has yet to be grasped, that of God and man working out together His design for mankind. To enlist men in that design we must look beyond economic, technological, political or ecclesiastic man and find Man, child and heir of God's love. That alone is the way to lead him to God.

7. Man, His Child and Care

'I would your Grace would take me with you: Whom means your Grace?'

William Shakespeare, *King Henry IVth, Part One*

'Man has very few friends in the world, certainly in contemporary literature about him. The Lord in heaven may prove to be his last friend on earth.'

Abraham Heschel, *Who is Man?*

Where and how shall we find Man? I had almost written 'find Man again' as if to suggest that yesterday surely men knew the answers, that ours is simply a temporary loss. Yet looking no further than to poetry it is plain that this was not so. Perhaps we still shy off meeting Him who thus comes to meet us there. It is easier, as those scrupulous executants of the Holocaust knew, to dispense with names and to burn numbers. So the question is better addressed to ourselves. Why do we conceal, disguise, play parts and mistake ourselves and others? It is a theme to which the profoundest drama since the earliest days of classical Greek theatre has constantly returned, and one which therefore we may expect to find in English drama too. Here is an example from elsewhere.

Marx was engaged with the time-honoured question What is Man? or more narrowly with what had happened to man in a certain historical phase. Marx reduced the field of his observation to the society of his time, and society itself to the conditions of the production of manufactured goods. The picture he saw and drew was thus narrowly selective but too accurately documented to be shrugged off. Describing the society about him he spoke in very precise prosaic terms. 'In exchange value, the social relations of individuals have become transformed into the social connections of material things; personal power has changed into material power.' He saw men therefore beholden to things to exist at all. He spoke of them as thus alienated from their own handiwork and even enslaved by it, entangled in a social network constituted by the tension between supply and demand, estranged from Nature, their fellows and themselves. As a humanist he found a word to make his point 'We have shown,' he wrote, 'that the worker sinks to the level of a commodity, and to a most miserable commodity'.

Commodities have a fluctuating value in the markets of the world. A society that could produce and burn commodities like coffee and wheat would not be deterred from burning men who ranked low in the scale of values. An opprobrious label, a star or a yellow spot, would be enough to secure their destruction. A world that, in Nietzsche's words, 'had killed God', would hardly hesitate to murder men. Men who found Man offensive were not likely to be restrained from self-destruction.

There is then a certain logic about the Holocaust as there is about the Gulag Archipelago. Unwanted commodities, unfashionable models, brands out of favour, go for scrap and in efficient economies are re-cycled to provide materials as well as room for their successors. Marx did not believe that mankind could be treated thus. The whole motivating force of his lifework was a passionate protest against it. His picture of man as a commodity, like that of Jeremiah's pots, served as an illustration of a searing vision. His aim was to challenge the contemporary practice of mankind which reduced human beings to the condition of a 'thing'. How to expose the nature of that practice in theoretical terms was the task to which he devoted his life.

In that he was, as has often been pointed out, very like a Jewish prophet, not least in that the bitterest of his attacks were upon his own people. No man more violently vilified Judaism as a religion of money. 'What is the worldly cult of the Jew? Bargaining. What is his worldly god? Money. Very well. Emancipation from bargaining and money, and thus from practical real Judaism would be the self-emancipation of our era.' This aspect of Judaism had gained 'universal dominion' and capitalism was its name.

Marx was however a prophet inverted, in that, devoting his whole attention to the cult of the money-god, he stayed within the circle of it all his working life. His enormous energy and industry were consumed in studying the features of the very god he loathed and the reification of man which he detested. He did not look beyond the fearful reduction of things human and divine so absorbed was he in the work, as he believed, of changing it. He was a man who elected to stay in Hell in order to overthrow it. His analyses and critiques, the theory of historical materialism itself, were painstaking observations of what he found there, the operative forces of its demonic powers. What he could not foresee was that his observations would captivate the minds of his students to the extent of turning his great negative vision into their positive programme of action. Marx had believed that the great negative which had become the god of the world would itself be negated, that mankind would be freed by acting upon the truth it had at last learned to see in its own handiwork. He did not suppose that men using his name would be tempted to turn the negation down.

Hence he did not continue to reflect upon the nature of man or religion. Marxist thinking until recent times has done little to carry this reflection further. Defection from such an arrested Marxism has therefore become a tribute to Marx, though it is not often accepted as such by the orthodox scribes. Marx had nonetheless achieved one hugely important thing. He had insisted upon the lostness of men and pointed out where they were to be found. It was a discovery made in very Hebraic terms. He went straight to men at work, to men employing others and being employed, to men making and selling goods. Hebrew religion gave primary place to both God and man at work. Jesus too had emphasized this side of men's lives, so that Marx, despite his much quoted words about the opiate religion, was on the same track of thought when he turned to examine men and their work.

There Marx stopped, and spent the rest of his life describing the basic economic relations into which men entered in doing their work. He endeavoured to do this in cool scientific fashion, to

observe and dissect, to trace and account for their features. It is
clear nonetheless that he knew very well that men and women
were more than workers. How much more, he was either compelled or chose for his work's sake to leave unsaid. He was too
involved in trying to show what had overtaken the workers to
have time to investigate who and what manner of men they were.
He found them being organized by an industrial process geared to
producing and selling goods, a process in which the machine
determined the way men should work and in which financial profit
determined its use.

The relations of men and women thus set to work were func-
tional and impersonal, designed to exclude whatever did not contribute directly and narrowly to the job. It was a picture of human
life quite insufficient to answer the question What is Man or to do
any justice to this 'pleasing anxious being', but it showed how the
question was being dealt with in practice. While 'Cotton was King'
men and women were his slaves – the psalmist's description of
God-given glory was wholly beside the point. Marx savagely
documented what the point was – that whatever men might be in
themselves or to God, in the working relations of economic life
they were hands at the looms, pens in the counting-house, genitals
in the stud farms breeding slaves to sell in the states of the American Deep South.

Inadequate as the real answer, his thought represented an insight
that was needed, and as such it has passed into the programmes,
the creeds, the theologies and the manifestoes of millions around
the world. It was heard because it pointed to things left unsaid by
the teachers of other faiths. There were in his words warnings that
oppression would become more heavy, there were facts which
passion could use to bring about hungered-for changes, there were
explanations throwing light on things from which the respectable
world averted its eyes. He produced an indictment of Church and
State which the common man had secreted in his bones. He
sounded a trumpet-call to those disillusioned with the life into
which they were born. Marx himself voiced 'the protest of man
against dehumanized life'.

Other voices joined in. The great nineteenth century novelists,

Stendhal and Balzac, Tolstoy and Dostoievsky, Dickens and George Eliot, looked more closely at Man and 'told me all the things that ever I did'. The great social reformers went to work with their inquiries and schemes. A new philosophical form of questioning came from Kierkegaard, Schopenhauer and Nietzsche to begin a new phase of self-understanding. Very soon the unconscious would be recognized as a terrain to be explored, and Freud would begin his investigations! More slowly than any of these, theologians stirred, often scared and reluctant to do so yet compelled by the thought of the changed world. Some indeed have rejoiced in the chance to do so and both as Christians and Jews contributed much to new vision of Man. As the faiths of the non-European world have become better known the range of inquiry has widened.

The questioning proved to be disturbing. Had both the Christian and Jewish faiths lost their way? While speaking of God with much learning had they failed to understand Man? Increasingly it appeared that the scenes of conflict in the Gospels and the comments of Jesus on 'blind guides' were relevant to the contemporary world. Thought processes in that world threw beams of unexpected light on men's beliefs and codes. Did religious teachers really know what was happening to men and women as the world shrank to a global village, as telecommunication invaded all places, as computerized technology took over more and more of decision in human affairs?

I have tried to stay with the event of Auschwitz in mind because I believe it must be allowed to prise open the ideological structures into which what should be a living faith has been allowed to harden. It is not by new ideas of God that our manner of life is going to be changed so much as by learning to look afresh on Him, the Man, whom we have pierced, rejected and slain. What God is in Himself we cannot know. What His relationship with mankind may be is the heart of Jewish and Christian faith. It is with that relationship we must start if we are to become responsible people at the level that the Holocaust demands. That means searching out the man whom God made in his image and for whom

Christ died. We cannot conceivably attach more importance to man than God has already done.

'We must find man again' becomes therefore the search for our fellows in the tower-blocks and the shanties, in the owner-occupier estates, inner-city streets, in villages and ghettoes. We must seek man and woman in relationships – marriage and love – in the fears of the sick and the guilty, in the meanings and losses of meaning that overtake and dismay. Auschwitz is not to be separated from the total condition of men's lives in the world today. It is to be seen much more as a fearful despairing rejection of what it means to be human, the frenzied attempt of dehumanized men to destroy rational thought and human relations. It was supremely a gesture of self-loathing. It expressed contempt for all and everything that man is or does.

With that in mind I turn first to a Jewish teacher, Abraham Heschel, who thinks in terms of Biblical man though he stands on New World soil. Human consciousness is formed 'like the bones in the womb of her that is with child' by man's relation to God (*Who Is Man?*). God seeks him out, puts questions to him, makes unqualified claims upon him. The Bible itself is a record of that divine initiative. Human dignity lies in thus being sought out by God as a personal act. Man is always 'not yet' what God would have him to be. The Biblical story of Adam declares that men can and do resist the calling that God has designed for them to work out, but the story did not stop there. God did not write off rebellious mankind but sought him with unwearying love. Rabbi Akiba once declared: 'Beloved is man, in that he was created in the image of God, but it was a special act of love that made it known to him that he was created in the image of God.' Hebrew religion is founded upon this revelation. God comes to and deals with men, reveals and makes himself known as a man would do with his friend, and as heart can speak to heart. He does not possess or use the prophet in an impersonal way, but rather kindles the spark within him, stimulates the whole soul to action, enables the man to speak for God.

Heschel speaks of the Bible not as man's theology but as God's anthropology, 'not man's vision of God but God's vision of man'.

Setting aside philosophical views of the nature of man he concen-
trates his attention upon prophetical utterance. This points to a
special relationship, at once as immediate and as dangerous as a
meeting with God on Sinai's slopes. What he has to say of Man
is in terms of living in a world in which men are accountable in
specific ways to God. 'The God of the prophets is a God of
temporal involvement' encountered in the history of this people,
and though the Bible preserves the record of Israel's prophets like
the vast alignments of the megalithic age, the true goal of Israel's
calling is that all the Lord's people should be prophets. One could
not say more of human responsibility.

Understandably then Heschel writes of Man in the tone of the
Song of Songs, and of reciprocal love as the key to the understanding
of the nature of man. All things flow from the fact of God's love
for man. Human life is the handling of sacred things and right
human relationships are those appreciative of this fact. Heschel
answers the question Who is Man? in a book of that title by
replying: 'a being in travail with God's dreams and designs, with
God's dream of a world redeemed, of reconciliation of heaven and
earth, of a mankind which is truly His image, reflecting His wisdom, justice and compassion'. Heschel has no doubts about the
importance of the sciences in enriching Man's knowledge of him
self, nor does he ignore the problematic aspects of human life and
the reality of suffering and frustration. He is equally concerned to
acknowledge the part which the concrete situations of man's world
plays in the working out of human responsibility. 'New in this age
is an unparalleled awareness of the terrifying seriousness of the
human situation.' Auschwitz and Hiroshima have defined certain
features of what it means to be human today and have heaped
heavier burdens on the spirit of Man in search of the meaning of
his existence, but they have not fundamentally altered the business
of living.

Yet it has been objected that Heschel's lyrical description of Man
as the loved creature of God, for whom He schemes and yearns
and suffers, has little to say to men who simply do not think in
those terms, who are bored by rhapsodies, perplexed by evil,
dissatisfied by theodicies. In much of his writing about Man's

nature Heschel ignores these feelings. Happy indeed the man who
loves and believes himself to be loved, but the shadows of turning
lie thick across human paths. What shall a man do when God, man
or woman delight him no longer or when meaning itself has seeped
out of life?

The problem has been faced by those Jewish thinkers who have
felt imperilled by the threat of a closed religious system; they have
insisted upon an existential Jewish theology sensitive to the pressures of the historical situation in which a man finds himself. Only
thus can the meaning of love be grasped. Man's condition in the
world is at all times subject to challenge. He must declare himself
as man to man, as man to woman, as parent to child, as child to
parent. He must from day to day work out afresh what it means
to be human. It was this way of thinking that caused Buber to
question what he observed in Israel in both religious and political
spheres. 'If a religion is to stay fresh,' he said, 'the only way for
it is to change itself constantly -- to renew itself in each generation,
from the inside.' Men must press on to discover what new levels
of meaning are waiting to be disclosed, what new obligations have
to be faced, what new ventures of faith to be made.

Heschel was not unaware of these demands. In his book *A
Passion for Truth* he examined them in the attitudes and life-work
of Kierkegaard and Rabbi Mendl of Kotzk. Both men saw with
sharp eyes how fatally religion could get locked in the past, both
fearlessly demanded that it be open to the future, to the as yet
unspoken word of God. Both sought to goad men to move out
from their spiritual entrenchments, and as such were disturbers of
Israel in the eyes of many. 'The Kotzker would call upon us to be
uneasy about our situation, to feel ashamed of our peace of mind,
of our spiritual stagnation. One's integrity must be constantly
examined. In his view, self-assurance, a certainty of one's honesty,
was as objectionable as brazen dishonesty. A moderately clean
heart was like a moderately foul egg.' What mattered most was
the stripping off of those things, whether present cultural attach-
ments or deepseated mythological conceptions, which hindered
the soul from waiting expectant upon God.

Both the Kotzker and Kierkegaard were deeply aware of the

disturbing demand made upon men's religious life by this summons to move. The Exodus was no incident of past history, nor
was Abraham's call an interesting event in the life of a nomadic
people. Both were moments of divine intervention, announcing a
new phase of life 'to the Jew first, but also to the Gentile' (Rom.
2.10); both were part of a chain reaction to be followed through
in the history of mankind demanding that in each generation men
be awakened to the need to forego the spiritual comfort so easily
provided by religion and to prepare themselves for the next stages
of their long march. Heschel himself spoke of it abruptly: 'Self-
satisfaction is the opiate of fools. Self-fulfilment is a myth which
the noble mind must find degrading. All that is creative in man
stems from a seed of endless discontent. New insight begins when
satisfaction comes to an end, when all that has been said, seen or
done looks like a distortion.'

Yet if self-satisfaction was thus summarily rejected it was equally
true that the Jew looked for joy, for the kind of delight that living
creatures could take from battling with wind and storm, from the
dangerous freedom that this escape from conformism and dogma
afforded. He looked for it in the most personal sense from direct
encounter with God himself. In the course of lectures given at the
Hebrew University of Jerusalem in 1938 under the title of *What is
Man?*, Martin Buber began by looking at the world situation at
the time. It could not have been a more forbidding, more unlikely
setting for the reception of spiritual truths. Judaism's understanding of Man made the Divine image, Man called into partnership
with God the Creator, Man the participant in God's revelation,
Man called to be holy as God is holy, all these things were implicit
in all he said, but he chose to begin with the contemporary scene.
It was not topicality that dictated the choice so much as a firm
grasp of how Judaism must see its relations with God, its point of
departure at any time. 'A new anthropological dread has arisen,'
he said 'the question about man's being faces us as never before in
all its grandeur and terror, no longer in philosophical attire, but in
the nakedness of existence.' Dachau had been set up in February,
1933, Oranienberg in March, and the Nuremberg Laws which
completed the disenfranchisement of Germany's Jews had been

adopted in 1935. The 'Crystal Night' came in November 1938, the
prelude to the horror to be released. In that year too the Nazis
silenced Buber.

How was it possible then to identify Man in such conditions as
these? Hitherto the inquirer had sought Man in the city, in the
temple, in the institutions of law or family life, in the conceptual
structures he had raised. Now two things called for immediate
notice: the first was the obvious shattering of the older organic
forms of community life which had, notwithstanding their often
crude standards, sheltered and nurtured men's lives: the second,
the manifest inability of men to master the world they had brought
into being, a weakness of human imagination and spiritual nerve,
which made them unable to cope with the problems created by
the powerful technological and poltical forces they had called into
being. 'Man faced the terrible fact that he was the father of demons
whose master he could not become.' The traditional integrative
forces of Europe's civilization had steadily lost power to contain
and control the demands of individuals and groups. Mere continuance of custom would avail very little to check or direct the new
movements at work. The resources expressed in terms of man-
power, horse-power and the powers of money and explosives were
about to dictate the shaping of human affairs and to enforce a
compliance of will in the absence of other factors. 'What else could
we do?' The words of King George V at the beginning of the
Great War typified a whole era.

In *The Eclipse of God*, Buber chose to turn for his text to the
work of Husserl; three sentences in which he saw the condition of
Man expressed in relevant imagery. In the first of these it was the
historical role of Israel that provided the illustration; 'wrestling
Jacob', the endless struggle of Man for self-understanding. Significantly, at that very time the theme was gaining a quite new
expression in Thomas Mann's novel *Joseph and his Brothers*. The
novelist reflected the mood of the time. 'Disquiet, questioning,
hearkening and seeking, wrestling for God, a bitterly sceptical
labouring over the true and the just, the whence and the whither,
his own name, his own nature, the true meaning of the Highest
– how all that, bequeathed down the generations from the man

from Ur, found expression in Jacob's look, in his lofty brow and the caring, care-worn gaze of his brown eyes. Unrest and dignity, that is the sign of the Spirit.' The Hebrew had turned the question from thoughts about God's nature to questions as to what He required. He did not doubt in the least that God did require things which must stretch the soul of Man to breaking point if he was to comply, but was that not what stamped human life with its title? Israel's God was not indifferent to Man. He had an appointment with him and Man must not fail to keep it. That kind of fear was the beginning of wisdom.

Did Man therefore know what God required of him? Israel's history had supplied an answer. It both did and did not, for what it knew was always the earnest of greater requirements to come. In that lay the nature of Man; he was called to go on from what was required in the past to that which awaited his service tomorrow. So in the second and third sentences Buber selected the human condition was given a more detailed picture. Its distinction lay in a quite personal sense of responsibility; a response to being addressed as a single person. Not the tribe, the nation, the crowd, but the person was the man God spoke to, not yesterday but today. So Israel's story, paradigm of all human life, was that of being sought out by the Divine Lover, confirmed in its being by the solicitude of God; this was the truth of Israel's history.

This basic responsibility for the individual soul was a challenge to commitment without which a man must be overtaken by boredom or loss of meaning. To the Jew the challenge stemmed directly from God. It established communion between mankind and its maker. 'We have seen this day that God doth talk with man and he liveth' (Deut. 5.24). This day could become this moment and response to it could be no other but celebration of the shared speech. Thus it carried into everyday life a full sense of human community, 'born not of the will of man, but of God,' since God was no respecter of persons but the God of all flesh. Man, named and known by the act of God, could be himself only so far as he recognized this and made it the pattern of human relationships for himself. Men shrink from such universalism, erecting their barriers to defend, as they judge, the values they prize. Neither Jews nor

Christians have found it easy to live in that way. Torah was for the Jew a sustaining of life towards that end, not an end in itself. In Christendom men like St Francis and Tolstoy did all that they could to honour its demand.

So when it came to summing up the nature of Man, Buber chose to express it not in attributes but in action, in a two-fold movement of persons with persons, without distinction. In *The Knowledge of Man* he called the first movement 'setting at a distance', allowing the other to be freely himself with space to grow up in. The second he described as 'drawing into relation', the coaxing or nurturing by which true shared iife is fashioned. With the materials and opportunities given by the natural endowments and cultural equipment of their circumstances men and women had to learn how best to provide for each other in marital, parental and the wider relationships of social life both freedom and the resources to be themselves. It was no man's business to stamp on his children, his wife, his fellows the image of himself, he should help and let himself be helped to forward the embodiment of the image of God in mankind.

The date, I repeat, was 1938. Few men could have been more conscious than Buber that what he was speaking of was not speculation remote from the critical scene of human affairs but an urgent immediate matter on which men with murderous intent were at work, a matter which affected the whole of human society. German streets, homes, schools, universities, churches, had been invaded by secret police, stormtroopers and experts in ideological warfare. Men surrendered their souls and demanded the surrender of others to the will of one man. Every day that intention was furthered with brutal and pitiless logic. Man was to be shaped in the National-Socialist image. Who could withstand such a purpose?

Buber saw it not as a sudden aberration in German life but as something prepared for and closely related to the question What is Man? which had held German minds so strongly. He objected that Heidegger's picture of Man was that of cold solitude in which 'apparently nothing more remains now to the solitary man but to seek an intimate communication with himself'. Man could but posture before a mirror to enlighten himself about his being. To the Jew who forever belongs to the children of Israel and to the God who surnamed him such a vision was simply 'an unblessed game of the spirit'. Buber sadly remarked that it sought to derive the essence of human existence from nightmare experience. His judgment was soon to be confirmed in the German extermination plan, Operation Night and Fog.

In his lectures a few years later, he returned to Heidegger's view of Man. He spoke of it as 'insurmountably empty', and urged that not that way could men come to right understanding of themselves. The mirror could offer no comment on meaning. 'The world is not presented to men', he said in *I and Thou*, 'by experiences alone'. Experiences belonged to and remained part of the world of objects whereas for the living man what mattered was the personal relationship, the relationship he called I-Thou. 'When Thou is spoken, the speaker has no thing; he has indeed nothing. But he takes his stand in relation.' The nature of Man was not to be grasped apart from the totality of the creation in which God had set Man apart from Himself but sought that He might draw him into a personal relation. The foundation of human life was this initiative of God. It could be described no otherwise but in terms of an unfailing divine solicitude – 'Where art thou?' addressed to man (*The Eclipse of God*). In Heidegger's world, said Buber, 'there is no such Thou, no true Thou spoken from being to being, spoken with one's own being'.

At first sight Buber himself stands apart from philosophers and theologians reflecting on Man, and is no less sharply divided from Israel's religious and political leaders. This prophet of human solidarity was treated with much indifference and even hostility by his own people. His theology was suspect to many, his political attitudes were often in sharp contradiction to those of the Zionist leaders. He rejected a good deal of customary religious practice and spoke roughly of mystical forms of religion, of visions of God's throne, of Kabbalistic speculations, of Messianic dreams, all of which he regarded as the byeways of the true life of the Spirit. He rejoiced, on the other hand, in whatever in Israel's long history had brought men into immediate intimate awareness of the presence of God in the day-to-day world, 'the world that is house and home'. Living was always the test of the worth of the doctrine. 'Judaism is sterile unless it tells us how to act.' Orthopraxis not orthodoxy was his concern. 'If we try to listen to its real voice, it can give us what we have lost: the link between our everyday lives and the absolute.'

To that link he always returned. Like the singer of his best-loved Psalm 73, he was often appalled by the sight of the triumph of evil men in the world. He clung to the faith of the Psalmist and faced men with compassion and courage. There are few more moving examples of that spirit than his speech to Germans when he returned to that country after the war. He could not be indifferent to any man's spiritual needs. 'Meeting with God does not come to a man', he wrote, 'in order that he may concern himself with God, but in order that he may confirm that there is meaning in the world. All revelation is summons and sending.' Man would come to his meaning-in-life by going where he was sent, by ungrudgingly accepting the privations it imposed, by foregoing the relations he now cherished in the faith that he would receive them again.

It was in virtue of this independence that he could speak both to Jews and Christians. Free to rediscover the fundamental Hebraic insights into Man, he could take his stand over against the impoverishment of spirit which both in interwar Europe and in Zionist Israel could lead men to feed on the fantasies of nationalism and racialism. A cult of racial purity, a *volkische* campaign to secure a people's identity, whether in Nuremberg or Jerusalem, offered nothing but prospects of disaster. It was not the true answer to the rootless individualism nor to the collectivities of the contemporary world, but a falling once more into an ancient trap. 'He who speaks the separated I, with emphasis on the capital, lays bare the shame of the world-spirit which has been degraded to spirituality.' It was but the newest enterprise to make gods to go before men and to brew the credulity to make them acceptable. Such a cult could produce nothing, it was a conjuring trick with religion and politics and art. Heidegger, in Buber's view, was not unaware of this and had therefore spoken of an age at hand in which a Coming One might once again initiate conversation between God and man.

Recalling it in the post-Holocaust years, Buber commented that such expectation had been seduced into hailing the advent of 'the most sinister leading personality of the then current history'.

Buber's own contribution to the finding of Man was made in the book *I and Thou*, and in a lifetime's exposition of it. Expressed in words that claim the attention of prolonged meditation, it tends towards the wordless kind of profound communication which obtains between human beings at rare moments in life. One hears the unspoken. It amplifies the relationship it quickens. The heart speaks and claims in so doing the heart's attention. It starts from and remains engrounded in that which is open to all, the God-given relationship of all human beings. It is lodged in the heart and needs to be sought there. It is all too much and too often asleep or imprisoned, its jailer most evil things. Yet this is the truth of human life. 'I possess nothing but the everyday out of which I am never taken. I know no fulness but each mortal hour's fulness of claim and responsibility.'

This 'everyday' is at once the conversation of man and wife, of parent and child, of friend and friend, together with three thousand years of the conversation between God and Man which Israel knew, which the Gospels overhear in the words of Jesus Christ. All that is truly human is caught from or awakened by that conversation, by learning from it to listen to speech beyond speech. 'It happens as speech, and not as speech rushing out over his head but as speech directed precisely at him.' The man whom Kierkegaard called 'the serious one' is the man attentive to it – Like a child who watches the face of his mother and learns from it to communicate with her, so man stands before God. All true education has but one proper purpose, to awaken men to attend to the mention of that which is common to all, to attend not as subjects who listen to proclamations but as members of one another who rejoice in that which they share.

To this common-to-all foundation Buber gave particular attention. In the individualistic society of the modern world the meaning of 'I' could be wholly misused and mistaken. All that was Hebraic in him rose up to reject the idea of the isolated individual self, the negation of the truly human. No less emphatically did he repudiate the search for more 'authentic' experience of human existence through the use of drugs or practices which heighten the consciousness of self. He resisted the flight out of self-hood and away from the conditions of social life and situation-claims. Engrossing and brilliant that way might be but it turned aside from the Exodus journey assigned to Man.

Buber grasped moreover the Biblical truth that Man must take words with him. Well aware that the man-made Night blurred words that they might become simply the instruments of the anti-humane degradation of men and women, he struggled to uphold the recognition of the sanctity of the word. In a world already far gone in the ruthless reduction of words to slogans or badges or drugs to provide sensations, he spoke for the integrity of words. The Word was no one's possession though men took it upon their lips. It partook of creative power and made possible speech between man and God and man and man just as the polarity of sex made possible the love between men and women. It needed an infinite space to dwell in and awe on the part of those who invoked it. Without these the Word could not kindle the relation 'We' embraced by its utterance, could not grow incandescent with the flames of Pentecost, could not contain a personal response to the Word of God.

Buber sought to affirm the true nature of human life by using what he called the two primary words descriptive of human relations, the 'I-Thou' and 'I-It'. He used them to clarify his own personal attempt to shape his life and also to describe the unique character of Israel's calling. 'I-Thou' does not disparage, deplore or minimize the significance of 'I-It'. To it belongs the charting of the relations of the objective world and the sciences that observe them. It was nevertheless to the dialogue of 'I-Thou' that he ascribed supreme importance. Man was the being addressed by God. His true life lay in the communion thus offered to him. He was the child of the Living Word. 'God does not want to be believed in, to be debated and defended by us, but simply to be realized through us.' That realization takes flesh through all the relations into which men enter in daily living when these are made open to God. 'Every particular Thou is a glimpse through to the eternal Thou; by means of every particular Thou the primary word addresses the eternal Thou' (*I and Thou*, p.75).

To speak in this way is to draw a map of human life as well as to set down in modern terms what Buber believed to have been the essence of Israel's vocation in history, a way of living so frequently lost to sight, so nearly abandoned, so often derided as leading nowhere. It was a hard way to follow, to be pursued on a narrow ridge, on the far side of the subjective, on this side of the objective, the realm of the 'between'. It lay waiting to be perceived as the land of authentic human life, as bold as that line of true portraiture which does not exist in nature but must be created by him who draws, as infinite in its possibilities of splendour as God himself. In that lay the mystery of Man's being. God did not invade the personal life of His creature. He chose rather to come as a guest, addressing the man as Thou. Man did not presume on his creatureliness but rather embraced it by exchanging the Thou with his maker. Out of that meeting or betweenness there came into being the genuine We, the We who are called to stand before God. 'Leaping fire', Buber wrote, 'is indeed the right image for the dynamic between persons in We.'

In such terms was Man's historical existence defined. The God of Israel required not any abdication of Man's humanity nor any effacement of separateness, but a greater, more difficult thing. It required him to make his way on that narrow ridge with such trust as only a personal relationship could envisage. The very separateness which it entailed carried with it the threat of a sense of forsakenness which could, as the Passion story of Christ insists, sound out the depths of spiritual agony. Who could keep his way without falling on such a dread path? The Hebrew scriptures were never more relevant to man's needs than in this: 'Nevertheless, I am continually with thee; thou hast holden me by my right hand.'

It was to the recognition of the precise task facing modern man that Buber sought to contribute in thus picturing man's nature and man's condition. He was well aware of the many competing views offered to men in the inter-war years. He contended firmly that neither collective man nor individual man could satisfy the innate desires and needs of the creature whom God had made. The 'creative freedom' of Sartre he rejected as being no more than a demagogic phrase, empty of real significance because it lacked roots in the more fundamental relationships which underpinned human life. He retained a severely critical view of the ordering of Israel's life in the Zionist state. The times were too deeply demanding to be dealt with in any but the most fundamental terms. Man's condition in the world was that of a displaced person, homeless and rootless and lacking in vision. For the sake of gaining power over things and of men as things, Man had come very near to bartering his birthright away. 'That peoples can no longer carry on authentic dialogue with one another is not only the most acute symptom of the pathology of our time, it is also that which most urgently makes a demand of us.' Buber did not doubt that the way to renewal of dialogue and the chance to carry it to as yet unguessed at richness of communion lay open to mankind. The great act of faith would need to be made. Men and women must venture to speak the truth in love, to speak it to fellowmen in hope, to speak it to God in trustful prayer.

8. Praying

'The loss of prayer would mean the loss of the person.'
        Maurice Nédoncelle, *The Nature and Use of Prayer*
'Prayer is the most essential of all human activities.'
                        Iris Murdoch, *Henry and Cato*

'Two men went up to the Temple to pray' (Luke18.10). The
parable is capable of infinite variation, whether men pray by twos
or by thousands, whether they pray in temples, synagogues,
churches, meeting-houses, homes or solitary places. If, in going
through vales of misery, men have learned to find in them pools
of sustaining water, if now with the dust of Auschwitz in our
mouths, and in our ears the sound of *The Waste Land*, 'voices
singing out of empty cisterns and exhausted wells' we experience
overwhelming need to do so again, it is to the recreation of our
praying that we must deliberately turn.

Both Christian and Jewish faiths stand in need of such a
regrounding in prayer. Both need to recover a deep sense of knowing before whom they stand. Both need to learn to pray for each
other as never before. Both must learn anew what it is that God
requires of them now. Their practice of prayer must be re-exam-
ined in the light of the events of our time and in terms of what
they begin to see of their tasks ahead. Each has much to learn from
the other.

To say this is not to lose sight for a moment of the great richness
of both traditions of prayer. No one could consider without sense
of awe the immensity of Israel's treasury of devotion, its liturgical
forms which express the Covenant between God and his people,

the Psalms and hymns that have never ceased to flow from Israel's life, the mystical movements of Hasidism and Kabbalism which give rise to literature as profound as it is boundless. 'To pray means to expose oneself to Him, to His judgment', and Israel has not failed to keep that appointment with Him.

Of Christian liturgical practice too we may make the same claim and marvel still further as we turn to the infinite diversity of the praying of saints and teachers; Augustine, Bernard, Francis, Ignatius, de Caussade and countless others. Yet men still stand in need of being taught to pray, need to be helped to understand what praying is, admit to the need for guidance to find in prayer a sure foundation for life.

The practice of Christian devotion has owed much to its Jewish springs. It found no better pattern for its liturgical prayer than Israel's recalling of participation in the life of a covenanted Body, of God's great saving acts, release from bondage, feeding of the flock, forgiving of their sins, directing of their hopes towards the Day of His Coming. It found no better means of sustaining and training the spiritual life than by using the Jewish scriptures, especially the Psalms, and adding to them its own distillation from Biblical sources in Canticles of its own. It took over Hosannas, Hallelujahs, Glorias to give voices to ecstasy in prayer. From the deepest of all its wells it drew the Lord's Prayer. Its use of Amen gave a firm foundation to words and silence alike.

How multiform and profound that legacy has been is to be seen in hymns and songs and poems within and outside church life or denominational uses. An extraordinary marriage of Jewish inspiration with felicitous English prose, to take but one example, begot in the sixteenth century a style of making melody to the Lord in words that continued to echo through the work of novelists and poets long after many of them had turned away from the Church. Hardy's poetry is inconceivable apart from the Psalmody of the Book of Common Prayer, an authentic continuation of the ironical and passionate questioning of Israel's God which down the ages has found its way into the prayer books of the Jews.

Yet having said this and acknowledged our debt to the legion of scholars of both faiths who have made known the wealth of

forms of prayer coming down to us from the past, we have now
to face what is required of us today. Has the learning process come
to an end or has it come to a specially critical time? Dare we say
that as Christians we have no more to learn from the Jews?

We live in a post-Auschwitz world. What demands does that
make on our praying? I have listened to Rabbi Gryn describe what
going with his father, mother and brother to Auschwitz was like,
how the millions died and the few survived, how he kept Yom
Kippur in his prison camp, how feeling he was already dead as a
human being he nonetheless prayed the liturgical prayers of his
people and asked for forgiveness, crying his whole soul out and
learning that God was also crying. Bearing in mind that at this
moment millions of men drag out their lives in similar misery,
how dare I do other than try to pray as he did? Auschwitz, said
Rabbi Gryn, is about Man and his idols. It is about abominable
things set up in place of God. This brilliant powerful, clever,
sophisticated world of ours stands so nearly in the grasp of inconceivable Evil and time is so short that no other talk can compare
in urgency with this. In a quite special sense the ancient Biblical
choice of Life against Death is ours today. We make the choice
only by learning to pray, by turning to God.

How urgent do we feel this to be? How truly committed to it
are we? How adequate is the response we are making? There are
in existence now a great many groups of people and representative
bodies set up by the churches to pray and speak together, to learn
to talk together as Christians and Jews have never yet done since
the parting of the ways. Many attempts are being made to sustain
an interfaith dialogue. All this is great gain, yet the matter is not
being set in the forefront of the day-to-day life of the Christian
Church. It is not spoken of as the most urgent task laid on the
Church today.

This means that as far as the praying of the Church is concerned
Auschwitz was not a 'crisis' at all. In attending my parish church
I do not hear my attention drawn to the fact of Auschwitz week
after week so that along with my fellow-Christians I am compelled
to think and pray about it. The fate of the Jewish people in modern
Europe is not connected with the crucified Jew who appears in the

stained-glass window above the altar. Newspapers tell me and those around me that Jews are a political nuisance in today's world. History tells me that they have through the ages been an ethical nuisance too. But how then are they to be prayed for? The problem of human suffering is never far from the hearts and minds of the congregation but no one speaks of the significance of the suffering of His people or suggests that something must be done about it. The reality of Israel's vocation to suffering, if one may dare to speak of it in that way, is accorded not the silence of awe but of disregard. It interrupts no habitual practice, challenges no custom, wounds no conscience. No one cries out 'Give your whole attention to this.' There is no one day in the Church's year when Christians feel obliged to come together to weep for our sins against the Jews. There is no feeling abroad that they should ask God to batter their hearts and make them new, or even invite the Jews to spit in the face of those who have thus put Him to shame once more. There is no fear that in our forgetfulness we outrage Him and His people while continuing to talk of love. 'This people honoureth Me with their lips but their heart is far from Me' (Mark 7.6).

True religion is about the reality of Man's life. True prayer is the celebration of it. It is not within human power to answer why all things are so, why suffering goes on at all levels of life, but it is in man's power to pray in the face of unanswerable things. In *The Essence of Judaism* Leo Baeck quotes from the Talmud 'Man must bless God in his affliction as well as in his joy,' even while he labours to bring suffering to an end wherever he finds it.

Great calamity is great opportunity. Auschwitz is perhaps for the churches in Europe their last chance to learn to pray responsibly for mankind. Its very occurrence reveals the extent of the poverty and blindness of their spiritual life hitherto. The gas ovens that burned human bodies could be, under God, redemptive did they also burn up the fantasies and false dreams of the world we have known. But it depends upon whether we see the task as a 'burning question' for ourselves too or whether we wait for the ashes, the ashes of death, to settle upon us.

'At this the Resurrected One turned His back on the speaker
and spoke out clearly yet with anguish. 'This cannot be true.
If I fail in this I fail in all else besides".'

(L. van der Post, *The Seed and the Sower*)

We shall not learn how to pray rightly about this calamity unless
we sit down in silence first and prepare to pray. The Hasidic
Rabbis were emphatic on that. There is a short story told of the
Rabbi of Kotzk. 'One day the Kotzker asked his Hasidim, "What
does praying in earnest mean?" They did not understand him. He
continued, "Is there anything that should not be done in earnest?".'
It was a remark in keeping with all that the Kotzker stood for with
regard to human life, in the audacity of his questioning and his
unwearied search for truth. It is also Judaism at its best. It is the
spirit of the great prophets old and new, of Isaiah and Amos and
Jeremiah, of Marx and Freud and Baeck, for it keeps before us the
dialectic of both Jewish prayer and Jewish thinking, the refusal to
try to avoid the polarities of human life, the anguish of living no
less than its delight.

I cite the Kotzker as but one example of the Hasidic teachers
whose work transformed the life of Jewry during the eighteenth
century in Eastern Europe, and which through the *Tales of the
Hasidim* has enriched man's knowledge of prayer today. Their
world has vanished but what has survived is the detailed record of
a movement among a despised and rejected people which brought
God in the most straightforward fashion into the entire fabric of
everyday life with wit and imagination and zest. It took hold of
the traditional practice of study and contemplation of rabbinic life
and brought them into everyday life with a shout of delight. The
Shekinah was expected to burst into flame in every bush. Every
word and event was a sign of the Living God. Man's job was to
offer God heart, mind, senses and words like so many vessels to
be used by Him; these laughed with delight, filled with proverbs
and jokes, with songs and wise sayings that testified to His Presence. It was a religion charged with the joy that had marked the
Baal Shem Tov, its earliest teacher, who saw the Divine each day
as Thomas Traherne did as he awoke in a daily Heaven, who

insisted that man's greatest sin was to forget that he was a prince, who could not forbear to dance with delight before God who had made Man a palace of glory.

The Kotzker prayed as one who tears up whatever pretentious piety would foist upon man's soul, whatever makes mechanical or trivial the response of the spirit to God. This kind of praying knows much self-loathing and rejects self-pity, while it strives to look open eyed at the world of brutal and criminal folly that men build. It checks itself on the threshold of prayer lest it chatter like apes and insists that the preparation for praying be purging, testing, solidly holding to things of God and not of men. The Kotzker waged war on praying by rote, on verbose repetitive prayers, on whatever obstructed the search for the truth in human relations with God.

His relevance to our post-Auschwitz world is plain. Like Kierkegaard (with whom Heschel compares him), the Kotzker was the singleminded serious man to whom God's word was law. 'You shall be holy, for I, the Lord your God am holy' (Lev. 20.7). It was a daunting demand but men had been made to meet it. God was the environment of Man. Right relationship with Him alone could give significance to man's life, could enable him to function in health, could build up through him the greater abundance of life to come. To turn away from it was suicidal and treason to God and man. The sharpest point of that claim, the goad that the Kotzker felt and bore witness to, was its emphasis on 'today'. To be holy today meant seeking anew the engagement point with this environmental God. No generalized devotion or piety could be substituted for the particular response it called for, for this would miss the point that God's work, like that of the artist, is unique and specific hour by hour, is in motion like the stars and the winds, and that praying must have the fine point of a moving pen.

Truly Jewish too, says Heschel, was the Kotzker's grasp of what it entailed. The Greeks ask: 'What is good?' The Jews ask 'What does God require of thee?' From these questions flew two different conceptions of life. For the Jew to be human meant finding out and observing the requirements of God with all the zest of a lover till the scope of requiredness embraced creation itself. So to the

Jew first but to the Christian also the primary task of prayer was
a resetting of sights from day to day to ascertain what the requirements of God were in a world which moved towards a new world-
order and common life, a world whose dazzling achievements
called for not only great intelligence but for a still greater measure
of charity. As men wrestled with the assets and the threats to
existence that their technology and science brought into use, with
politics, political theology and political education, with the hungers
and fears of men and women who now found themselves exposed
to themselves and others as never before, they needed even more
help in learning to pray. For praying is the process of transmutation
of the elements of the world that they may become the materials
of the House of Life. Can that process cope with an event like the
Holocaust? Have Jews themselves learned how to do this and
therefore given Christians a chance to learn once more how
Hebrew spirituality stands up to such testing?

This raises in the profoundest way the question of the growing-
points of our attempts to pray in the modern world. It is right that
the basis of all our praying, the great fundamental acts of God that
have disclosed His will and His love for His people, should be
rehearsed again and again. It is right that the language through
which a people have been made most deeply aware of these things
should be cherished and constantly used. Liturgical prayer stands
too near to the bedrock requirements of human faith in God to be
treated without a due sense of awe. We ground our feet in these
things that we may stand firm in the present-day world, in the
darkness that falls across it, in the glare of the searchlights that
expose and distort. Our praying has to take hold of the things of
our time that challenge belief in the goodness of God and flood
people's hearts with dismay and horror. If the maturing of humanity demands that we carry our faith in God into this new world
we must learn how to pray with the knowledge of what this faith
entails, of what it must face and surmount, of what it must hold
before God.

Not all our attempts to do this will succeed. Most of them will
fall short of the spirituality that should work in and through them.
We are nonetheless constrained to go on. There should be an

untiring effort to grasp and embrace new and difficult things. The
process of transmutation can scarcely be other than painfully
experimental. What matters is that the process should go on, that
the Spirit should be at work in these unwelcoming fields, that the
words to express what is sought should be found. It is the business
of prayer to try to penetrate to the reality of human experience.
Reality should be known, and prayer must endeavour to hold it
to God. Buber wrote: 'Everything is waiting to be hallowed by
you; it is waiting for this meaning to be disclosed and to be realized
by you. . . . Meet the world with the fulness of your being and
you shall meet God.'

Auschwitz marks a crisis for the attempt to face reality, not only
for Jews but also for Christians. This may have been recognized
by certain leaders of Christian thought, but it is not something
that has made an impact upon the prayer life of the Church. The
reason is painfully obvious. The great bulk of Christian congregations have lived so long without feeling any need to acquaint
themselves with Jews and their history that Auschwitz does not
have any great bearing upon their lives. Religion has actually
insulated them from any possible sense of pain arising from what
has happened. Without some new effort to establish a relationship
of concern enlightened theologians will have little effect. Congregations will go on using the Bible and singing the Psalms and
Canticles without realizing that a new and greater degree of unreality has been added to what they do.

By contrast it should be remarked that Israel has throughout its
history suffered for the sake of its singularity as a nation and been
compelled to use its prayer as part of a continuous learning process.
'The best which God gave to Israel, He gave through suffering.'
Through prayer, suffering Israel turned necessity to glorious gain,
for it meant not resignation to fearful and evil things but a constant
questioning of God. 'Why hast thou thus dealt with they people?'
Baeck spoke of 'Why' being used as a word of prayer and declared
that this 'Why' was a keynote of Israel's praying. A note of daring
was thus introduced which challenged those involved, both God
and Man. Why does God keep silent, why does He countenance
the fearful injustices, is it really because of their sins that men

suffer? (See Chapter 4 – 'An Account of our Sins' – in Petuchowski's *Theology and Poetry*.)

If we are to appreciate Jewish praying we must begin by seeing
the importance of the liturgical basis first of all. Jewish prayer is
supremely 'common prayer' to an extent that few Christians can
understand. Coming to it they may feel something personal lost
to sight in the absence of 'Christ and his mother and all his Hal-
lows' (Gerald Manley Hopkins) but closer acquaintance with it
must bring home the truth that in prayer the Jew participates in a
relationship established between God and His people of quite viv-
idly intimate character. The personal aspect of prayer is in no way
diminished; it is raised to true dignity and vastly extended by being
set in the context of God's dealings all down the ages with His
people. A man praying within that shared experience of the community of Israel learns how to pray. Things of ultimate concern,
tried, tested and proved by all Israel's history are the educative
media he learns to observe.

Since Israel has not been permitted to forget the terms of its
Exodus calling, its prayer carries with it the full weight of community purpose. Christian liturgical prayer has preserved community language but rarely succeeded in matching it with the
shared life in the Body of Christ. Hence it has not been able to
withstand the encroachments of the spirit of individualism fostered
by modern life. Those who come together to pray in churches do
so as aggregates loosely assembled rather than as conscious communities. Having known for so long the favoured circumstances
of establishment or social approval, the Church has rarely felt
obliged to school its members to pray from the stark premise that
'We are Christians because . . . .' and thence to pray for the life of
the body thus defined. Israel knew no such privileged place. Its
separateness was invariably costly and therefore Jews learned to
pray: 'You chose us from all peoples and tongues, and in love
drew us near to Your own greatness; to honour You, to declare
Your unity, and to love You. Blessed are You Lord, who chooses
His people Israel in love.'

This has been the strength of Jewish liturgical prayer and it has
sustained the personal praying of men and women in the face of

intolerable hardships. By what means can a new dimension comparable to this be given to Christian praying? It must be effective
at parochial levels and it must be treated as of overwhelming
importance for the integrity of Christian witness in the world
today. There are two new focuses of attention in this witness. The
first of these is for a serious study of Christian-Jewish relations in
the past and a patient attempt to understand Israel's special condition today. Without this Christian prayer will be unrealistic. The
second is the specific question of how to pray in this post-Auschwitz world and we must look to the Jews for help in setting about
it. This will sound quite strange to many Christians and there is
no easy process of learning how to achieve it. Yet we might well
begin by asking what a Christian should try to do after reading or
hearing about the death-camps. His Good Friday liturgy is not on
the face of it helpful but after a view of the event through Jewish
eyes, he will look at the Passion as an event in the contemporary
world.

A *Yom HaShoah* liturgy was planned for Christians in 1972. It
consisted of readings from diaries, poems and novels written during and after the years of the Holocaust together with choruses and
prayers. It sought to allow the voices of the victims themselves to
be heard; thus we stand with them, and Christians can know
themselves to be the survivors, spared by the mercy of God and
compelled to ask what He would now have them do. 'Help us to
hear the voices which you send today.' Grant that we do not forget
them. God Almighty is called upon 'to raise up a man who will
go peddling through the world', that familiar Jewish peddler who
will offer the cakes of soap that a million lives have been destroyed
to make, a peddler who will disturb the conscience of mankind,
bring into our streets and homes and council chambers and
churches the reek of the concentration camps, bring to our ears
the screams and weeping of mothers and children, old men and
boys, bring us to a halt in the midst of an otherwise forgetful live.
Dare we protest and plead to be left undisturbed? Auschwitz
assembled millions of outstretched hands because those of Jesus of
Nazareth had left us unmoved.

This asks for a radical overhaul of Christian praying, not to imitate Jewish forms but to learn from Israel's experience how to look at human life in the presence of God. All too often we have looked away. Now we need to find a new focus for prayer. There is a fear today that the Church may lose itself in the pursuit of good works, that its clergy may see their job simply in social-political terms closely geared to the politics of the day. The temptation is nothing new. In Jewish eyes it was not the good works that diverted attention from God but the compromised political attitudes of Christians in years gone by which defiled their service of God. What is called for is not a turning away from the world but a finding a new kind of direction in it. This discovery must be little short of monumental. There can be no real sense of direction without it.

The truth about the Church's life in the modern world is that it has lost this sense of direction. It has steadily lost contact with the life of the world. Men's consciousness of what the Church was for and how it should be prayed for have grown confused. They could not conceive it in terms of a moving column of men on the march nor see the events and circumstances of the contemporary world as a challenge to their devotion. The Church's liturgical forms were too anatomical, wondrous structures indeed but with bones of theology that lacked the flesh and blood that life in the world should supply. Its hymns and its canticles were fixed in traditional modes. All too rarely a poet broke through the accustomed forms and grasped theological truth in words that gave it an imaginative power. Writing of the Vexilla Regis hymn, David Jones said tersely: 'It is the sort of thing that poets are for; to redeem us is part of their job.' We likewise need new poetical forms to continue that work of redemption. The Benedicite must be newly embodied; if we sing David's Psalms today they challenge us to look for a writing of psalmody that is our own. Charles Wesley's hymns were not the greatest poetical works but they were the most serviceable kind of poetry for multitudes of souls that thirsted for it.

The two things that a changed style of praying call for are: a new vision of the involvement of Christianity with the history of mankind and a new readiness to use poetry, drama, dance, music

and all the arts to express what this involvement means. At the
moment a Christian congregation is likely to be unaware of the
tumultuous majesty of the scene in which it is called upon to play
a part. It hugs its accustomed paths and forms and sees little or
nothing of either abysses or mountain tops. Its glimpses of green
pastures get more vague and conventionally tricked out. Yet this
impoverishment in our churches is the outcome of choice, of a
standing aside from the historical, interrogative and lyrical participation in a vast cosmic drama into which God has called His
people.

Judaism has met with difficulties too. Down the ages it has
known its own special temptations to become absorbed in mystical
teaching, intricately vast as only the Jewish mind could make it,
or to be rigidly ruled by the Torah and Talmudic interpretation.
The disputes and tensions between Orthodox, Reformed and Conservative bodies are real issues and indicate where human needs
have to be reviewed and consulted age after age. Further Christian
and Jewish forms of devotion to God in prayer are not to be
thought of as doing the same thing in slightly different ways. On
the contrary it is their two-fold task that should be constantly kept
in mind. They can learn of each other but learn in their own ways.

Both will have to face the problems which beset any such effort,
that spring from the root sin of indolence of heart. For the most
part Jews have not, throughout history, had much leisure to fall
victims to sloth of body or spirit, but in the world of today the
conditions are altered. Crises are unavoidable. 'I do not envy a
Jew', says the great Talmudic teacher to the youthful David Lurie,
'who goes into Bible today. Goyim will be suspicious of you and
Jews will be uneasy in your presence. Everyone will be wondering
what sacred truths of their childhood you are destroying.' Yet the
Jewish intention of pursuing the truth has impressive power. In a
passionately-conceived small book entitled *Why I am a Jew*, written
in 1927, Edmond Fleg expressed his faith in such striking terms
that one section was later included in the Reform Synagogues'
Prayer Book as material for study. One phrase ran: 'because the
faith of Israel demands of me no abdication of mind.' Because
Judaism has been so much a programme of action it has required

its adherents to think out what it means to serve God at this or that time and thanked Him for demanding the effort to do so. 'Blessed are You, Lord our God, King of the Universe, who makes us holy through doing His commands, and who commands us to devote ourselves to the study of His teaching.' But study can get lost in the mountains of scholastic learning and some Jews have grown impatient with this. The remedy lay in pressing on and the Rabbis have never lacked courage to keep options open and make it clear that submission to God does not mean resignation but a readiness to expect Him to act. A people that can retain this hope in the shadow of the Holocaust have learned much of what is at stake in the Creation and redemption of the world.

When we turn to see this in Christian terms there is much less ready response or experience to draw on. We can look at it with the reflections once made by Matthew Arnold on just such issues in mind. Arnold was no great prophet but he was sufficiently disquieted by the society he lived in to express his misgivings. What he saw and wrote was light-years away from the Final Operation but he shivered like a man who feels without being able to name it that something threatens. He knew that the gaps were there and were probably widening.

Arnold was not deceived about the thinness of contemporary spiritual resources and the likelihood that they would soon be sorely tried. When he pleaded for a recognition of the service of God in terms not only of right conduct but also for art and science he was asking for something that he believed to have been greatly neglected in the Christian Church of the day. In *Literature and Dogma* and in *Culture and Anarchy* he sought for a wider recognition of these things and posed his problem in terms of prayer. 'I find that with me, he wrote, 'a clear most palpable intuition is necessary before I get into prayer'. He knew that he could not pray as he believed prayer should be made because he was cut off from any sense of direction shared with his fellow-Christians. The mainsprings of praying were weakened by a lack of shared purpose.

In his mixture of diffidence and earnestness Arnold was anything but Hebraic. One canot imagine him dancing with the Scrolls of the Law or fiercely supporting some little back-street synagogue

whose roots were in Galicia. He was neither a leader of men nor
a stricken deer. He was a popularizer of ideas, a propagandist
rather than a man of creative imagination, but his instinct was sure
and he stood near to the cultural life of the time, even if his voice
was not clearly heard or remarked. It was nowhere more telling
than in his reflections upon the divorce of religion from poetry and
the arts. There is still no more eloquent manifesto of poetry's
contribution to human life than his essay on the *Study of Poetry*.
'The future of poetry is immense', he wrote, because in poetry,
where it is worthy of its high densities, our race, as time goes on,
will find an ever surer and surer stay.' Arnold was not able to
make very clear how poetry would fulfil this task, how the criticism of life which he claimed it embodied could be brought to
bear on the actual scene, but what he contended has since that time
been more commonly recognized. Expecting the poets to do what
religious teachers were failing to do may have been a misplacement
of hope, but he knew in which direction to look.

What was largely missing, he felt, was an adequate understanding of the nature of language and poetry and notable of its relation
to religion. He was raising the problem which has since occasioned
a great deal of anxiety to numbers of earnest Christians, unprepared
for the kind of criticism of religious statements which are commonly made today. Little had as yet been done in Arnold's time
to help them to see how the language of poetry was used, and still
less to recognize that language employed to speak about God was
being used in a specially poetical fashion. No great religious teacher
in England had followed up the hints of Newman, no great use
had as yet been made of what Coleridge had said of the work of
Imagination. Christian theologians, like their Jewish counterparts
were inclined to be suspicious and even vituperative when their
members began to find fault with the traditional modes of
expression.

More important still there was widespread indifference to the
question of the nature and quality of human responses to critical
moments in life, to the degrees of sensitivity and fineness of discrimination involved in relations between human beings. No great
sense of concern was expressed for the emotional immaturity, the

poor standards of ethical judgment, the confusion of values, that
clung to and even flourished in the life of organized religion. One
may trace in nineteenth century novels a mixture of an attempt to
be just and generous to the Church as a venerable institution with
an increasing note of exasperation and even contempt for its
crudely immature grasp of what was already revolutionizing
human life in the world and its inability to equip its members to
face the change.

Blunted susceptibilities were no good condition in which to
register the facts or the meaning of the gathering storm. Their
bearing upon spiritual vision and vitality received little attention.
The reduction of life to what has been called that of the One-
Dimensional Man was not seriously challenged by the churches
because their own standards were not outraged by it.

When the Great War broke up the facade of this 'civilized' world
it revealed the kind of spiritual impoverishment which a steady
decline in prayerful grasp of the challenge being made to the
Christian faith by the world being fashioned could have made
almost certain. The strain of the war made it only too likely that
the moral and spiritual issues would get little attention. 'Today',
wrote David Jones (in *The Tablet* in 1941), reflecting upon the role
of religion and poetry in such a world, 'we live in a world where
the symbolic life (the life of the true cultures, of institutional
religion, and of all artists, in the last respect – however much we
may disavow the association) is progressively eliminated – and the
technician is master.' It would have seemed wildly mistaken to
have spoken of Germany as a land from which institutional religion
was being rejected, and in the event there were numerous brave
individuals and small groups of Christians who resisted the Hitler
régime, but the speed and ruthlessness with which the Nazi tech-
nicians went to work bore out the truth of the observation. The
hooked cross proved to be stronger than the once-powerful symbols of Germany's cultural and religious life.

So today's problem is one of spiritual re-creation, of enlisting
the common man and the artist, the youth of the counter-cultures
and the women seeking new understanding of the place of wom-
anhood in society, the saddened and baffled, the hopeful and the

visionary, in a rebuilding of spiritual purpose of which praying is the dynamic factor. It has been the singular genius of the Jews in history to demonstrate to mankind how new beginnings may be made. Christians may once again need to look at the Jewish experience of renewing a people's devotion to God and put themselves humbly to school. It was a misapprehension of disastrous consequences that led them once to suppose that this people who had led them to Christ could then be turned off with scorn as having nothing more to give. That error has been very heavily paid for.

What matters today is our willingness to begin again. The psychologists and scientific inquirers of social problems can help us to understand something of what went wrong and brought European Jewry to the gas-chambers. They can offer us technical help. What they cannot do is to supply what great faiths have existed to do, the true education of the spirit of Man. The Holocaust was the fruit of miseducation and it will happen again unless the processes of such miseducation are undone and replaced by a new beginning of spiritual life more serviceable to humanity in this present perplexed condition.

Judaism still lives in the world despite all the efforts of demonic men to destroy it, because it has never abandoned a willingness to begin again. Chaim Potok's words at the opening of the novel to which I have already referred are precise : 'All beginnings are hard.' They get harder the more we are led to make them in fundamental matters of faith and commitment and self-knowledge. Whether it is a new way of understanding the Bible or ourselves, all beginnings are hard. 'Especially a beginning that you make by yourself', that is, the effort to think and to pray and live in a new direction. Rebirth was the Gospel's description of it. Dying daily was to give new scope. What the churches are faced with today is no less a momentous choice.

The new beginning must take hold of both public and private prayer. Jewish praying is supremely something done by 'the children of Israel'. In that prayer they renew the corporate relationship already defined by and rooted in God's election of them. The personal aspect is in no way diminished but vastly extended by this sense of community, of belonging to the holy nation. Jews

have rarely been allowed to think of themselves as anything but
a separated people, a painful condition for personal experience but
not without strength-giving help. By contrast, there are some
features of Christian church life and devotion that appear to have
forgotten that 'it is not good that the man should be alone' (Gen.
2.18). Men come to their full stature only by drawing upon the
sustenance of that common conversation between God and His
people. 'Private prayer will not survive,' wrote Heschel, 'unless it
is inspired by public prayer', and public prayer in its turn will not
continue unless it directs the attention of heart and mind towards
that which gives meaning to Creation itself, a part in the working
preparation for the Kingdom of God.

There is then an immense field for mutual assistance between
the two faiths for shaping a new sense of corporate calling to bear
witness to God in the world today. Since all the worth and truth
of liturgical worship depends on right relation with him who will
be present in His own way, the traditional forms must needs be
flexible enough to allow for discernments of things newly-revealed
and newly required. We must offer the best that we have. We
must also be ready to meet new requirements with new recognition
and profounder awareness of obligation. With the Holocaust constantly in our prayers, we must be ready to put into His hands
such contrition as only He can turn to more glorious gain.

9. The Kingdom of God

'I must own to you that I shall never give up looking forward to the
day when all discord shall have been silenced. Try to imagine its
dawn.'

Joseph Conrad, *Under Western Eyes*

'By the Kingdome of God is properly meant a Common-wealth,
instituted (by the consent of those which were to be subject thereto)
for their Civill Government, and the regulating of their behaviour,
not only towards God their King, but also towards one another in
point of justice, and towards other nations both in peace and warre.'

Thomas Hobbes, *Leviathan*

Not many years ago Missions to Jews, organized attempts to
convert Jews to the Christian faith, were part of the working
missionary activity of Christian Churches. At Stuttgart in 1930
four such German missions invited a Jew to address them. This
was a remarkable venture of faith or one of the most ironic gestures
in history. Today it looks like a gathering of the blind inviting
someone to join them at the price of his eyes. It is reminiscent too
of the Gospel passage about the sighted and blind (John 9.40).

Martin Buber spoke to the meeting under the title *The Two Foci
of the Jewish Soul*, dealing with the two central beliefs round which
the faith of the Jews had turned from time immemorial. The first
of these he described as the experience of God high and lifted up
beyond man's comprehension who yet chose to seek out His creature Man that his life upon earth might reflect the holiness of his
Maker. The second he called a consciousness of God's redeeming
power at work in the world, drawing men into a participation in
that redemptive work. Jews felt the world's lack of redemption,

Buber said, like something tasted by the tongue or like a burden heavy to bear.

He then turned in a courteous fashion to make clear why and how he was opposed to Christian missionary work directed towards the Jews. It followed, he said, from his understanding of the Kingdom of God. He had spoken to them 'as a Jew, that is, as one who waits for the Kingdom of God, the Kingdom of Unification, and who regards all 'missions' such as yours as springing from a misunderstanding of the nature of that Kingdom, and as a hindrance to its coming.'

It was clearly and bravely said. Half a century later, with the fires of the Holocaust burning between, we see a little more clearly, we are a little more disturbed by what we see. Who has a right to talk of the Cross in a post-Auschwitz world? What credibility now attaches to a church or churches that were silent when that event occurred? And as for the Kingdom of God, how seriously do we in public and private prayers and in our discussions about the life of faith set the Kingdom of God at the heart of all? Does it mean that much? Do we even pause as we say, 'Thy Kingdom come'? We speak of it as a world hereafter. A few still believe it to mean the Church. More rarely do we come across those who await its coming on earth. The lead-story of the Gospels, that the Kingdom of God is at hand, is not news for most Christians today. It has no significant place in the way they look at the world.

They still repeat the Lord's Prayer, and hearing the Scriptures they are constantly reminded of the sayings of Jesus concerning the Kingdom, the basis of many sermons. But prayer for the Kingdom's coming does not figure largely in Christian liturgical practice. The foci of Christian faith are elsewhere, in the Person, the work and the presence of Christ, in the Spirit and in the life of the Church. Neither the traditional collects of the Book of Common Prayer nor the many revisions of the Holy Communion service nor the Mass in the vernacular have set prayer for the Kingdom's coming at the heart of devotional life. No great sense of urgency, no yearning or longing for it, no summons to turn once again expectantly towards it, no joyous conviction that come it will because God has willed it, marks the practice of most of our churches.

By contrast, of course, Jewish practice does, with good reason, do just those things. In Leon Roth's words; 'Judaism may be looked upon as the concern with citizenship in the Kingdom of God.' When you have spent several millennia trying to establish a foothold on God's earth you either cling very tightly to the hope of that Kingdom's coming or you find existence a very sick joke. If the Kingdom on earth is not to be God's it may well be that of Darkness crowned. The Prince of Darkness is a gentleman to those who know their place. He has no objection to religion. He has not, save in the case of the Jews, found it a serious source of disquiet.

What has not been uppermost then in Christian theology, practice and prayer has been a joining together of personal involvement in building the Kingdom on earth and a sense of the part this great hope has played in man's history until now. Thus it has neither impressed itself deeply upon the minds of worshippers of God that the work of the Kingdom is something of daily concern, nor has it enabled them to look at the history of mankind, in hopeful but realistic terms. Much of that history has been compounded of idealized versions of the work of the Church and servile attention to the Powers of the World. Christian devotion has tried to by-pass the world and to lose itself in an O Altitudo, as Sir Thomas Browne remarked.

Today there are signs of change. Most churches have become more involved in the social-political problems of mankind as a whole and have taken some part in work to alleviate poverty, disease, disasters and political oppression. A shift in the make-up of the Christian Church from white to black and brown peoples has played an important part in this change. But we can neither lose sight of the fact that a great many Christians are profoundly opposed to what they regard as a turning away from the Church's true task, a 'spiritual' affair, nor ignore the extent to which what has been called Culture-Christianity, a faith that accommodates itself to prevailing social conditions, holds its place in the life of the westernized Churches. It is here that the Jewish question is the issue still to be faced. The Holocaust is the reminder that the Churches were silent when challenged by evil men and that Israel was once again the central issue in the question of who should inherit the earth. That many brave Christians risked their lives to help Jews must be gladly declared, but in so far as the Holocaust's lesson is unmarked by churches, church leaders and the great mass of churchgoers there is no reason why the same evils should not be repeated. Unless that lesson is learned, it will be easier to repeat evils, for the credibility and integrity of the Church is so weakened by what has been done that without *metanoia*, the searching of soul, it will have less resistance to offer.

The issue is theological. Is the earth the Lord's or not? We ask: is God dead, is he down there, is he improperly described in doctrinal language and avoid the great question once again put to mankind in Golgotha-Auschwitz. What Christians are failing to do when they thus look away from the Scriptures and see the Jews only as stubbornly anomalous people is to understand their own history and themselves. If they are not Israel, joint-heirs with Jewry of the promises made to the fathers, what are they? Their attempt to exclude, convert, assimilate, and even assent to Jewry's destruction, has brought them nothing but stained hands and confusion of soul. They will not do better than this unless they return to their true calling, to the service of Him who called their forefathers not to assimilate with the world but to wait and work for His coming Kingdom.

It is not surprising further that the movements for Christian Social Action, Christian Socialism and the like stemming from the mid-nineteenth century's awareness of the new problems facing the Church have flickered and faded. They did so because they lacked roots where the roots must be. They were almost wholly contained within Christendom's soil. What they lacked was something foregone when the Christian Church turned from the hope of the Kingdom of God.

The erudition of Troeltsch is needed to trace the development of the world-outlook of the Christian Churches from their beginnings in the teaching of Jesus to the achievement of the great Mediaeval Church and the challenges which Protestantism levelled against it. He concluded that the Church absorbed into its elaboration of doctrine the original message of Jesus of the Kingdom at hand, and presented itself in His Name as the Kingdom of God in the world. But this presentation did not wholly convince although its teaching was widespread and was reinforced with fire and the sword. It fell to heretical sects to retain a hope of redemption through the Advent of Christ and the ushering in of His Kingdom on earth. The attempt to project the Kingdom in ecclesiastical-spiritual terms resulted in the creation of lay secular powers who quickly brought into being a social, political and technological world independent of and far stronger than anything that the Church could control. To the problems of that enterprising and tormented world it could offer even less help. 'The main historic forms of the Christian doctrine of society and of social development' wrote Troeltsch, are today, 'impotent in the face of the tasks by which they are confronted'. The Holocaust and the post-Auschwitz years have left that judgment with us.

By contrast with what has thus become the rather vague worldliness of Christian public devotion, Jewish practice has been more explicit about the coming of God's kingdom on earth, more insistent upon the worshippers' part in what it involves. It has rooted this hope in the soil of the earth. The closing prayer of a synagogue service puts it thus: 'Let us magnify and let us sanctify the great name of God in the world which He created according to His will. May His Kingdom come in your lifetime, and in your days, and in the lifetime of the family of Israel – quickly and speedily may it come, Amen.' God is constantly addressed as 'our King' and 'King of the Universe', and the hope expressed that 'the world will be perfected under your unchallenged rule; when all mankind will call upon Your name and, forsaking evil, turn to You alone.'

The prayer issues from Judaism's age-old concern for the Kingdom of God. If today Christians need Jews as a model, as a community from whom to learn something of how a people may serve God in the historical political process, it is vital that they understand something of Jewish wrestling with the hope of the Kingdom, recognize what part it played in the teaching of Jesus, and what problems it confronts men with now. This is not a one-way affair. The people of God as a whole stand always in need of renewal. They must learn from and teach each other. Christians represent the universality of the Kingdom over against the Chosen People who stand apart; both have a necessary witness to make to the Kingdom of God in the world. One day what we now regard as the separate vocations of the synagogue and the Church will cease. Paul's vision is of the triumph of God's saving purpose for all Israel and not simply Israel after the flesh. No less significant is the fact that it is by a Jew that the promise of God is conveyed and opened to mankind. 'It is from the Jews that salvation comes.'

It is for this reason that we must think of missions to Jews as a hindrance to the Kingdom's coming. Representing the age-old attitude of triumphal Christian rejection of Judaism together with the assumption that the Christian Church is the sole agent of God's dealing with mankind in history, such missions could not but popularize views which lose sight of the realities of the world-situation and the teaching of Jesus himself. For to the Jews the Kingdom, however it came, could not be described save in terms of the life of a holy community in which the laws of God express-ing His delight in mercy and justice prevailed. Assimilation via Christian baptism might make it easier for European Jews to find a place in society but could scarcely commend to them that society as an example of such holy community. For Christians themselves it meant a continuing confirmation of anti-semitic thought which lent itself to a worldliness that would prove to be quite unable to resist political and cultural programmes issuing at length in the Holocaust. 'That slide into damnation started, like the credibility crisis in Christianity, with Christian lies about the Jewish people, with abandonment of the essential Jewishness of Christianity, with the murder of those who could be identified as signal representa-tives of a counterculture the world hated and most of the baptized betrayed with enthusiasm.'

Jesus came announcing the imminence of the Kingdom of God and calling on men to repent that they might be in readiness for it. Both announcement and demand were, on his lips, of more radical character, more profound in their grasp of the spiritual issues involved, than all that had gone before. 'Never man spake

like this man' (John 7.46). However much the religious and philosophical and cultural contributions of the Mediterranean world of
the first few centuries of the Christian era shaped Christian faith
to become of universal scope, it nonetheless sprang into being
from the life of a Jew, and it did what no Jew had hitherto done.
But Jesus the Jew stood in the Jewish experience of relations with
God. He did not invent the great themes of the Kingdom, God's
Law and God's Grace, but took what was Israel's learning process
about these things and carried it to the next and conceivably final
stage. It was done with the authority – 'ye have heard it said, but
I say unto you' (Matt. 5.21) – of one who knows that this is no
sudden disclosure of spiritual truth but the flowering of God's
immemorial concern for His people. He can count on foundations
laid and therefore build higher and greater the true temple of God.

The announcement of the Kingdom of God at hand is a call to
reality in the terms in which Jews had learned to conceive what
reality meant. The kingdom meant human community subject to
God, the ultimate Truth. It meant theocratic community. God is
called King to express in quite personal terms the reality that
underlay, sustained, destroyed, recreated and brought it its consummation all that had been created, a reality that made its own
energizing and loving Will known to mankind through revelation
to man. So personal indeed were the terms that while He is of such
Glory that men cannot look upon Him and live, He argued with
Abraham, wrestled with Jacob, talked with Moses, endured His
people's unfaithfulness like a lover. He was at all times the Father
who yearns for His sons.

There is then an objectivity about this Kingdom, an objectivity
of circumstance, of history, biology, economics and psychology,
with which men must come to terms if they are to live at all. They
must come out of the world of magic and the pitiful idolatries that
represent stages of arrested development and the caste systems of
frozen social relationships, for this King is alive, a Law-giver who
takes account of people's behaviour, a person who loves mercy
and justice and sets dignity on the brows of his children. Men did
not attribute these things to a God of their making but they met
them or were met by them, were summoned and driven by them,

judged, punished and raised up again by this King who for His own purpose had taken them into His hands.

When the prophets said 'Thus saith the Lord', they meant therefore that this revelation – tried by experience – did in quite personal fashion speak to the children of Israel, requiring them to live in response to His will. It made nonsense of idols that could but express the lusts or the fears of those who made them. Human life for this people – and ultimately for the whole world – could not be on the basis of 'do what you will'. The Kingdom had laws to be learned and kept, but the process of learning too was as personal a matter as the life it was given to serve. In Jewish understanding of the Kingdom of God men were not subjects ruled over by and at the whim of an inscrutable despot but witnesses to and co-partners with the Lord God whose purpose all things were designed to show. That purpose was being achieved here and now just as its Law was a contract made not with past generations but with 'you who are here this day', so that the Kingdom itself was already present. It did not have to await the end of all things as so much later apocalyptic writing came to suggest, but was to be realized on earth for 'the Lord your God is your King here and now' (Deut. 29.10–15). But neither is it a static affair completed and finished. It is always coming, always 'not yet' achieved in its fulness and beauty, for its reality does depend on and must wait for the true response of love coming-to-be in men's hearts. It cannot be brought into being by fiat or imposition.

It was with this dynamic and earthy character of the Kingdom of God that generations of Jews were set to wrestle. Always in danger of being lost to sight, abandoned by men unwilling to gird themselves to it, formalized by the unimaginative, it remained their calling among all nations. It made them the most restless people on the face of the earth, the most disturbing to those who sought to set up substitute kingdoms of their own. Hitler rightly decided that for the Third Reich to succeed the Jews must be wiped out, just as ages before men killed Jesus and John and Stephen and multitudes of forgotten men and women who bore witness to a quite other Kingdom that claimed the earth and all that human life means for the service of God.

The Jews came back again and again to their basic commitment, to the conviction of the Kingdom's reality which gave them the strength to endure and repent and seek it again. They learned the hard way that this Kingdom is achieved not given, chosen not stumbled upon, willed not conveyed like a piece of real estate. 'The soul must pray for it,' Rosenzweig was to write, 'for it is no other than that which consummates what in creation God began and what in revelation He does not cease to make present to us. All prayer, even the individual lament, subconsciously cries out for the coming of the Kingdom, the visible representation of what is experienced only in the soul's holy of holies.'

Israel's understanding of the Kingdom of God is a process of distillation, lengthy, laborious and harsh. The Psalms are the songs of the human soul learning to see itself thus involved, grieving, rejoicing, enduring and waiting in hope. The job of the prophets was to bring to renewed recognition the terms of its own relationship which Israel as a people had with the Kingdom. They were there to provide the kind of critique which Marx in his own way sought to bring to bear on mid-nineteenth century life in a limited socio-political field. Israel's prophets had wider terms of reference set to them in God's Covenant and the Torah. Being practical men drawn from no single class or school of thought or circumstance, they made their critique in terms of all that was being done in the day-to-day life of the nation. Since the Law covered all sides of personal and social life it gave them the standard they needed to pronounce on Israel's faith or lack of faith. It cut clean through the political and religious idiom of the contemporary world. It enabled a Nathan to challenge great David himself, an Amos to speak unabashed in Bethel, an Isaiah to pronounce God's judgement on Israel and Judah. It moved Micah to denounce both priests and judges for their shameless corruption of justice and religion.

For something like half a millennium this critique was built up. Its truth was subjected to history's test. The Jewish scriptures are a strange compilation of accounts of a people's *Pilgrim's Progress*, a journeying through a long night, sustained by the hope of dawn. They are wholly realistic in their assessment of human behaviour and their insight into the heart of Man. They counter the recidivist folly and wickedness of this people with an obstinate defiant conviction that the goodness of God will prevail. The prophetic word is always a defiant 'And yet' set over against the obvious triumphs of deceit and violence and the glaring apostasy of kings, priests and people.

Behind Jesus there stood men who had countered the very real victories of evil with still more determined insistence upon the ultimate triumph of God's Kingdom on earth. He spoke to a people who had mocked and betrayed even more than they honoured acknowledgment of it, but who nevertheless still knew, now uneasily, now with passionate hope, that its truth still stood. He spoke to a people in great distress yet possessed of a conviction that they could not abandon. 'Although the fig tree shall not blossom, neither shall fruit be in the vines, the labour of the olive shall fail, and the fields shall yield no meat; the flock shall be cut off from the fold, and there shall be herd in the stalls: Yet will I rejoice in the God of my salvation' (Habbakuk 3.17–18). Because of that 'Yet', the later Isaiah would not flinch from describing the bruised suffering Servant as Israel's calling and out of the grief-laden thought exclaim: 'Thou art my servant, O Israel, in whom I will be glorified.' Such men built up the expectation that the Day of the Lord would dawn and that its coming would transform the life not of that nation only but of the world itself.

Human illusions die hard, killing those who hold them. Israel survived because, under God's hand, she turned from them to reality. The Exile, the invasions, the seductions of Hellenism, the cruelties of Herods, the internal warfare of sects and kings, winnowed out the grain from the chaff. In the years that followed the ending of the line of great Biblical prophets, years that brought more and more cruel blows to Israel's will to endure, a yearning for God's intervention and the birth of a wholly new age must have been almost all that many could still retain.

Into that world came John the Baptist and Jesus of Nazareth 'preaching the Gospel of the Kingdom of God and saying: the time is fulfilled and the Kingdom of God is at hand: repent ye and believe the Gospel' (Mark 1.14–15). That Messiahs and pseudo-Messiahs had come and gone took away nothing from their appeal

to the turbulent Galileans. Preaching the Kingdom in that countryside meant taking the risk of being wholly mistaken and the
Gospels have little to say of the content of what was preached; but
they suggest that Jesus did turn directly to the poor, the sinners or
people who knew not the Law, and claimed from them faith in
the Kingdom at hand. To hold them Jesus must have put into
words the hopes that such people already cherished, whatever
recasting of these He intended to make. He came in the great
tradition of Jewish prophets, His words have their characteristic
freedom, seeking not to destroy nor to bring about any reform in
the current religious practice but to carry the faith of this people
to a new level of relation with God and man.

It was therefore a dangerous enterprise from the start, and this
Jesus knew. To talk of kings and kingdoms, to announce the
imminent upsetting of the social-political order of Galilee at such
a time was to cast fire on the earth in no uncertain fashion. Excited
men hear things at crude levels of what is acceptable or repellent.
Partisan expectations must from the outset have made the distinctions Jesus sought to define a hazardous affair. He was followed
by crowds who thought of the Kingdom not as a spiritual state in
men's hearts so much as a violent upheaval which would topple
despots from their thrones. Many flocked to Him as to a possible
king who would lead them to revolutionary success. The title
Messiah was bandied about before and during and after His trial
and execution. It was to be on men's lips, as a word of inquiry,
derision, expectation and fear, and to stay in their minds as a
source of still greater perplexity after His death. 'We trusted', said
some, 'that it had been He which should have redeemed Israel',
and others are reported to have asked Him outright if His purpose
was to restore the kingdom to Israel. Since Messianism meant a
transformation of human life, whether it involved the Kingdom
of God or not, the scene in which Jesus worked could give rise to
the widest variety of hopes.

Before we look further at what the Gospels did set down it is
important to make clear the Jewish conditions into which Jesus
came, if only to offset the attempt which the Gospels so often
appear to be making to emphasize the Jewish rejection of Jesus.

What could men have understood of the Kingdom in the situation they knew? A generation earlier the war between the last Maccabean king, Mattathias Antigonus, and the Edomite Herod had drenched the land with blood. Unspeakable cruelties were practised to crush the people. Herod's capture of Jerusalem in 37 B.C. with the aid of the Romans is said to have left not only the royal city but the land round it a wilderness for years. The reign of terror continued as long as Herod had reason to fear either friends or foes. The story of the massacre of Bethlehem's children may or may not be true but its like and worse was in keeping with Herod's behaviour. While he lived the population grew weary of oppression. When he died they rejoiced. Some drew apart into communities like Qumran. Others took to the hills and waged warfare as Zealots against the authorities as best they could. We cannot say what the relations of Jesus with these men may have been, for the Evangelists were not directly concerned with them. What we must do if we are to entertain Jesus's words and work in the life of mankind today is to hear them spoken and done in circumstances not of theological study but in a countryside that saw cities burned to the ground, men, women and children sold as slaves, and rebels crucified by the roadside. The words 'The Kingdom of Heaven suffereth violence and the violent take it by storm' (Matt. 11.12) are beyond explanation but serve to remind us of the background of Jesus's work. The sectaries of Qumran do not mention the Kingdom of God in their scrolls but they lived as men on the alert, prepared to do battle with the Powers of Darkness when the time came.

What then did Jesus mean by the Kingdom of God? The Gospels themselves represent a shift of attention from the news of the Kingdom's coming to which Jesus summoned men to attend to a number of views about Jesus, such as His being the Christ, the personal embodiment of the Torah, the Way, the Truth and the Life, through whom by faith as by a rebirth men would enter the Kingdom. How far Jesus did preach Himself in that way we cannot know, for the Gospels were plainly written to guide and strengthen the convictions of the early Christian communities in the faith in their Lord. Yet they show a remarkable unconcern for Himself compared with his emphasis on the Kingdom at hand. The note of authority that they assign to His words has been given great personal power. To whom else shall we go? 'Thou has the words of eternal life' (John 6.68) speaks of a trust in Him which has surmounted the failure to understand much of what He had said. But the words do not hide the fact that the news of the Kingdom was the core of His work, whatever men came to think and believe about Him in the years that followed. Nor do they fail to suggest that Jesus found it difficult from the outset of His work to focus the attention of hearers upon the expected action of God rather than upon their own expectations as to how their time of oppression might end.

'Today', Jesus is reported to have said (Luke 4.21) after reading in Nazareth's synagogue the words of Isaiah describing the release of captives, relief of the bruised and poor, and the Jubilee Year of the Lord at hand, 'is this scripture fulfilled in your ears.' The note of dramatic announcement is clear. A voice that had not been heard for a long time was speaking at last. It brought all that the Law and the prophets, the Psalmists and Teachers, had pointed forwards to a moment of recognition. The tradition that the Evangelist knew made it clear also that the news brought confusion. Men's hopes were fanned into flame but was this the fire on the earth that was to be kindled?

For the announcement meant that a crisis in human affairs much graver than men had ever yet known was coming about. It was to involve all mankind but for the Jews it had a special concern. They had had at all times a particular task to perform. Now it had special urgency attached to it. The crisis would be a disaster to those unprepared for it, a disaster greater than they could imagine. It would grind them to powder. For those who were watchful and ready to meet it, prepared by penitence to await God's act, it would be the beginning of a wholly new course of life, a transformation of all that had ever been. What mattered then was a watchfulness on the part of men.

Such an interpretation may put too great an emphasis on the eschatological character of the Kingdom, even if we regard the references to portents and cosmic disturbances as being the embellishments added later. It appears to lessen the importance of the actual work of Jesus, to depreciate the spiritual content of his preaching, to ignore the significance of his Passion and Resurrection. For John the Baptist could have announced the coming establishment of the Kingdom and prepared the way for its coming. But the Christian communities plainly saw fundamental a difference between John and Jesus; the Fourth Gospel makes John's salutation of Jesus as the Lamb of God a key to the drama enacted in human terms.

It is possible even so to combine the experience of the first Christian groups that led them to speak of Jesus as they did with the undoubtedly eschatological descriptions of His work which they inherited from earlier days. A world-shattering event that caused stars to fall from Heaven had not taken place, but they saw no reason then or for a long time to come to abandon the imagery which had been used to describe the circumstances in which they themselves had come to their life in the Body of Christ. For them it was certain that an old world had passed away and that all things were made new. They were not pretending that life was easier or that martyrdom was less likely, but they were convinced that the New World had begun. 'We know that we have passed from death unto life because we love the brethren.' They did not speak of it as the Kingdom come upon earth as much as they talked of it as rebirth or incorporation into His Body, but they knew it had happened. 'If I by the finger of God cast out devils', He had said, 'no doubt the Kingdom of God is come upon you'. For the followers of Jesus there could be no doubt that the Kingdom had come upon them; they could look back and rehearse the signs of its coming in the stories of casting out devils and healing the sick. They knew now in their own lives what the signs had portended.

What had emerged from the total experience of being with Him as witnesses to the mighty works done, to His passion and fresurrection and the outpouring of the Spirit was the new life in the community that was to become the Christian Church. That Church was not to be equated with the Kingdom of God but known rather as a foretaste of its ife, an earnest of its triumph to come. Jesus had spent no time in speculating about the nature of the Kingdom of God, still less in organizing the Church which was formed in His name. There are good grounds for believing that the idea of organized mission, preaching salvation in His name, was itself a later development. What did take place was nevertheless a quite fundamental religious event whose nature, known in the experience of those who continued in the fellowship, strained and almost defied attempts to describe it. The New Testament writings represent these attempts, and though Paul attempted to provide theological exposition of it his imaginative and reasoned effort to do so sprang from the life of the Body and the problems to which that life gave rise. What men were moved to say about God and His Christ issued from the religious conviction of those unlearned and ignobly born artisans and peasants who surrendered themselves to the Gospel which Jesus had preached and to the certainty of His Resurrection.

What may be said to characterize that new life was neither a programme of action nor a creed to be taught but a waiting on God with an open and fearless attitude towards mankind. The disciples exercised an improvization of faithful living which was destined to be more revolutionary than anything that mere men might have invented. 'Knowing not whither he went' which had been the experience of Moses was carried to far greater lengths by these men whom Jesus had drawn together. They also went out, and this new exodus disclosed for brief moments at least that Israel's faith could indeed embrace the whole world. The Kingdom of God was disclosed in their utterly trusting acceptance of what God would have them do and their refusal to be frightened by threats. But there is also a Pisgah-like feature about their great venture. What was destined to follow was not that great world-embracing fellowship in which Jews and Gentiles were at one with each other, but a rivalry of faiths, a setting asunder of that which the Spirit had joined, a great loss of vision as the Church and the Synagogue took their respective ways. The radicalism of the Gospel of the Kingdom would give place to a compromise with the world.

In earlier chapters some of the reasons for both that parting of ways and opposition of faiths have been discussed. We know how rabbinic Judaism endeavoured to close the ranks of a sorely stricken people and to begin the rebuilding of Jewry's life in the years that followed Jerusalem's destruction. We can likewise imagine what efforts were made by Christians, Gentile and Jew alike, to extend, define and consolidate the life of the churches exposed to the threats and temptations of the surrounding religious and political world. In extreme times the extremist teaching tends to be heard most keenly. The trustful openness to which I have referred gave place to attitudes less consonant with the hope of the Kingdom coming on earth. It is in relation to that reshaping of thinking about the Kingdom that Buber's remarks, with which we began this chapter, have now to be understood. The hindrance he spoke of – the misunderstanding of the nature of the Kingdom as the Jewish prophets had divined it to be and as Jesus had preached and embodied it in his own life – grew out of the choices men made in dark times and under the influence of apocalyptic thought. The range of temptation was wide. It stretched all the way from the desperate desire to survive in a hostile world to an unrealistic grasping after status in worldly terms. The bartering begins in small things, in exchanging the prophetic insight of Israel for the philosophical and religious ideas of the Roman world.

Buber traced the progress of this change in terms of the distinction between the prophetic and apocalyptic modes of thought. A good deal of the latter had found expression in Jewish psalms and prayers. Geza Vermes (In *Jesus the Jew*, p. 131) and other have adduced examples drawn from writings like the Psalms of Solomon as illustrations:

Behold, O Lord, and raise up unto them their king, the son of David;
And gird him with strength, that he may shatter unrighteous rulers. . . .
With a rod of iron he shall break in pieces all their substance,
He shall destroy the godless nations with the word of his mouth..
And he shall gather together a holy people. . . .

It is never easy in following the use of traditional imagery to distinguish that which retains its world-rooted character from that which expresses flight from the doomed earth. 'The prophetic belief', Buber wrote, 'promises a consummation of creation, the apocalyptic its abrogation and supersession by another world, completely different in nature; the prophetic allows "the evil" to find the direction that leads towards God, and to enter into the good; the apocalyptic sees good and evil severed for ever at the end of days, the good redeemed, the evil unredeemable for all eternity; the prophetic believes that the earth shall be hallowed, the apocalyptic despairs of an earth which it considers to be hopelessly doomed; the prophetic allows God's creative original will to be fulfilled completely, the apocalyptic allows the unfaithful creature power over the Creator, in that the creature's action forces God to abandon nature.' From day to day choices made by men and women under the stress of confusion and persecution the direction of the two faiths was to be projected.

It would be foolish to suggest that Judaism maintained unblemished witness to the prophetic interpretation of Israel's faith during the long and bitter experience of the 'Christian' era. In the centuries during which the Talmud was put together and rabbinic Judaism charted the course of dispersed Jewry, many gusts of mystical speculation, fervid messianism, secular rationalism and the appeal of cultural assimilation threatened to destroy the proud witness which the Jewish faith was pledged to declare. Yet it kept its course not simply as an upholding of a creed but as the bond of a nation whose language, ways of living, law and expectations enabled it to retain identity and hope. It could still embrace the fundamentalism of Hasidism and the rationalism of philosophers when the attacks of anti-semitism forced upon it the renewed recognition of Jewishness set in a hostile world. 'Jews today', said Chaim Potok,' are engaged in an effort to create a third civilization', for Israel's emergence as a state three years after the end of the Second World War was a portent of a new phase of Jewish witness to God, even if atheistic Jews play a large part in its upbuilding. Such witness points forward to a world of nations whose interrelationships and styles of life we can at this moment barely conceive. We lack symbols to give us direction towards it. Once again men need the watchfulness of the hope of the Kingdom of God. Once again we need Jewish vision.

It is in relation to the concept of the kingdom of God then that the past history of the Christian Church must be seen. Cut adrift from its Jewish foundation the Church clung for some time to the thought of the speedy end of the world, some Fathers allowing two centuries, some more, for its progress towards the end. Men's attention was turned towards a Heavenly Kingdom, towards a theology of Heaven, Hell and Purgatory, to notions of immortality and a life after death. The Church, like an Ark of God, preserved the souls of those appointed to life till the time of their trials should cease.

Establishment as the official faith of the Roman Empire gave its own twist to this severance of Christian faith from the hope of the Kingdom as it had been proclaimed in prophetic terms. From this time onwards it knew two worlds intermingled, a condition so perilous to salvation that the saints counselled withdrawal from the secular world that men might devote themselves to God. The sense of the Kingdom as the Old Testament writers had known it – a kingdom of materialist expectations of oil and wine and rejoicings in God's bounty – gave place to mystical contemplation of life freed from temporal desires and concern. Yet, continuing to live in the social-political order, the Church also defined and tried hard to control the secular world as a servanthood with its appointed task. The compromise with the World Powers took various forms as the dualist position became defined. Anti-semitism significantly entered them all for the Jew continued to represent a dissent in the name of the God who created and loved the world.

The Holocaust may be said to be witness to the breakdown of human effort to maintain the compromise any longer. Though wrought of the sufferings of the Jews, it spells the defeat of the Christian pretension to stand up against the powers of the world. We shall wholly mistake the Holocaust's nature if we fail to recognize its universal significance. Failure to understand what the Holocaust means puts humanity itself in question.

It is the Kingdom of God which is at the heart of the problem. The long effort of compromised Christianity to give to God the largely unreal service of an idealized Kingdom elsewhere has come to a disastrous condition, though once it proudly claimed the Keys of the Kingdom, the control and direction and even a convincing challenge to the sensual, intellectual, material and political intentions upon which men set their hearts. For men learned in pursuing the things that they loved, as scholars or merchants, troubadours or soldiers, politicians or craftsmen, to set aside all other claims. The reckless expressed themselves ready to risk Hell itself for the sake of a kingdom, a woman, wealth or their evil desires. Bold spirits would first murmur and then cry aloud that religion was naught but a man-made device to keep cowards and fools in subjection. There is today a whole generation to whom the Christian Church finds itself unable to speak with conviction, Nor will it do so until it has faced the event about which it kept silent a generation ago.

It is all our theology, Jewish and Christian, which is under scrutiny now. We have nothing with which to weigh up the issues we face save the crucial disclosures of Scripture itself in the bruised and rejected servant of God and the crucified Christ, neither of which it would seem has been recognized in the crisis of the Holocaust in our midst. For both faiths have affirmed their belief that God acts in history, that His agents are all-unwittingly men bent on pursuing their own sinful ends, that His servants have laid on them the iniquity of a recklessly Godless world. Both have struggled to hold fast to God who would yet redeem and raise to new life those who trusted Him. As a Christian I cannot say to the Jews that God punished them for their iniquity, for I do not believe that to be true. I am compelled to believe, by the scriptural faith that we owe to the Jews, that the iniquity of us all, including the specific iniquities of Christians like myself, was laid on the Jews. I am an onlooker at the crucifixion. I have heard of a faith in God which survives that event and carries men on to new life set down in scriptural words but I now know it to be true in the history of our time. I know just a little better what the Jewish election means. I tremble with apprehension that the Christian Church to which

I belong and which has contributed its own evil behaviour to the sufferings of that people has not yet learned to see itself thus involved. I am forced to admit that this suffering is indeed what men inflict when they turn their backs on the Kingdom of God. The warnings and pleadings of Jesus and all the prophets have found confirmation in this grim event. But I know that the Church I belong to has not taught me to see human history in that light.

What Jews will do in this new phase of their existence in the world will concern mankind more intimately as the world shrinks to a global village and the thoughts of men's hearts are proclaimed instantaneously among all peoples. But what Christians must set about doing because of the Holocaust is an immediate matter. We cannot afford to grow careless to what it revealed of ourselves. We cannot neglect the reminder that the earth is the Lord's and that our real business is to prepare for His coming. Only so far as the Kingdom of God is made central to all Christian thinking and praying may we hope to be faithful servants.

Buber has put it: 'I recall an hour', he wrote, 'that I spent forty years ago with Albert Einstein. I had been pressing him in vain with a concealed question about his faith. Finally he burst forth. 'What we (and by this "we" he meant physicists) strive for,' he cried, 'is just to draw lines after Him, to draw after – as one retraces a geometrical figure'. The Kingdom of God stands for the figure that God has already drawn for the life of His people on earth. It is our most pressing business to set ourselves to follow His drawing. For too long Christianity has connived at the destruction of Jewry, whether by outright murder or by missions. If we are startled at finding these two things set together, it may help us to see how both have hindered the Kingdom's coming.

10. Israel and the Nations

The Queen's Hotel, Manchester, is not an exciting building and is unlikely to stir the imagination of the passer-by. Few places however in England in modern times have been the scene of a more momentous meeting, of a conversation more fraught with consequence. It was here in 1906, in the midst of a General Election campaign, that Arthur Balfour invited a young Russian Jewish scientist to meet him, and heard from him a reasoned and passionate exposition of the Zionist cause. 'It was from that talk with Weizmann', he said later, 'that I saw that the Jewish form of patriotism was unique.'

The Zionist movement was still in its youth. A pamphlet written by an Odessa Jew, Leo Pinsker, denouncing the Russian May Laws of 1882 which imposed new heavy disabilities upon Jews in Russia, demanded that the Jews must have a land of their own in which to become once more a nation. The air was charged with thoughts of land and people for it was in that year that Thomas Masaryk joined the staff at the Czech University at Prague, and there was much stirring among Czechs, Slovaks, Serbs, Croats, Slovenes,

and other peoples in Europe. A few years later a Viennese jour-
nalist, Theodor Herzl, attended the trial in France of Alfred Dreyfus, and reacted to the anti-semitism which he saw there in action
by conceiving the simple political project of the setting up of a
Jewish state. It attracted enough support to bring into being the
first Zionist Congress held in Basle in 1897. 'Zionism aims to
establish a publicly and legally assured home for the Jewish people
in Palestine.'

Herzl's movement met with opposition from prominent Jews
and his efforts to win support from the German Kaiser and from
the Sultan of Turkey came to nothing. He himself had no illusions
about the need to expropriate land for the settlement of the pioneers
and to withstand the theocratic pretensions of the rabbis. He was
thinking in terms of the liberal-revolutionary outlook that had
become an active force in nineteenth century Europe, but his
scheme had to make its way in fields where the imperialistic policies of the great powers were grinding towards a conflict. The
British, circumspect with regard to political tactics but with less
regard for African rights were later to offer territory in Uganda
for a Jewish National Home, an offer which was actually accepted
by the sixth Zionist Congress but subsequently rejected. The mys-
tique of the holy soil already counted for much.

In the minds of others more mundane thoughts were at work.
That eccentric freebooter, Laurence Oliphant, to take one example,
had addressed Lord Salisbury in 1882 with plans for a Palestine
Development Company which would have applied the methods
by which the great British trading companies had reaped rich
dividends in India and Africa to the dominion of the Sultan of
Turkey. His articles on the Land of Gilead read like the glossy
brochures of the pedlers of real estate. He overlooked nothing
from vast mineral deposits, cereals, wines, fruits, to medicinal
waters and tourism. The Sultan of Turkey was alarmed, Lord
Salisbury was not impressed, and the project came to nothing. It
was already clear that the land of Palestine was becoming a piece
on the chessboard of international politics.

Balfour did not forget his conversation with Weizmann. By
temperament, upbringing and intellectual outlook he was predis-

posed to look favourably on the claim of the Jews to a special position in Palestine. No doubt he also saw it as having political value, since his Government had felt it necessary to restrict the immigration of Jews from Eastern Europe into Great Britain. He had long detested anti-semitism, and the indebtedness of the Christian world to the Jews was at the forefront of his thinking.

His sympathy grew to conviction as World War I threw into stark relief both the need to secure the support of the Arabs and the problem of deciding upon the political future of the territories shaken loose from the Turkish Empire. From the words exchanged in the Queen's Hotel there was born just over a decade later the promise made by Balfour, now Foreign Secretary in Lloyd George's Cabinet, which is known as the Balfour Declaration. 'His Majesty's Government view with favour the establishment in Palestine of a national home for the Jewish people, and will use their best endeavours to facilitate the achievement of this object. . . .' Its text was to be incorporated in 1922 into the ratified Mandate of the League of Nations under which Great Britain had taken over the administration of Palestine. It established a National Home for the Jews in that land, and three years later, in 1925, Balfour went as a guest of the Zionist Organization to open the Hebrew University in Jerusalem.

The scheme was then, as it has never ceased to be, the subject of acrimonious debate. Within the British Cabinet, Balfour faced the sharp opposition of Edwin Montague, then Secretary of State for India, who voiced the dislike of British Jewry for the project and the belief that it would only intensify anti-semitism throughout the world. It was clear furthermore to many observers that the moral and cultural aims of the scheme were bound up with the tortuous politics of the powers competing for furtherance of their own interests in the East. Already pledged to support certain nascent Arab states and critical of French designs in Syria, the British Government was about to embark upon a policy from which it would withdraw some thirty years later baffled and humiliated by the problems which this Hydra-headed monster presented.

For the moment, however, the auguries looked propitious. King Feisal who spoke for the Arab peoples wrote: 'We Arabs ... look

with the deepest sympathy on the Zionist movement. We ... wish
the Jews a most hearty welcome home. We are working together
for a reformed and revived Near East, and our two movements
complete one another.' Not only were Arab leaders as yet unop-
posed to the scheme, but the expert on Middle-Eastern politics
Mark Sykes, who championed Arab liberation also warmly
endorsed the Zionist cause. 'It might be the destiny of the Jewish
race', he said, 'to be the bridge between Asia and Europe, to bring
the spirituality of Asia to Europe, and the vitality of Europe to
Asia.' Just what Europe had been doing with the spirituality of
Asia for the last nineteen hundred years or what the vitality of
Europe had in store for Asia went unremarked, but the years were
to write a cruel commentary upon that hope. It is important even
so to recall that the Statement of British Policy, issued by Churchill
in June 1922, spoke of the need to make clear to the Jewish people
that while the imposition of a Jewish nationality upon the inhabi-
tants of Palestine as a whole was not to be contemplated, it was
'in Palestine as of right and not on sufferance'.

Balfour's own views still deserve attention. Speaking in the
House of Lords in 1922, he said: 'I do not deny that this is an
adventure. Are we never to have adventures? Are we never to try
new experiments. . .?' Surely, it is in order that we may send a
message to every land where the Jewish race has been scattered, a
message that will tell them that Christendom is not oblivious of
their faith, is not unmindful of the services that they have rendered
to the great religions of the world, and most of all to the religion
that the majority of your Lordships' House profess, and that we
desire to the best of our ability to give them the opportunity of
developing in peace and quietness under British rule, those great
gifts which hitherto they have been compelled to bring to fruition
in countries that knew not their language and belong not to their
race.'

Experiment, but whose, to what end, and under what conditions? It fell perforce into the hands of men whose vision and
policies were often quite other than those which either Balfour or
the Zionist leaders had had in mind. Even before the Mandate had
been ratified Great Britain had cut off a large portion of the terri-

tory and handed it over to King Abdullah to form part of the kingdom of Transjordan. In a matter of a few months certain wealthy Arab families led by Haj Amin Husseini, soon to be called Grand Mufti of Jerusalem, not only declared their opposition to the project but spoke openly of the destruction of the entire Jewish community.

Attacks upon the new settlers began at once. Violent pogroms took place. By 1936 the whole Arab community was in revolt. The British Government replied with a series of Commissions of Inquiry but gave little protection to the Jews. Treating the new state more and more as a colonial possession and as subject to the dictates of policy aimed in the first place at securing Arab support, the British Government in the year of the Nuremberg Laws imposed strict quotas on further immigration. In Weizmann's words: 'Six million people were doomed.' The Evian Conference convoked by Franklin Roosevelt in May 1938 made clear the unwillingness of all major states to do more than offer expressions of sympathy.

Worse was to come. In a White Paper issued in May 1939 the British Government wiped out the Balfour Declaration. 'His Majesty's Government therefore now declare the unequivocally that it is not part of their policy that Palestine should become a Jewish State.' Though the Mandates Commission condemned this as not in accordance with the agreement that had given Great Britain the mandate in the first place, and though Churchill, Amery, Morrison, Sinclair and many others rejected it as a cynical repudiation of 'a pledge given not only to the Jews but to the whole civilized world', the White Paper was approved in Parliament. The Grand Mufti who had taken himself to Berlin received in an interview with Hitler in 1941 an assurance that when Germany had destroyed the two citadels of Jewish power, Great Britain and Soviet Russia, the Führer would liberate the Arab world and eliminate the Jews then living in the Arab sphere. Confusion however still reigned in British policy. In the post-war period the British Government rejected an Anglo-American Committee's report that the White Paper be abolished and failed to maintain by military methods any semblance of peace in Palestine; it had shed responsibility. In January 1947 the whole matter was turned over to the United Nations Organization which ended the Mandate and recommended that two states be set up. The Jews immediately accepted this. The Arabs rejected it and talked once again of a holy war to drive out all Jews.

On May 14, 1948, the independence of the new State of Israel was proclaimed, recognized by the Great Powers, and greeted by the Arab League with threats of unremitting warfare. Aided by large gifts of money from American Jewry and later by reparation payments made by the West German Government, the Israeli people began to reclaim the soil, to build houses and schools, to provide for a population of Arabs and Jews both rapidly increasing in numbers. The violence continued and the 1960's saw large-scale support being given by the U.S.S.R. to Egypt, Syria, Iraq, to all who were in the words of Colonel Nasser determined 'to wipe Israel off the map'.

The Six-Day War, the Yom Kippur War, continued terrorist acts have added their own grim chapters to the unfolding story of this experiment. Jews who had survived the Final Operation, Jews who had been expelled penniless from states like the Yemen, Jews who 'returned' from all parts of the world to live on the holy soil, were exposed to a life of unceasing military and terrorist threats. Israeli politics, economy and culture were perforce dominated by the question of survival. The great experiment which wise Rabbi Judah L. Magnes had in mind when he called Israel 'a laboratory in which the supreme experiment is being carried out', that a nation should be a witness to God in the world, was once again involved in a test of endurance.

Half a century of diplomacy, intrigue, warfare, economic pressures and terrorism only brings us to the threshold of questions which Israel raises both for the Middle East and for the world. In *To Jerusalem and Back* Yehoshafat Harbaki, a specialist on the Arab-Israeli conflict, said: 'We Westerners do not understand the Arab problem, nor do the Israelis, unfortunately, know much about it.' It has been the misfortune of Zionists, the majority of whose leaders in every walk of life have inherited advanced Western European cultural ideas, to have been thrust into the conducting of this experiment in a quite different world. The Arab problem

could be seen as one more example of the traumatic experience
which peoples in Africa and Asia had known, the consequence of
sudden exposure to the impact on traditional modes of living of
a powerful alien culture. The Palestinian question, part of a much
larger one embracing States from Iraq and Kuwait to Morocco, is
a cauldron in which seethe the political infightings of very diverse
Arab groups, the religious fanaticisms of ancient faiths strained by
contact with the modern secularized world, where folklore is
exploited to serve class-conflicts and economic rivalries and where
power politics are made explosive by armaments and oil and
superheated by nationalist self-consciousness. Such factors disrupt
attempts to bring understanding and peace to this part of the
world.

The adventure, the experiment, as Balfour called it, touched off
more deep-seated human reactions than had been foreseen, and
this in a world already strained by the upheavals of war and
economic disaster, by a situation which revealed the moral and
spiritual poverty of the leaders and peoples concerned. Adolf Hitler
was not wrong in seeing Germany's problem as 'the Jewish question'. It could even be said that he saw further down to the roots
of humanity's problem than did most of his contemporaries. The
crisis indeed posed the question What is Man? and the Jew represented an answer not simply in terms of a man's individual life and
faith but in those unspelled-out matters of national existence.
National Socialism was the crude brutal formula devised to answer
the Jewish question in a wholly inverted way. Its logic demanded
the extinction of the Jews.

When we turn then to consider the problem of nationalism in
the world today we do well to bear in mind Saul Bellow's warning
that we can be seduced at times into thinking 'that anything that
can be studied and written up is also susceptible to reasonable
adjustment'. We are dealing with matters in which the least-known
and most irrational forces of human nature are at work. There is
something in the Jews that arouses a fearful insanity among other
peoples. Neither the great international religions like Islam and
Christianity nor their secular socialist counterparts, nor the new
nation-States of the post-War world have been untouched by this

insanity. The condition of the Soviet Jews is but one illustration of the problem. Nor must we lose sight of the question as to whether Jews inside and outside of Zion have understood what Zion requires of them in the world today. If their Biblical mission still holds, then this present time has its own share in the creative-redemptive act of God. Do they, do we, see this as the underlying significance of the national question? The generation of Weizmann, Ben Gurion and Golda Meir has been compelled to think in terms of national survival and the end of that struggle is not in sight, but some of their contemporaries and many more of their children ask what that survival is for, a question not new in Jewish history but one which always needs to be asked. A religious nationalism not prominent in the formative years of the Zionist movement, is a part of Israel today. Masada could be repeated or this nationalism could lend energy to a wholly new venture of prophetic faith. No Christian can be indifferent to this new wrestling of Jacob with his historical task.

Few people in 1922 could have foreseen the forest-fire course of nationalism in the twentieth century world. Racism rightly commands attention today in social relations but beneath and beyond it lurks the more fundamental problem of nations and the relations of nation-states with each other. The problem is at once old and new: old in respect of Israel's calling, new in the proliferation of nations the world over pressing claims for recognition, independence and seats at the Assembly of the United Nations Organization. It is old in the light of Israel's task of working out a pattern of human relations that bears witness to God, new in that modes of living have changed and are changing so fast that those patterns have constantly to be redrawn.

Yet it would be shortsighted to treat all the conflicts and tensions in which Israel has been and is presently involved as a political matter of a nation involved in a struggle for power and survival. We mistake Israel's role in human history if we fail to see it as what has been called 'a system of communication'. Just as the language of great poets, the music of composers, the drawing of artists, the plans of architects and the skills of many others extend, embody and nourish the human spirit, it has been Israel's task to compose, define, celebrate, give form to, the true community, the right relationships of men in society, to be a holy nation. The pattern which Israel has been required to seek to honour down the ages is that of mankind growing up to its true stature. Leon Poliakov has called it Israel's 'ungrateful social role', an obligation 'to symbolize the great ethical values, to personify the forces of moral conflict ... and as scapegoat, to serve as a barometer of the tensions in Christian society'. The Bible never hides the fact that Jeshuran has kicked against this obligation and times without number betrayed it. The Holocaust might suggest that the burden is too heavy to bear. But Israel's history insists that God does not let her go nor leave her. 'Thou art Mine' is the pledge of her continued life. God's Covenant is, not was, the inescapable truth of this nation's existence.

It was as a nation, as *the* nation, that Israel confronted the world. Its mysterious character grew more not less impressive as its peoples in Europe became more conscious of the ties of language, custom, race and common interest which united them and of their differences from others. Nationality proved hard to define but easier to quicken. It was able to establish itself as a rival of older religious appeals. As the French Revolution and the changing conditions of nineteenth century life swept men into new ways of living it was as a religious force that the spirit of nationality gripped men's hearts and minds. It could offer much to those in pursuit of political power; equally it could excite the multitudes who as yet had none.

From the first stirrings of this awakening nationalism in Europe the Jews were not excluded. While the French Revolution gave the opportunity to them to become in 1791 'the first full and equal citizens of any state in Europe', the spirit of nationalism quickly turned to attack them. In the German states where romantic imagination and political necessity combined to inflate national dreams the Jews were at once suspect as an alien body. From J. G. Fichte, the idealist philosopher, there came the suggestion in 1793 that the Jews form a state within the state and as such could never be other than enemies of it. Since the State was to be regarded in Hegelian terms as the supreme manifestation of the Spirit, the Jews could scarcely be thought of as anything but destroyers of all that was sacred. Prevailing opinion was utterly hostile to them.

Despite the efforts of Jews to assimilate to German society which went on almost to the days when Hitler began his campaign, the German nationalist movement, headed by Prussia, consistently excluded them. In the brief period of the Stein-Hardenberg administrations Jews were granted full freedom as citizens and the same rights as Christians. Almost at once a reaction set in, all concessions were revoked, and year by year for some twenty years down to 1841 fresh legal disabilities were heaped upon the Jews. Then in 1841 came the notorious draft law which proposed to exclude them from any profession or office in which they might exercise authority over Christians or enjoy any rights which might diminish those of Christians. Though protests were strong enough to ensure that the plan was not enforced, controversy itself was enough to maintain the continuing exclusion of the Jews from social affairs and to keep alive the crudest mythological ideas of the nature of the Jewish faith.

What that could mean was shown in the infamous Damascus affair in 1840 when the Jews of that city, men, women and children, were arrested and tortured at the instigation of the French consul and of the Governor of the city, allegedly for murdering a Capuchin friar to secure blood for ritual purposes. All Europe soon learned what had taken place, and though the French Government under Thiers defended its consul, the outcry was of sufficient force to enable leading Jews like Adolphe Crémieux from France and Moses Montefiore from England to visit Turkey and to secure by personal intervention the release of the prisoners. The Damascus affair showed, as did the Dreyfus trial fifty years later, that popular Christian feeling could be whipped up into hysterical outbursts against the Jews to a point where rational behaviour could be swept aside. The point was not lost on Heine who saw it as a brief disclosure of powers that could be loosed to annihilate humanity itself.

If the nationalism which was to form one part of the title of Hitler's party was anti-semitic to the core, the socialist movement, though it attracted many Jews, added its own weight to the rejection of Judaism. It took various forms in the political and philosophical works of Marx, Moses Hess and Bruno Bauer. Bauer claimed that the alienation of man from freedom and true sociality, though connived at by Christianity, was basically the work of the Jews. They were the traders of mankind. Their outlook was dominated by the pursuit of gain and their intolerable egoism was both an affront to mankind and destructive of human progress. His writing was symptomatic of the learned nonsense soon to be spread throughout Europe.[1]

Marx made his views known in the two essays he wrote on the Jewish question and in his polemical pamphlet *The Holy Family*. There is no evidence to suggest that Marx, though he quoted liberally from the Scriptures, ever studied Judaism or any other religion or indeed objected personally to Jews with whom he mixed freely and to whose collaboration he owed much. He used the word Jew very freely to express contempt – Lassalle was 'a Jewish nigger' – but he was neither anti-semitic nor anti-Christian in aim since he directed his attacks to other fields. Nonetheless he used the word Jew to personify the enemy. Judaism was equated with Capitalism. 'Let us not seek the secret of the Jew in his religion but let us seek the secret of religion in the real Jew.' That creature, nowhere presented by Marx in terms of history, had made money the world great world power and made it the god of the Christians too. As such the Jew was the enemy of mankind, acknowledging only legal relations – 'my bond, I'll have my bond' – and contemptuous of art, philosophy, history and humanity itself. Perhaps only an immensely learned man could have been so immensely wrong.

The outcome of that failure on Marx's part to take seriously the history and the social condition of the people from which he had sprung was to be seen in the treatment accorded to the national question by Marxist leaders. Few of these thought this question important enough to subject it to an extensive critique or to ask why the workers of various nation-states were more inbued with nationalistic feelings than with concern for the Socialist Interna-

1. J. Carlebach, *Karl Marx and the Radical Critique of Judaism.*

tional. So the International failed to check the rivalries which led to war among the great Powers. The Third International ignored native working class traditions in favour of Soviet policy; it paved the way for anti-semitism in the Soviet Union, and it made no progress towards a satisfaction of the national aspirations of the peoples of the world.

Christian churchmen were no clearer or more at ease about the national question. The Papacy was at loggerheads with the Italian struggle for national unity and independence. In France a highly conservative clerical party was at war with the newly emerging popular and democratic parties. Germany claimed to be a Christian nation; religion was looked upon favourably when it supported the State, and Christian leaders were for the most part ready to do this. The Kulturkampf showed that there were limits to acquiescence but did not seriously challenge the nationalistic fervour. In Britain an established Church and a variety of minority denominations showed no desire to consider the question of nationalism deeply. In the pre-Christian pagan era nationality and idolatry went together. Christendom had drawn a great diversity of peoples together under a common creed and paved the way for the emergence of a new concept of nationality.

As the Roman imperial structure broke up the one-time small sect became the Church whose disciplined faith gave cohesion to a more comprehensive social order, to a fellowship rooted in small communities embracing both slaves and freemen into which the sole condition of entry was the baptismal rite.

The presence of Jews neither converted to nor assimilated into this society did not worry the architects of the Christian order. Intent upon saving the Empire as a political structure the Christianized Emperors readily acquiesced in the substitution of a theoretical fellowship for the common life in the Body of Christ which the primitive Church had known; they gave to the clergy an authority to shape the new order by doctrinal and moral teaching. The dualist thought and practice accepted into the Christian faith during the time in which it became the official religion of the Empire extended to all aspects of its life. There was but one society upon earth, one goal for mankind hereafter, but it was expressed in a dualism of Church and State, each with its organized hierarchy of administrative officials and systems of law.

In practice it could hardly hope to hold together. Built into its structure was a struggle for power; religious and secular leadership claiming for itself the allegiance of men. For a time it appeared as if the Church with its sanctions embracing the world to come could not but achieve this, but in its bid to do so by assuming temporal and legal power it forced the State into claiming authority no less extensive.

This sense of nationhood makes its appearance then as a factor in Europe's development long before the modern divisive political map was drawn. In the latter half of the twelfth century imaginative vernacular literature embracing both Biblical and secular history was fostering a keener awareness of national distinctions. In the following century 'nations' made up the student body of universities and voting by nations became the accepted practice in the Councils of the Church. These were pointers to what was to come.

The great nation-states proceeded to partition not Poland only but the whole world and to take steps to suppress whatever might question or weaken their powers to do so. As far as they could they sought to tribalize churches and the moral and spiritual teaching they gave. In the aftermath of the Napoleonic wars the polarization of men's lives went on apace. Pietistic thinking turned away from the worldly concern of the great churches and their manifest acquiescence in the disparities and social injustices of contemporary social life. Self-esteem and self-interest became the substance of nationality. This was the immediate background upon which the nature and policy of the Fascist and Nazi states were projected. Much is to be learned of both from the discussions conducted by Mussolini with the Church. Religion, it appeared, still served a useful purpose: 'Catholicism can be used for national expansion.' There was much to be said for morality too provided it was seen as a part of men's individual lives. Supreme authority nevertheless belonged to the Nation. 'Moral laws held only for man as an individual, not as a member of a nation, and nations as such led their lives apart from the moral law of Christianity' (D. A. Binchy). The Nazis provided a cruder version of these views. Thus the fragmentation of Christendom had reached the point where the Church could enter a Concordat with nation-states who claimed precedence for their political aims over all human rights and obligations. In the words of Buber: 'Something without precedent is taking place in this era. Some of the national egoisms which have been held in check by Christianity as by a common and supreme truth have freed themselves not only from Christianity, but from all inhibitions whatsoever. In their eyes, truth is nothing more than the function of the nation, and the 'prince' proclaims himself God (*Israel and the World*).

It was no accident then that the deification of the national interest and the planned extermination of Jewry should come to a head in Germany. To say this is not to imply that the Third Reich was the inevitable outcome of German history. What we can point to are the many factors which made Hitler possible so that, in Peter Gay's words, he 'was neither an unwelcome invader nor an uncaused accident' (*Freud, Jews and Other Germans*). Coming later than all its rivals to political unification Germany compounded its nationalist strength out of a powerfully emotive mythology, a philosophical systematization of thought, a highly developed educational practice, efficient and authoritative social administration, technological power and pride in military success. Its religious and political divisions served chiefly to confirm the sense that national well-being must be purchased by total assertion of unified purpose, by total surrender to what it demanded. National Socialism sprang not simply from Hitler's imagination but from the conditions of Europe in which Germany struggled to realize its national identity. Among the conditions affecting the Reich must be placed the anti-semitic strain, the index of baulked nationality's pride.

To understand Judaism in relation to the national question we must realise that German Jewry had for a long time experienced intolerable internal strain. Jews were often prominent among Jew-haters and ready to join in the most scurrilous attacks upon Jewish institutions, ideals and behaviour. The success with which some had become good Germans made them anxious to repudiate the alien intrusion of others. For the sake of that Germanness many paid dearly in personal terms. The Jewish conductor Hermann

Levi bore for the sake of the master's music all the crudely offensive
and contemptuous anti-semitism of the Wagner family. There were
others who, like Walter Rathenau, openly expressed their determination to prove themselves wholly German in culture and lay-
alty to the State. 'We are endowed as no other people is for a
mission of the spirit. . . . We can and,must live by becoming what
we are designed to be, what we were about to be, what we failed
to become, a people of the Spirit, the Spirit among the peoples of
mankind.' The 'we' of that declaration was not that of Judaism but
of the German nation, for Rathenau went on to say: 'I have and
know none but German blood, no people but the German. If I am
driven from my German home, I remain German and it alters
nothing. You speak of my blood and race, meaning the Jewish.
With the Jews I have no bond but that which all Germans share,
the Bible, memory and the formation of the Old and New Testament.' We may likewise recall that it was with such a conception
of the larger German culture and not a little animosity towards the
Jewish faith that Freud spent the greater part of his working life.
Only when the true nature of anti-semitism forced itself upon him
during the 1920's did he elect to call himself a Jew rather than a
German.

The nationality problem, Christian and Jewish, faced Herzl and
the pioneers of the proposal to set up a Jewish state. *Der Judenstaat*
(published in 1896) examined and dismissed the idea that the Jewish
question was simply a social or religious matter and that, given
time, it would die away. Herzl foresaw increasing pressure upon
them. He put it plainly: 'It is a national question which can only
be solved by making it a political world-question to be discussed
and settled by the civilized nations of the world in council.' The
great nations were at the time ill-prepared to discuss and settle
their problems in this way. Nevertheless the proposal could be
said to anticipate some of the work which the makers of the Treaty
of Versailles and the League of Nations undertook. What preparation had there been on the Jewish side towards achieving an understanding of what was involved? The Jews admitted their right to
be accorded what other nations enjoyed; but did they, deprived for

so long of such things, know what would be involved in securing them, and was something more at stake in the Jewish question?

Jewish teachers had from the earliest times been concerned with the national characters, this nation above all others had been instructed in the right conduct and meaning of a nation's life, and had fought long since the battles of the idolatrous misuse of national feeling and well-being. But was it in its Dispersion prepared to translate that ancient teaching into the idiom of modern life?

Modern Jewry had not lacked information about anti-semitism. The founder of the philosophy of Jewish history in the modern world was Nahman Krochmal. While he lived and wrote in his Galician town the mass armies brought into being by the French Revolution marched across Europe destroying the last bastions of the medieval world to make way for the new Nation States with their plans to transform the world. He saw how recklessly and arrogantly the newly unleashed nationalistic powers dealt with the citizens of their own states and of others and asked how the mad rush to destroy human beings could be halted. Jews living on sufferance in lands where they were despised and persecuted were in no position to change the policies of the powers any more than Israel, poised between Egypt, Assyria, Persia and Greece had been; but that weakness did not negate Israel's obligation, it rather confirmed it. It was still Israel's task to open men's eyes to idolatry, to resist the demands of the absolute State, to insist that God only could rightly demand the final allegiance of men.

The test would come when the character of the Zionist enterprise was being defined. One aspect of this was outlined by Aaron David Gordon in 1920 in an address to a conference held in Prague to discuss immigration into Palestine. The signs of trouble were already there, even though the number of immigrants was still small. In defining Zionist aims Weizmann had spoken of Palestine becoming 'as Jewish as England is English'. Gordon had been among the pioneer entrants into that land in 1904. Though already a middle-aged teacher he was determined to work on the land; he was filled with a profound conviction of the need to restore a living connection between men and the earth which God had made. He realized quickly how deeply Arab opinion was alarmed and offended by Zionist aims. Gordon wholly believed that the project of establishing a Jewish National Home, internationally guaranteed and formally recognized by the great powers as having an historic title, could, if wisely pursued, contribute to something even more important than the satisfaction of Zionist political hopes. It was a sine-qua-non of Israel's own achievement that it should do so, though the cost would be high.

Gordon saw Israel as committed to discovering how a passionate love of the nation could be harmonized with a recognition of wider obligations. Mankind as a whole needed to grasp more firmly the principles of true community living. It needed a more truly religious sense of the nature of life. The stark individualism which had characterized European life since the Renaissance, whether in terms of men or nations, had brought it to the brink of chaos in which freedom depended precariously upon a balance of power, in which wealth was measured increasingly in terms of the consumption of goods, and where moral standards were made less and less explicit. 'What was fading ... was a certain concept of freedom, based on that "preservation of an inner sphere exempt from State power," in which, all liberty consisted.' What would be needed, not simply in Israel but in modern society as a whole, was a more realistic, courageous and hopeful attitude towards the future, a renaissance of a profoundly religious conception of human life. Only so could this or any other nation participate in the renewal of human life.

'Without the nation that is part of humanity there can be no humanity; for the individual cannot be a human being. Who should know this better than we, the children of Israel? We were the first to proclaim that man is created in the image of God. We must go further and say: the nation must be created in the image of God, not because we are better than others, but because we have borne upon our shoulders and suffered all that which calls for this. It is by paying the price of torments, the like of which the world has never known, that we have the right to be first in this work of creation' (A. D. Gordon, Address to World Conference of Hapoel Hatzair, Prague 1920).

Here was the clearest enunciation of Israel's calling made in twentieth century conditions. Here too was Israel's title linked to her record of suffering. Here the religious component in human life was shown as the foundation and ultimate sanction of the social order.

For a Christian trying to think and pray carefully over the meaning of Israel for Christians, Muslims and Jews, and for the whole world today, there can be no question of telling the Jews what they ought to do. Remembering how much Christianity has contributed to the sufferings of the Jews, they must rather learn to bring greater understanding to the problems now facing Israel and pray that Jews themselves may tackle them from the deepest levels of their historic calling. They must likewise bear in mind that Israel has known no respite from the challenge to her very existence long before and after Hitler decreed the Final Operation. 'On this speck of land – an infinitesimal fraction of the surrounding territories – a troubled people has come to rest, but rest is impossible. . . . At this uneasy hour the civilized world seems tired of its civilization, and tired also of the Jews. It wants to hear no more about survival. But there are the Jews, again at the edge of annihilation and as insistent as ever, demanding to know what the conscience of the world intends to do. . . . And the civilized world, or the twentieth century ruins of that world to which so many Jews gave their admiration and devotion between 1789 and 1933 (the date of Hitler's coming to power), has grown sick of the ideals Israel asks it to respect' (S. Bellow, *To Jerusalem and Back*). It is not on political grounds only that we Christians must see Zion today as a world problem.

For Israel is an armed camp. She is reminded daily that her survival depends upon unceasing vigilance and the readiness of her citizens to bear the brunt of attacks of an enemy many times greater than she is in numbers and resources. To the generation of Ben Gurion and Dayan and Begin these are the priorities. There have been outstanding Jews who have urged that Zionism means much more than this and that Israel's present problems are not going to be solved unless their connection with her age-old calling is observed. In Israel's history men have always been tempted to judge all things touching the life of the nation from the angle of its survival; even religious comment has been approved or disapproved according to its supposed contribution to national morale.

In the earlier formative period the question of Israel's future could not be judged on grounds of economic or political expediency but only upon those cosmic foundations which accounted for Israel's presence in the world. By any other reckoning she should have perished long since. More important than her political stature was the purity of her witness to the divine intention. The mystery of Israel was proclaimed in the fact that in spite of the crimes of her oppressors and the follies and sins of Jews themselves, Israel still existed as a nation. As Buber reflected upon Psalm 73, it was but by the mercy of God that the Jewish nation had not long since turned wholly away from its calling and concluded that God had ceased to care.

Can this interpretation stand up to the challenges of the twentieth century? Israel's mystical teachers had conceived of her role in relation to the great cosmic drama of a once-shattered primal unity redeemed through the action of God who had chosen this people to effect it. To the end of time Israel must live among other nations to play an appointed decisive part in the world's redemption. From the great events of history like the Exodus and the Exile, from the Torah as a whole down to the single letters of sacred words there gleamed the shafts of the light of his glory. To less mystical minds Israel's role was more pragmatic. She continued because she represented a grasp of something essentially human, something which underlay the thinking, feeling, creative spirit in man, which but for Israel's costly witness would be lost to sight by other men. Gordon himself made use of the phrase, 'a people-incarnating-humanity'. It was Israel's business to see that the image of God was truly expressed in the life of a nation. The Messiah would come to the nation through whom all nations were to be blessed.

In the political arena then in which the great powers and the nations of the world are now participants. Israel struggles not simply with her neighbours but with herself and in the depths of the nation's soul. As we pray we must recognize that truth, and honour it. Unless we pray with that kind of awe we betray our own insensitivity to Biblical history, for what is being worked out in Israel today is a part of the titanic strife that embraces Jacob and Moses, Amos and Jeremiah, the Passion of Jesus Christ and the Holocaust. We fail wholly if we fail to see the radical relation of the struggle to these things. We are involved in it. It is part of our own salvation-history.

It is significant that Jews who have played an outstanding part in the world's diplomatic affairs – Nahum Goldmann and Buber, for instance – tend to speak with one voice about the momentous choices that Israel must make. Goldmann indeed, while bluntly declaring that 'there is no hope for a Jewish state which has to face another fifty years of struggle against Arab enemies', goes on to say 'We unquestionably took the wrong direction from the start, and did not pay enough attention to the warnings of a far-sighted Zionist minority... who sensed what a false step it was.' It is not simply a matter of military success; what has been happening in Israel has been the elevation of State power to supremacy over all other aspects of national life, the politicizing of human life. This could destroy Judaism no less deliberately than the anti-semites have endeavoured to do.

There is a common note then in Goldmann's insistence that the real challenge is how to make Israel different from what it is today, to make it the champion of a war, not against Arabs, but against poverty, illiteracy and inequality, for the abolition of the sovereign state, and for peace', and Buber's definition of the nation's task 'We talk of the spirit of Israel', he wrote, 'and assume that we are not like unto all the nations because there is a spirit of Israel. But if the spirit of Israel is no more to us than the synthetic personality of our nation, no more than a fine justification of our collective egoism, no more than our prince transformed into an idol – after we had refused to accept any prince other than the Lord of the Universe – then we are indeed like unto all the nations; and we are drinking together with them from the cup that inebriates. And when we grow drunk after their fashion, we become weaker than any other nation, and find ourselves entirely defenceless in their hands.'

This is the thinking inherited by a new generation to whom the Holocaust and the founding of the Zionist state are events of the past. The children of those who suffered so much and those who saw the miracle of Zionist dreams take place will soon take over the leadership of the nation. Throughout history Judaism has attached outstanding importance to its children. The unfinished, often mistaken, often rejected, task of Israel's calling may be yet accomplished through them. Not simply the biological or political continuity of a people but the steadfast hold of a Godgiven promise is what has sustained Israel. It is now being called to make choices deeply significant not only for Israel but for the whole of mankind. The last word on what is at stake was expressed by Buber: 'Let us awaken this Zionism in the hearts that have never felt it, in the Diaspora as well as here. For here in this country also we need a movement which strives for Zion, aspiring towards the emergence of the rebuilt Zion from the materials at our disposal. . . . A Messianic idea without the yearning for the redemption of man-kind and without the desire to take part in its realization, is no longer identical with the Messianic visions of the prophets of Israel, nor can that prophetic mission be identified with a Messianic ideal emptied of belief in the coming of the kingdom of God.'

'We also go with you' (John 21.3).

11.   I Am Joseph Your Brother

'If this people which is not a people is the people of God ... a nation without equal, then what becomes of the rest of us?'
Karl Barth, *Church Dogmatics*

'Before God, then, Jew and Christian both labour at the same task. He cannot dispense with either. He has set enmity between the two for all time, and withal has most intimately bound each to each.'
Franz Rosenzweig, *The Star of Redemption*

Men have always been ready and adept to build up walls within and without their minds to defend themselves, to exclude others, to wall up nations and their own souls. China's Great Wall would be the only human erection perceived by eyes from another planet. Perhaps more penetrating vision might see the wall of partition designed to exclude the Jews as something more symbolic of the human condition, something which throws darkness across this world as nothing else has done.

This is the wall of partition whose breaking down the Epistle to the Ephesians announced so long ago (Eph. 2.14). It has had nonetheless an obdurate history of continuance. Today we are conscious at least that there are some chinks in the wall through which Christians and Jews may talk to each other. We are awkward about it. What do we now want to say? What are we ready to hear? What do we think in our hearts of the one who has stood through millennia of human history on the other side of the wall ? Why did Christians and pagans so feverishly build up the wall? What were they trying to keep out?

For a moment it appears that the wall was once not there. The

Christian scriptures, the Acts of the Apostles and the pastoral epistles, suggest that an effort was made by the young Christian Church to see that the wall should not be raised. What was possible once can be done again, given the will to do it. Why not a Council of Jerusalem now to write its own chapter of the Acts of Christ's Body in the world of today? At this we are likely to pause. We may recollect that St Paul reminded the Gentile members of the Church that they owed their life in God to the fact of having been engrafted onto Israel's stock, that they would otherwise have been without hope, without God, in the world, that their riches in Christ had come to them through the Jews. It was not easy to confess that to turn against the Jewish people was to turn against God Himself, who had chosen to be represented by this people. Marcion, for one, could not stomach the thought. The Jews, he insisted, were the creation of some other god. Others, including Hitler, have said this too, but have they really believed it? Perhaps they expressed only a wish that it might be so; what they really despaired of was the thought that Jews did represent God, and they hated them both.

These thoughts have been with the Church throughout history. We may trace the awkwardness in the Gospels. Yet if we look to Jesus, the Fourth Gospel, a book by no means tender to the Jews, records Him as saying that salvation was of the Jews. This suggests that we too must seek Him among His own people and not claim that because some of them cast Him out, He was parted from them for ever. Israel's God was not only the God who had chosen this people but the God who had said that He would not let them go. They were graven upon the palms of His hands. To seek Him elsewhere would be to run the risk of being beguiled by Christs of men's own making, by Christs of much theological subtlety. The obvious difficulties of Christian work in the world today sprang from just such confusion of mind, from this image of a Christ detached from His people. Pious imagination sinks into vain imaginings unless checked by constant reference to the Jesus whose flesh was Jewish.

For the greater part of its history the Christian Church saw no reason why it should try to talk with members of other religious

faiths, save in a polemical or apologetic fashion. It alone possessed
the truth. It alone was guided by the Spirit. While it might use the
philosophy and literature of the pagan world to illustrate the saving
truth it was not beholden to any of them for its knowledge of
eternal things. Yet unconsciously absorbing and wilfully appro-
priating much that was pagan it solaced its pride by proclaiming
its unique commission.

Today it is possible to see how impoverishing, self-deluding and
morally destructive this attitude has been. The immensity of the
missionary work of the Church and the heroic faith of the pioneers
of the great outbursts of Christian devotion is not to be doubted.
Men carried the knowledge of the Gospel of Christ to many nations
and the great concept of Christendom bearing His name was
brought into being. But the facts of the world-situation arrest us.
Neither Jews nor Muslims have yielded to Christian blows or pleas
nor has advanced education or higher standards of living made
men more willing to accept what the churches have to say. Its
history has become a dubious asset for the Church today. In learning to look with more chastened mind at its own record, the
Christian Church may well begin with the most terrible item of
all, its relations with the Jews.

How may we set about this new beginning? I have referred
elsewhere to the history of the parted ways, to the build-up of an
anti-semitism that is almost taken for granted in Christian thought.
In theology, to take but one example, we find in Bultmann's
thinking not so much an exclusion of the history of Israel from
decisive exposition of Christian faith but a cutting asunder of that
faith as a whole from revelation in historical terms. On the other
hand there have been striking re-assessments of the relationships
of Christian theology with Jewish sources. These offer at least the
ground upon which a new kind of understanding may be
attempted. Reinhold Niebuhr, for instance, recognized with great
humility 'the strange miracle of the Jewish people' and remarked
that it had no analogy. 'It must be appreciated for what it is.'

I wish however to look elsewhere. While the great anti-Jewish
campaign was being set in motion in Germany in the inter-war
years, Thomas Mann began to write the sequence of stories entitled

Joseph and his Brothers. In the foreword to the whole work he described the conditions under which it was written, conditions which raised questions in sensitive minds not simply about the fate of the Jews but about the future of civilized Europe and mankind. Something like a shiver of cold apprehension passed across the cultural scene. Mann took the Jewish story and told it again.

There have been greater novels written during the past fifty years but few which have more sensitively touched the foundations of human life in terms of vision and the effects it has on the soul of man. 'Men saw through each other,' he wrote, 'in that distant day as well as in this.' They also saw what men down the years would turn away from and refuse to see, what in pride and anger and folly they would choose to be blind to. But to Jacob and his house, to see into the things of God was their commitment. The pain and the joy, the good and the evil, of living itself were the fruits of what they saw. 'Not for nothing was he the pupil of old Eliezer, who knew how to say "I" in such an ample way that Joseph's eyes grew dim with musing as he beheld him. The transparency of being, the characteristic recurrence of the prototype – this fundamental creed was in his flesh and blood too, and all spiritual dignity and significance seemed to him bound up with awareness of it.' This Joseph, symbol of something reaching down to the depths of the mystery of God's ways with mankind, would be cast into the pit by his brothers, rejected and spurned and enslaved, till the finger of God moved on to that moment when, standing before his brothers in Egypt he would not only make himself known to them but find words to say what the relationship with God meant to them, to himself and to all men to come.

The words of the Biblical story are brief. 'You thought evil against me; but God meant it unto good, to bring it to pass as it is this day, to save much people alive' (Gen. 50.20). The irony of the circumstance, the drama of recognition, the tumult of human emotion – all charge the moment with rare intensity, but the sense of dimension imparted to human life that it gives is more important than these. The Jew will affirm from the pits and the prisons, the ghettoes and camps all down the years that God has indeed said this thing and brought it to pass. Through the fire and the flood, through pain and through death, He would do so again. There is nothing comparable to it elsewhere. It is certain that men will need it again and again.

We must pause on that evil. If the Holocaust is to do for mankind what the story of Joseph in Egypt suggests, what the Passion of Christ exhibits, we must see the evil for what it is. Bettelheim and Wiesel, Frankl and Kaplan and others have tried to warn us that this is not easy task. Words – Holocaust, genocide, mass-murder – can blur the sharp image of that which the eyes of the spirit must see; and yet must try to comprehend the incomprehensible, the men with a hatred of life, of love, of light, with a hatred of all that is human and divine, who desired the darkness and death of the spirit itself. Egyptian records tell us nothing of Joseph, Roman history has scarcely an unassailable genuine word on the Passion of Jesus. Our news-service is better. The facts have been told to the world. Our danger lies not in our lack of knowledge but in our not knowing what they meant and must mean today. To miss out on that is to share the fate of Hitler's victims.

What is to be kept in mind can be illustrated not by dwelling upon the Holocaust but by looking a little more closely at the words of two Jewish prophets of our time. The Biblical Joseph not only made himself known to his brothers and received them with love but declared to himself and them that the hand of God was at work in such things. In an hour of need they were brought together. 'He had sent a man before them, even Joseph, who was sold for a slave.' From that act of deliverance and reconciliation there flowed the formation of Israel as a nation to bear witness to God at all times. What lay hidden in the history of centuries to come were more grievous acts of oppression, more stark confrontations of separated peoples, till God should 'bring it to pass as it is this day' that a reconciliation of profounder implications for the whole world should be made. The two men that I speak of have stood apart in many respects from the mainstream of Jewry's life but have spoken as prophets from the deeps of its calling. They are Franz Rosenzweig and Martin Buber.

Of some men it may be said that they appear to embody in their own existence the movements and crises of a whole people. Rosen-

zweig was such a man. Though he died before the great waves of
Nazi violence had broken over German life his choice to remain
a Jew and his life-work, the re-interpretation Judaism and Christianity to each other, make him in many senses a man sent before-
hand by God to prepare the way for the revelation of long-needed
truth. To do so at all he had to come face to face with his own
personal recognition of that truth. He did so at Yom Kippur in
1913.

Like so many Jews of his generation in Germany he had made
up his mind to abandon the nominal Judaism of his family background, 'the empty purse' as he called it, and to become a Christian. He had been greatly influenced by his friend Eugen Rosenstock, a Christian of Jewish descent. He had also thought long
about the Christian nature of contemporary German culture. 'I
began', he wrote, 'to reconstruct my world, and in this world
there seemed to be no room for Judaism.' He felt himself unable
to go on with a life which appeared, as he said to his mother, 'to
disregard all reality which lies beyond the purview of the *Frank-
furter Zeitung*'. Even so he resolved to make it a truly religious
choice and to enter Christianity as a Jew. He went therefore to
synagogue on the Day of Atonement as he supposed for the last
time. He remained a Jew.

He himself has written in a note on a poem by Judah ha-Levi a
most moving account of the significance of the Day of Atonement.
We meet in this note the word 'dialogue' which was to play so
influential a part in both Jewish and Christian thinking in later
years. Rosenzweig described the dialogue between God and man.
Year by year the Jew must stand before God in these depths, the
soul before Him who made it. 'Does God take the first step, or
does man?' Does not God insist that man take it while setting
between Himself and His creature depths that must make at-one-
ness seem quite beyond our grasp? Of course the last word could
only be God's but God could choose to be silent. Man cries in that
silence, 'Forgive'. This is the germ of Jewry's life. Israel's intent
on the Day of Atonement is to bring both national and personal
existence to the threshold of death, to receive them again at the
hand of God.

From then onward Rosenzweig sought to make clear to himself
and his readers what he now believed of the nature and the relationship of the two faiths. Many eyes besides his had looked at the
mediaeval statues at Bamberg and Chartres where the blindfolded
Synagogue grasping her broken staff contrasted Israel's condition
with that of the Church clear-eyed and sceptred.

It was not with uncertainty that Rosenzweig looked at the symbols. 'The synagogue which is immortal', he wrote, 'but stands
with broken staff and blindfolded, must renounce all work in this
world and muster all her strength of preserve her life and keep
herself unsullied by life.' The task of bringing the world to salvation she must leave to the Church, yet before that Church she
must bear her own witness to God, renouncing all worldly ambi-
tion, and learning through suffering to hallow God's name, enduring all things for His sake. At this witness the Church could look
only with awe.

What Rosenzweig said then amounted to this: that both faiths
were to be seen as manifestations of one underlying religious truth.
Each needed the other. Each carried a part of the truth as the
ground and title of its existence. Each must honour the other as
the servant of God. Each stood answerable to the one Lord and
Master who had called them and given them their work. A wholly
new relationship between the two must be seen and upheld. Here
indeed was revolutionary demand. Looking back to it in the light
of all that has happened in the churches in recent years we may
well see it chiding our dullness of vision.

More was to come. In the wartime correspondence with Eugen
Rosenstock, in a number of essays and finally in his great work
The Star of Redemption, Franz Rosenzweig undertook what has
been described as 'the first attempt in Jewish theology to understand Judaism and Christianity as equally true and valid views of
reality'. Jewish teachers had long complained that Christians had
made little attempt to undo the misrepresentation of Jewish faith
that had been the great wall between them. It was not usual for
Christians to think of themselves any poorer for that. Rosenzweig
set out to try to find ways through which the dialogue could begin.

Rosenzweig did not come easily to his thoroughgoing Judaism.

It was through a battering dialogue with Rosenstock that he clar-
ified his position. The correspondence between them represents
the true dialogue to which Buber and he came to attribute the
formative relations of human life. It carries the hallmark of true
real spirituality. 'I believe', wrote Rosenzweig, 'that there are in
the life of each living thing moments, or perhaps only one
moment, when it speaks the truth. It may well be then that we
need say nothing at all about a living being, but need do no more
than watch for the moment when this living being expresses itself.'

Was the Holocaust such a moment of truth for Christian-Jewish
relations? Rosenzweig was not prophetic in the popular sense of
foreseeing the future but he looked searchingly at the situations
facing both faiths. His judgments were often pointed. He attacked
fellow-Jews for 'toying with Christian and pagan ideas'. He
rejected entirely the idea of Israel becoming a political entity like
other nation states, remarking that 'it is this rootedness in ourselves
and in nothing but ourselves, that vouchsafes our eternity'. True
Judaism was therefore no academic affair and it was an intensely
personal and lonely struggle. It was nonetheless quite inseparable
from the age-old Jewish obligation to return to Israel's calling. 'It
is how Christian Jews, national Jews, religious Jews, Jews from
self-defence, sentimentality, loyalty, in short "hyphenated Jews"
such as the nineteenth century has produced, can once again without danger to themselves or Judaism, become Jews.' Did he reckon
the cost of the process rightly?

What he saw and foresaw was published in his great book *The
Star of Redemption*. It is a strange difficult book; it takes off from
death and ends in life and wrestles throughout with the question
of how men may speak to each other. It is a prophetic book. Not
inappropriately it was first written on postcards from the battle-
fields of the first World War. It was shaped to equip the Judaic-
Christian faith for its conflict with an increasingly hostile world.

Rosenzweig believed that the time was short. He saw European
culture approaching the point of collapse and he saw its need to be
rescued by powers from outside, for by itself it could only grind
towards a chaos of self-destruction. The rescuing powers must
include Judaism, but all of them stood in danger of being secular-

ized and Europeanized by their intervention, corrupted by contact
with that which had sapped the spiritual resources of Europe
already. Yet the task was laid on both Christians and Jews, and
what mattered above all else was that each faith should work at its
proper task, not ignorant or jealous of the other, but conscious of
a joint calling to serve God and His people. It was the Jews' task
to live in the world and to hallow God's name there. To Christians
it fell to go through the world to make disciples out of every
nation. 'The mission of Judaism was to endure till the end of the
world as the people of the King before whom one day all the
nations will bow down. The mission of Christianity is to preach
to the heathen, to christianize countries of the world and the souls
of the people.' How pitiful that down the ages men of the two
faiths had wasted their lives so recklessly in hating each other.
Both were needed. Each needed the other.

The Star of Redemption is not a literary nor theological master-
piece. Theories and speculations stick out like awkward bones,
detours in the argument consume attention, the scope of the work
overwhelms its unity. Yet it holds together, as do all great books,
like a galaxy and wheels with the same astounding motion. It is
a cosmic vision. Ever and again some supernova within it flares
up with brilliant intensity. Rosenzweig believed profoundly that
the subject itself was like that. It could not be treated 'as though
it were a Platonic dialogue, not murder and manslaughter'. Too
many had left their bones in the wilderness or died in torment in
prison, in fires or on crosses, to permit easy writing to grapple
with faith or life.

The ground plan of the book lay in the six-pointed star. Man,
World and God were linked with the three expressions, Creation,
Revelation and Redemption. Life meant becoming aware of these.
It meant finding that the light which blazed at Creation now shines
to herald the dawn of the kingdom of light. In the pagan world it
shone in the darkness unseen. The two faiths perceived and bore
witness to it. Judaism was 'the eternal fire' at the heart of the Star,
Christianity the rays issuing from it.

The language might seem at first sight to belong much more to
a world of mystical vision than to the conditions of twentieth

century life, but Rosenzweig made immense claims. The historical fact of the Christian Church in no way annulled Israel's calling to sanctify God's name in the world. No one could ever usurp that role. It was time that Christians affirmed it and ceased to look upon Jews as unaccountably stubborn in maintaining the ancient faith. It was time too that Jews learned to recognize that the covenanted relationship of God and man had been opened to all mankind and that the Christian Church must win men through Christ to participation in it. Both faiths were involved in an unending struggle to preserve the purity of their service to God. For Judaism this meant seeing its history contrasted with that of all other peoples, buying its eternity at the cost of temporal ease and success. For Christianity it would for ever mean being committed to the preaching of the crucified Lord, resisting the attempt to substitute for it a gospel of aggrandisement and cultural success. For ever it must bring every thought into true subjection to Him who thus died.

What then of Joseph facing his brothers? In the two final sections of *The Star of Redemption*, Rosenzweig dwelt on the two faiths seen together. He would not set one above the other but called upon both to 'cleanse the doors of perception' in a spirit of penitent renewal. He probed for a genuine readiness to come clean from the pride and contempt that had poisoned relationships in the past. Before ever the Holocaust came to set the whole matter in terms of survival for both Jews and Christians, he tried to get men to see that the time was one of crisis.

Few books in the modern world have attempted so much. Rosenzweig was emphatically Jewish in insisting upon the weight of Israel's 'no' to the pagan world and human idolatries, a 'no' that was scored deeply into Israel's history and beyond. The gods of the heathen and the gods of the philosophers were patrons of easier appeals and syntheses of ideas. Israel's God required a 'no' to them all. From Israel Christianity too must constantly learn to say 'no' to worldly appeals. It had been weakened in learning to do so by its failure to apply to itself the lessons of Israel's past, by its narrow interpretation of Old Testament scripture as no more than a foreword to its own life. It would need Israel's gesture of firm resistance if it was to say 'no' to the 'ghosts of the tribes' and all the new versions of Moloch, Astarte and Caesar.

But the 'no' of the creature is swallowed up in the great gesture of God's giving life to His world and His people. It is likewise transcended in the love towards which his creatures are drawn. 'As He loves you, so shall you love.' In loving, Redemption takes flesh and embraces the beloved that they may know themselves in an eternal 'we'. The 'no' of the separated brothers is transfigured by the great leap of yearning love which testifies to the quickening spirit of God. Not lightly did Rosenzweig speak of the Song of Songs as 'the focal book of revelation'.

So, he continues, 'we find ourselves'. We come to the point which is central in all great drama, the point of recognition, the *anagnorisis*, not of tragedy but of the Divine Play, reversing men's choices — 'you thought to do me evil' — and crowning them with a Godgiven choice of Life. For both faiths it is the miracle of rebirth. It is this alone which can give, must give, room for mission, not of one superior to the other, but of each to the other. 'The people of God, on both sides, stand in perpetual need of renewal.' The tragedy of the past nineteen hundred years lies in the separation of these brothers. The Holocaust must bring home to them both that only through mutual recognition of each other with no other motive but that of love may they play their appointed part in the world's redemption. Now is the time. Christianity has come perilously near to accepting the kingdoms of Church and State in lieu of seeking the Kingdom of God. The Jew has come near to thinking that outside the Jewish there is no valid consciousness of the world. Now, the one must recall the other to the share which each has in the overall task. The Christian must honour as he has not yet done the people called out by God to be 'a kingdom of priests and a holy nation'. Unthinkingly he has applied it to himself and failed to read the Scriptures aright. He must now learn truly to recognize what implications arise for him from the presence of a people bearing God's law in the world. This brother was, in the strange mercy of God, sent before him. He must humbly ask why. He must furthermore begin to prove what his own calling 'through Jesus Christ' really means in this total scheme of Divine Redemption. The Jew, so wronged, so tortured, so persecuted, in this Name, must forgive. It is asking a miracle of love.

Both then have their tasks to perform in disclosing the truth that blazes out in the Star. The Christian must wrestle with a world in the making, the Jew keep unsullied an appointment with God. In the night sky that covers them both it is to the Star of Redemption that both must turn. 'Yea, we now recognize the Star of Redemption itself, as it has at last emerged as a figure for us, in the divine visage' (*Star of Redemption*, p.418).

Such understanding is yet to be found. In Egypt, the story says, it was through interpreters that Joseph first spoke to his brothers. Revelation waited until he could speak with them face to face in their common tongue, till their souls were ready to hear at the deepest levels of need. Interfaith dialogue is likewise a matter of personal recognition, not easily arrived at but to be sought for with tears. It calls for much greater awareness of what the relationship asks of and offers to men than has been commonly understood yet. True religion means not the exalting of spirit nor the mystical vision but a response to being sought out and addressed. Both Christians and Jews have long known that God came unexpectedly to His own people in that way: 'By the starlight naming a dubious Name' (Browning). It is time that they learned to keep watch together.

It was no easy task that fell to Buber. While he thought and wrote indubitably as a Jew, in Israel he was treated with great indifference and even with active dislike. Scorn for the dreamer does not die easily. His words were more often listened to by outsiders than by men of his own people. Yet he quite deliberately chose 'to remain standing in the door of my ancestral home'. The bridge-building he attempted rested firmly upon his faith as a Jew. Thus, while he had much to say of Jesus, claiming even that no one could know Jesus from within as Jews could know him, he was adamant in rejecting the Christian doctrine of the Divine Son and the suggestion that Jesus was the Messiah. Not that way would the kind of understanding he sought be established. 'We will never recognize Jesus as the Messiah come, for this would contradict the

deepest meaning of our Messianic passion.' The words are harsh;
so are other words used by Buber in distinguishing the two faiths.
He is not infallible, but we may learn that in making such sharp
distinctions he sought to establish a real response in the meeting
of those set apart. The truly religious instant lay in the moment in
the everyday life of the world when a man wholly responded to
another, God's image to God's image.

The dialogue that he sought was no easy option. 'By far the
greater part of what is today called conversation among men', he
wrote, 'could be more properly and precisely described as spee-
chifying.' The speeches belonged to a world of slogans and cynical
rhetoric, of newspeak and doubletalk. The telecommunication
medium was about to reinforce the one-sidedness of public utterance. Few at that time could have guessed at the extent to which
true communication was threatened. Thomas Mann left Germany
to assert the writers' responsibility for human values expressed in
language, believing, as Buber did, that the death in the pot of the
German régime was not simply the vile brutal treatment of men
but also the falsification of speech, the devaluation of words, the
corruption of language, which destroyed the relations of persons.
The dehumanization of political life was projected in words that
brought darkness to a whole people.

What then was dialogue? It might mean an exchange of views,
chance conversation, inquiry or flirtation. It could be as famous as
the dialogues of Plato, as studied as the imaginary conversations
devised by men of letters, as infamous as conspiracies to murder.
In Hebrew usage it meant the expression of the most profound
relationship in terms of the Spirit. It was that which both prophets
and psalmists knew, as they themselves were drawn into the purging and quickening of this expression. It was in itself a manifestation of God's love for His people that such dialogue could take
place. 'They shall hear my voice' and in hearing and answering
would become truly His children. It was what the Johannine Gospel implied by the 'I-in-You, You-in-Me' community of being. It
was not bounded by words or times or places but being entered
upon partook of the boundlessness of God and confirmed man's
creaturely existence.

In post-Auschwitz days it has come to be seen as fraught with a new significance. Viktor Frankl has given it enduring expression. He cites as an illustration of it the choice of an inmate of a concentration-camp not to 'run into the wire' and put an end to the misery he underwent day by day, but to engage in 'imaginary dialogues' with his mother as an act of love. 'The fact that I did not even know whether she was alive hardly disturbed me.' 'The true intending of another personality as such', says Frankl, 'is independent of the person's physical presence, independent, in fact, of the person's bodily existence altogether.' Love outlasts and outreaches the death of the beloved and opens to those who love a deathless relation.

Buber believed that Hebrew religion remained unique in preserving its dialogic character, in holding fast by its conviction that God Himself had established this relationship with His People, not in any mechanical sense but as a factual thing which came into operation when men held themselves free to respond to a possible transformation, rebirth or exodus-like self-giving. Jewry could grow careless to it, could wantonly 'go whoring after other gods', but the Covenant gave this foundation to Jewish life. Looking at the world situation around him Buber therefore concluded that the future of man depended upon renewal of dialogue, and that the Jews were called upon in this critical moment of human history to undertake this dialogue at profounder depths than had ever been reached before.

It is now just over a century since Matthew Arnold concluded the preface to *Culture and Anarchy* with the words: 'Our race will, as long as the world lasts, return to Hebraism; and the Bible, which preaches this word will for ever remain, as Goethe called it, not only a national book, but the Book of the Nations.' It is in a light very different from anything Arnold knew that we look at Hebraic and Hellenistic culture today but his instinct was right. He was seeking for right foundations for human life, for order, intelligibility, reason and human dignity, without which all culture must certainly wither away. He was conscious of forces at work that jeopardized access to these sustaining things. Buber contended with similar conditions, grown more emphatic, and in this respect he is the greater humanist.

He did not come easily to his own understanding of Hebrew *humanitas*. Attracted early in life to the cultural side of the Zionist movement, Buber went on to study Hasidism, an enchanted wood from which some shy off with contempt, in which some get bemused and lost, and from which others return having learned a great deal of the springs of spiritual vitality which Jews have from age to age come across in their exodus journey. The Hasidism of Eastern Europe renewed Israel's grasp of righteousness; it was embodied in everyday life as a lyrical thing. It re-enacted the mood out of which the Psalms had once come. Buber learned from it the sense of encounger with God in the world; the expectation that the Shekinah would disclose itself in its glory through the multiform daily life of men and women. Buber's collection *Tales of the Hasidim* is a store house of such insights.

So Buber approached this Hebrew *humanitas* without illusions. On the longstanding cleavage between Jews and Christians he spoke with careful but hopeful words. 'What then', he asked, 'have you and we in common? If we take the question literally, a book and an expectation. To you the book is a fore-court; to us it is a sanctuary. But in this place we can dwell together, and listen to the voice that speaks here. That means that we can work together to evoke the buried speech of that voice, together we can redeem the imprisoned living word.' The invitation was not enthusiastically welcomed on either side, but Buber pressed on. He addressed himself to his 'dear opponent' not in sentimental fashion, for the issues were to a Jew too brutally paingiving for that, but with the conviction that conversation should be attempted as part of the peacemaking towards which men are called. Several times in the post-war world Buber undertook to speak to German audiences as a matter of duty in what he called 'the final battle of *homo humanus* against *homo contrahumanus*.' Not 'waiting till Messiah comes' but now in the very tempestuous currents of anger and hatred the truth must be spoken in love. 'I am not concerned with the pure;' he wrote, 'I am concerned with the turbid, the repressed, the pedestrian, with toil and dull contrariness – and with the Breakthrough.' He did not doubt that the break-through would come in these same unlikely unlovely conditions, that the halting words of today might become the springs of Adamic conversation tomorrow. 'If our mouths succeed in genuinely saying "thou", then, after a long silence and stammering, we shall have addressed our eternal Thou anew. Reconciliation leads towards reconciliation.'

The difficulties to be faced were immense. Neither diplomat nor philosopher, neither mystic nor politician, neither traditionalist nor sectary, he sought ways to ground his teaching in living itself, in simply asserting life in the face of the harsh and repellent conditions of Europe and the Near East. He chose to pit education against propaganda at a time when the latter appeared to have well-nigh conquered the world. He was to find his message increasingly difficult to deliver within the Israeli state. He did not waver from his lifelong purpose; the search for a personal relationship with all men, He believed that only in free, open, fearless encounter could the forces of hatred, deceit and darkness be overcome.

Buber's *I and Thou* is the manifesto of that faith, a manifesto of Joseph our brother sent ahead in the darkest of times to open men's eyes to the truth of our human condition. Set beside the *Communist Manifesto*, *Le Contrat Social,* Hume's *Treatise on human nature* or Hobbes' *Leviathan,* Buber's work looks a little drab. It provides no all-embracing philosophical structure, no solutions for the problems, but rather an indication of an attitude and an approach. Its foundation is not in ideas so much as in actual relations between man and woman, neighbour and friend, and its reach embraces the world. Its worth lies in the openness that it brings to Everyman's response to living. It would fail the moment anyone said in formula fashion Buber says '... Expressed in frequently awkward terms, it resembles those wordless or brief modes of communication which take place between a mother and baby, between lovers in moments of understanding, between the dying and those they love. It reveals, it confirms, it sustains. What it communicates is what is needed for personal growth.' Man wishes to be confirmed by each man as he who is, and there is genuine confirmation only in mutuality.' What John Macmurray taught in his Gifford lectures on *Persons in Relation* lay at the heart of Buber's treatise.

He used human experience as his basis and chose two primary

words, as we have seen, to describe the relationships that men knew. The primary I-Thou signified a relation of person to person, I-It a relation to things, of subject to object, of planner to plan. I-Thou meant the meeting of persons, each affirming the other. I-It underlay the vast enterprise of mankind in making, using and manipulating things, structures, materials, ideas and people as means to an end. Buber spoke of these things as he himself sought for a true foundation for living.

I-Thou was therefore the heart of man's true relation with God, but in Biblical writing it came in significant fashion with the Thou set first. 'Thou art mine' says God, affirming His creature's being. Man is a 'Thou' to the Living God who ordained him to learn to say Thou to his maker. Only this calling could give man freedom to grow as a person, only in this thou-saying could he know a community of free persons. On this basis alone could the day-to-day life of mankind know continuing joy and delight in a common existence. 'I possess nothing but the everyday out of which I am never taken', Buber wrote, 'I know no fulness but each mortal hour's fulness of claim and responsibility.'

No more was needed. Human life was nothing less than an invitation made by God to man and the response he offered to it. That was the meaning of the election of Israel and the Torah, a meaning disclosed to the Jew first that it might be embraced by mankind. The world and Time are but the stage upon which men take their cues and respond. Now, at this moment, God speaks and is heard by the attentive man, by the man who faces creation as it happens. It happens as speech directed precisely at him. The test of all true religion lies in its ability to help men to hear themselves so addressed, and to hear beyond Joseph's voice and the voices of brothers the One who speaks through the moments of meeting, whose voice is that of rebirth.

To write in this way is to draw a new map of human life, or to walk on what Buber described as a narrow ridge, on the far side of the subjective, on this side of the objective, the realm of the 'between'. Like the ancient ridge-ways of primitive men it linked man to man, to the natural world, and to a transcendent sense of their calling. In such moments of meeting 'the mystery of the coming-to-be of language and that of the coming-to-be of man are one'. Communication means going that way together.

Yet as Buber freely admitted the primary I-It could not be, ignored. The world of things encroaches upon the world of persons, and the I that masters and uses them, accumulates powers to extend them, and sees itself grown vast in its capacity to deploy them. Human history records the augmentation of the world of this It. Technology, science, the arts, religion itself are made the objects of its manipulation. With the threads of doctrine Lilliputian men define the nature of God, put masks on the face of the living, make formulae of the intents of the heart. The gains of these empires are so assured that men grow giddy in their pursuit. The mystery of man's ability to make gods to go before him presses hard on his glimpse of himself surnamed by the Living God. On Sinai's slopes he can turn betrayal into a festival of religion and reduce even a Moses to near-despair.

Nevertheless the I-Thou is the truth to which mankind must return. Suffering attrition and rejection, perversion and abuse, there is at the heart of man's experience of living a knowledge of the Thou who speaks to and is spoken to by him. The meaning of the Exodus name of God is a declaration of His presence not on our terms but on His. 'I shall be present as I shall be present.' The walls that men in their fearfulness and pride raised could shut out the light of His glory, their shouting could drown His words, but He remained faithful. He would not forsake His creature nor could the creature find his fulfilment in anything, any 'It', that usurped His place. The empty heart of man yearns for the 'Thou' that gives meaning to man's existence. Israel's trust is in Him who fills hungry souls with goodness.

Buber's great life-work was to declare the presence of God in every relationship that transmitted the 'Thou' to mankind. Every meeting, event, perception of ordinary daily life could mediate such a disclosure. Human life he described, as I mentioned earlier, as a two-fold movement involving what he called 'a primal setting at a distance' and a correlative 'drawing into relation'. Life began as a relation in process of being perceived. It grew in the distancing enacted and re-enacted by births and rebirths. Man was addressed

by God across the great divide of things human and divine that he
might come to know the ineffable Love which filled all things.
'There are not two realms, that of spirit and that of nature; there
is only the coming Kingdom of God.'

The deserts through which the hungry soul passes, the darkness
that conceals the glance that confirms our being, the wall that parts
lovers, are real but they are not the whole truth. By living his life
towards God who has spoken the 'Thou' man finds himself met.
'All revelation is summons and sending.' The God of the Hebrews
is met at the point where He gives men a new part to play in
creative Love at work. God is gone before him to prepare for his
coming. It is for journeying man to keep the appointment along
the road.

One who thus gave distance and the 'between' so important a
part in the scheme of Divine intention could not have ignored the
separation of Christianity and Judaism. It too had its work to do.
Both faiths had yet to be purged of the things which hid and
obstructed the 'Thou' in their standing before each other. Could
they now begin to see at long last the brother long parted from
them? Buber minimized nothing of the contradictions that set
Christian and Jew apart. The lines must be drawn not in hatred
but love. What was called for was the artist's approach, not commanding but coaxing the form of it into light. It meant being
humble enough to rejoice in the otherness of the brother, in the
singular otherness to be loved. To the two faiths fell the one task.
'It behoves both you and us to hold inviolably fast to our own
true faith, that is to our own deepest relationship to truth. This is
not what is called "tolerance"; our task is not to tolerate each
other's waywardness but to acknowledge the real relationship in
which both stand to the truth. Whenever we both, Christian and
Jew, care more for God Himself than for our image of God, we
are united in the feeling that our Father's house is differently
constructed than our human models take it to be'. The walls of
that house do not divide but unite.

12. In the Time of God's Eclipse

'Unreal City
Under the brown fog of a winter noon.'
                                        T. S. Eliot, *The Waste Land*

'Never shall I forget that nocturnal silence which deprived me, for all
eternity, of the desire to live. Never shall I forget those moments
which murdered my God and my soul and turned my dreams to
dust.'
                                        Elie Wiesel, *Night*

In a now largely forgotten novel of the Victorian age there is a not
unmemorable description of darkness descending upon and envel-
oping human life. On a June evening the small Burgundian city of
Semur is plunged into darkness and its streets reoccupied by the
ghostly dead. In the surrounding countryside warm summer sun-
shine lingers on the fields but at the city gates the chill of night
and mist takes over and in the streets 'desolation seemed seated in
all these empty places'. Mrs Oliphant's *Beleagured City* is not by
any stretch of imagination a great novel. Its fantasy wears thin, its
characterization is commonplace, but in its genteel Victorian way
it made its point. Worlds away from the reality of the horrors of
Operation Night and Fog, it hinted at something no bigger than
a man's hand which might soon make black the heavens and bring
darkness at noon into our streets.

It is not easy to keep a check upon our metaphors or upon the
romantic imagination that employs them. In this we face a considerable danger. The real questions that the Holocaust should raise
can be distorted or hidden away from us by the imagery we are

led to use. The word Holocaust itself is suspect. The reality we must face can impose too great a burden on our sensibility so that we fall back on words and images that are already worn and dulled. We have no language adequate to our need. We are outraged by the event, we feel constrained to speak, but how can we speak of the unspeakable? The words take over and in using them so often we cease to think or go on thinking about the significance of the event. The occasion slips away. Yet now, more than ever, it is important not to let ourselves be seduced from the fundamental task imposed upon us.

What we first need to see is that the Holocaust happened because men and women in Europe failed utterly to understand the situation in which they lived. Neville Chamberlain failed lamentably to comprehend the mind of Hitler during his talks at Godesberg and Munich, failed even more to realize the nature of the Nazi purpose taking shape. Was he more insensitive than others, more ignorant than the rest of us? Dare we claim today that we now take much more trouble to be truly informed about our situation because we have learned a lesson from this dreadful past? Our television screens tell us instantly of a number of events occurring round the world, but do we look more comprehendingly at them?

What is it that we have learned? Is it more than a hope or resolution that Christians and Jews should now begin to be 'nicer' to each other than they have managed to do for almost two thousand years? If more, then how much more? What does the 'more' involve? In this book we have looked briefly at a number of things that are called 'religious' such as the Kingdom of God, the question of prayer, the differences that historically divided Jews and Christians, the concept of man that has been influential in our respective cultures. Do we see these things as being of supreme importance for the future of mankind, for our children's children? Is it conceivable that in failing to take them more seriously than we did in the past we have doomed generations to come to a bloodier and more cruel fate than even the victims of Auschwitz knew? In other words, does it matter so much how we stand before God? Are we convinced that radical change in Christian thinking, behaviour, teaching, church-life and mission will be needed if Christianity is to do more than repeat the sad spectacle of the churches of Europe looking helplessly, tongue-tied, on the triumph of Evil spelled out in the murder of Jews?

It is because I believe this to be supremely *the* religious question that faces us and one that is even now gathering weight and momentum to give it an urgency we dare not neglect, that I take up the metaphor of the eclipse of God. Simply to use it gives no guarantee that we use it rightly but use it we must.

The phrase began to be used by both Christians and Jews some years ago. 'The vast body of Christian people', wrote Gregor Smith, 'are suffering from an eclipse: they do not see the sun, they walk in shadows, and have almost forgotten what it is like to live in the full splendour of light. To say that they are suffering from an eclipse means that between God and them something has been interposed. It is really God who is in eclipse'. Martin Buber's voice echoed that thought: 'Eclipse of the light of Heaven, eclipse of God, such indeed is the character of the historic hour through which the world is passing.'

This imagery has been common in both secular and theological uses. The outbreak of the Great War in 1914 came as a shock. Grey spoke of the lamps going out all over Europe. Like Burke's recollection of the dazzling splendour of Marie Antoinette at Versailles, the words caught men's imagination. They suggested the darkening of once bright skies. This was fond delusion; the darkness had always been there. It was men's artificial lights that flickered or were extinguished. As soon as they could they lit them again, lit even more brilliant lights. They kindled those lights 'brighter than a thousand suns' and cast the shadow of Hiroshima round the world. They took pains to develop the bright art of the film and the television screen to extend men's vision to seemingly infinite lengths. They brought into every home the shades of the black and merciless things that crouch in our streets, the darkness that falls across the relations of men and women, the fading out of beliefs that were charged to give an assurance of light.

Theology likewise took up the image. It has frequently used such terms as the death, the disappearance or the eclipse of God. His silence, His hiddenness, His whereabouts, have all been studiously discussed. It is more common to speak of Him in the depths than in the heights. Men have repeated Pascal's words with a new respect as their cosmological knowledge has extended the picture of the dark immensity of the Universe in which they live. They perceive a little more surely the brief nature of the play in which they perform their parts. They are not unaware of the spectacle of a darkened theatre in which no one watches and no one plays.

What we have always to ask is what lies behind the imagery that we use. Has the Holocaust helped us to identify in a surer way the great issues that as human beings we now face?

We recognize how faint a light our Christian beliefs throw on the world in which the Holocaust could take place, fainter, that is, than the many competing lights that men kindled for other ends. We have noted earlier in this book that Christianity could not but appear to Jewish eyes as a romantic religion, illusion-producing when what was desperately needed was knowledge of truth. Its romanticist aspects gained greater appeal as the numbers of half-believers grew. Men can be sentimentally attached and affectionate towards that which makes few demands upon them. The churches of Europe were scarcely disposed to question the splendours of imperial glory or commercial and technological triumph or race and racial purity. Romance extolled for a season the White Man's Burden and then shifted its gaze to his culture, his technology and even his genes. Studies of life in the rural parishes of Lincolnshire and elsewhere, together with famous surveys like that which Charles Booth conducted in London in the closing decades of the nineteenth century have shown that 'the stronger influence on the individual in his everyday life' was pagan and not Christian at all, that such paganism was 'incurably earthbound and pessimistic'. No great sense of alarm was occasioned by it. Life in the great cities and towns of industrial England sloughed off a good deal of primitive folklore and gave little but new superstitions to replace it. Lower-middle class religion flourished. New churches were built, new missions sent out, new clergy recruited. What did not take place was the shaping of radical religious critique of where men were going. Religious Germany was in like case. European

Christianity had a false impression of its influence in the political world.

To say that is not to suggest that men were hypocritical about their faith or that there were not a great many men and women who lived lives of true honest service of God. It is to contend nonetheless that the trends in society, both technical and political, were against them. The Churches tried hard to strengthen their influence by making long overdue reforms but they did not set out to study the situation with which they were faced as an urgent immediate matter. They addressed the world on behalf of God in terms which grew less and less meaningful to the people they hoped to reach. They could offer less and less evidence of corporate living to question and challenge the life of the society in which they were set. They tended to foster a religion of pious, respectable and unadventurous enclaves. There were brilliant minds and devoted lives at the service of the Churches but the process of the eclipse of God went on because the more obviously influential factors at work in social life, whether cultural, economic, political or intellectual, pursued ends quite other than those of ecclesiastics. The Churches paid dearly for having for so long committed the direction of their witness to clergymen whose education had been increasingly out of touch with the emerging world.

Eclipse was a fitting symbol of what took place. It was a slow inexorable process, part wilfully determined, part unwittingly allowed to happen, in which the reality of relationship with God had been obscured and in which the ways of serving Him were blurred into general unspecific terms. To ancient faults new dangerous factors were swiftly being added. We must count in the legacy of superstition, of cursings, spells and witchcraft, of hideous exploitation of the fears of ignorant minds. We must include in it the scarcely-challenged cruelty of men to women and children, the shadow cast upon the very springs of human love. We must add in the persecution of heretics and the barbarities of religious wars. These things breed other evils of suspicion and intolerance that infect the body of believers, growing to fever-heat under conditions of stress. The Church failed to deal wisely with the Enlightenment, itself resisting new ways of thinking about man's life on the earth and giving grounds to its opponents to describe it as the enemy of human progress.

Worse was to follow. The French Revolution so frightened men that politicians both lay and clerical courted the churches and used religion to buttress the ancient régime and to brand discontented persons with charges of atheism and free-thought. The political exploitation of religion meant further alienation of the industrialized populations of the great cities and towns. God was being eclipsed by the fearful folly of professed disciples who so often spent time and energy and resources in sectarian battles.

To do so was to abandon great areas of human life to the influence of other agents. The nineteenth century was to see the rise to power of artists and writers and secular teachers whose work at best evoked imagination and at worst played with the sentimentality and crude fantasy that a largely disinherited populace required. It was soon to put to both crude and clever use the increasing knowledge of human psychology which research in that field was to produce. In the absence of acceptable religious symbolism still coarser substitutes would be used. The more primitive appetites of mankind became the object of quasi-religious practice.

It is with these movements of men's souls that we have to deal if we are to understand either the background to Operation Night and Fog or our own problems today. Men cannot live in a void. The messianism of Hitler met a need felt by millions of men and women. In him they felt they encountered not simply the political saviour of a society threatened with collapse nor even a prophet of a new social order so much as an incarnation, a personal embodiment of their own deepest selves and needs. They sought in him the assurance of their own identity as persons, and a tangible bond uniting the German race.

That so crude a substitute faith could carry such power was a witness to the impoverishment, moral and spiritual, that had overtaken German society at the time. The Nazi attempt to rejuvenate ancient Teutonic deities and mythology might be considered ludicrous in the twentieth century, but it represented something more satisfying to men in their mass than the philosophical reflections or outmoded symbols they met in traditional religious

circles. The swastika on the armband carried more conviction than
the crosses inside the churches. Religious leaders were not unwilling to acquire a new charismatic authority by wearing the hooked
cross and hailing Hitler. 'Ours is an age', wrote Buber in *The
Eclipse of God* 'in which God is absent', and at such a time men
turned to the makers of idols, to those who provide ersatz religion.
'This is a time,' said Heidegger, 'of the gods who have fled and of
the God who is coming; it is indigent because it stands in a double
lack; in the no longer of the departed gods and the not yet of the
Coming One.'

This hatred was soon to be answered in kind. The black peoples
found a voice in the arts that drove deep their message into the
white man's world. Malcolm X, James Baldwin, Eldridge Cleaver
and a host of often shrill, bitter and scornful tongues made clear
the confrontation now inescapable in the cities throughout the
world. 'At the centre of this dreadful storm, this vast confusion,'
wrote James Baldwin in *Notes of a Native Son*, 'stand the black
people of this nation that has never accepted them, to which they
were brought in chains.' The white man who had entered Africa
to reduce its peoples and resources to serve only his own will
found tides of rejection rising to challenge him in the most vulnerable areas of his psychological and spiritual life. White consciousness damaged already by age-old rejection of Jews could not
but feel still more insecure in the face of the coloured man's claim.
In America confusion was doubled, for, in Baldwin's words, 'the
Harlem Negro could identify himself with Jews from Moses to
Jesus Christ yet hate and despise the Jews whom he met and lived
with because he saw in them the expression of his own humiliation
and desperate attempt to live a human life in the white man's
world. The structure of the American commonwealth has trapped
both these minorities into attitudes of perpetual hostility.'

It is in those words that we might find the fears of mankind
today most truly expressed. Everyman feels himself in danger of
being both trapped and exposed in a minority, a minority of one.
This spells lostness to him. The lostness increases in horror as the
impersonal world presses ever more heavily on him.

It would be foolish to attribute all the ills of mankind today to anti-semitism. Human lusts and fears are more diverse in origin and scope. Nevertheless the problems now facing mankind as a whole cannot be grasped apart from an understanding of the significance of anti-semitism in human affairs until now. The Jewish question is universal. It is the question of Man's nature, relationships, work and purpose in life. These questions were once covered by religious beliefs that were largely owed to Jews. The Jews gave to the world the conviction that life could only be rightly lived out as an act responsive to God. God Himself required men to respond in terms of mercy, love, freedom and truth. The weakening of that conviction brought the confusion and loss of direction already described as an eclipse of God. Man was losing his way.

Thus Israel's role in history, to confess the truth and presence of God in the world, and Christianity's charge to carry this truth to all mankind were both jeopardized by the enmity that was engendered between them. Both were committed to say 'No' to attempts to build human life on other foundations than this. Both were charged to subject all purposes whatsoever to the test of whether they hindered or helped men to come to the knowledge of God not in terms of ideas but in actual living. Both were likewise committed to building up a palpable visible community expressive of God in human terms, in the personal life of its members.

These tasks were impossible of achievement but for the guidance and help of God and the constant willingness of the faithful to seek renewal of the direction of life in penitent return to Him. The conceit that they might be achieved by those who rejected each other could only witness against them. Anti-semitism is a fatal flaw in Christendom's long attempt to serve God in this way, a flaw which in time has been expressed in the growing confusion of its apparently successful life. The magnificence of its achievement cannot hide the pathos of its evident failure. The culture it nurtured broke away from its spiritual basis and challenged it with an ever-increasing scorn. For some time at least a dazzling success attended this culture. The idea of progress which gripped men's minds could hardly keep pace with the enterprise it inspired.

Knowledge made a god of technological man; he needed no other. The lights of heaven might be safely put out.

What broke across twentieth century Europe and involved the whole world in its storm was the realization that the basic relations between men no longer obtained. The lostness of men was a social fact. To whom else could he go? 'This is a moment of potential anarchy when the community lacks any explicit principle of order which can be effective under the conditions of the time. This is the night of violent and bestial release, the opportunity of the inhibited perversions which can now ally themselves with technical power. The dominance of the dissociated idealisms is over, and the two remaining active principles, sadistic vitality and technical power, join forces in a brief period of dominance' (L. L. Whyte, *The Next Development in Man*). This Lancelot Whyte called 'a short reign of Anti-Christ', but for those who sit in its darkness it can be a very long night. Thirty years after Auschwitz we may well ask whether the principles of Europe's social-political-intellectual life have been changed. How far have Christians begun to see how they helped to bring the Holocaust about?

The Bible spares nothing to those who call God good. It records crimes, tyrannies, disasters, cruelties falling upon all men. It dares say that God creates Good and Evil, Darkness and Light. It says He both hides and reveals Himself, that He speaks and is also silent. The dumbness of God is a source of devout complaint. The biblical writers saw no reason to make light of the fury of God. They bowed to it in the full knowledge that His ways were not those of men. Even so they held fast to their trust in Him. 'Though He slay me yet will I trust.' Modern Judaism has not gone back upon that. In a Conservative Jewish prayer-book published in the United States the places of horror – the concentration camps – are deliberately named in the affirmation of faith. If indeed Jesus of Nazareth dying in agony upon the cross recited Psalm 22, it was wholly in keeping with Israel's maturest faith. 'Every religion', wrote Pascal, 'which does not affirm that God is hidden is not true', and in affirming that faith he himself committed himself to the God of Abraham, Isaac and Jacob. Port-Royal's spiritual strength was nourished upon such food.

Nevertheless the darkness and silence appall. The darkness and light are alike to Him, in the realm of darkness his wonders are known, but man is not God and but for His help could not endure it. Those Jews and non-Jews who in the dark years took their lives were no cowards but men and women whom the darkness destroyed. It was not the unthinking or shallow who measured the horror but those who in fineness of spirit were overwhelmed.

This night sky of the Lord that has become the condition of our time and has been experienced in the anguish of the death camps and the bewilderment of multitudes of sufferers round the world is still, so faith affirms, the darkness where God is. The great tradition of Christian religious art did not fail to bear witness to the darkened skies. Today it is likely to find its continuance outside the realm of religious faith and symbol. Writing of one of its most striking examples in our time, Picasso's *Guernica*, Anthony Blunt saw fit to relate it to the long line of European art which ran from eleventh century Spanish manuscripts 'through the tympana of Burgundian Romanesque churches to Durer, Michaelangelo, Jean Duvet, Bruegel and El Greco in the sixteenth century, all of whom painted the Apocalypse or the Last Judgement as symbols of the evil of the world and the doom which must befall it'. In Picasso's world the heavens are empty and no ear will hear the prayers of those stricken down beneath a pitiless sky. Men and their cities go into the dark. Warsaw, Dresden, Guernica, Hamburg, Beirut, Hiroshima, Hanoi, are enveloped. Villages like Lidice and Oradour sur Glane bear witness to uncontrollable destructive lust, to a hankering after the Abyss, to the fury issuing from man's darkened heart.

> He who wept for Jerusalem
> Now sees His prophecy extend
> Across the greatest cities of the world.

He sees the death-camps erected to build Hell on earth and seat Darkness crowned in the midst of tortured and dying men where He looked for the Kingdom of God to come.

It was such a situation seen close at hand which caused Dietrich

Bonhoeffer to comment: 'Surely there has never been a generation in the course of history with so little ground under its feet as our own.' He was speaking of Man's relation to reality, religion's business, and went on to describe the time as one of no religion at all. He went on further to ask, as one who would not turn back in the darkness, how Christ could become the Lord of such displaced disinherited people. Where and how could light be sought for such men? He could be curtly severe about churchmen hastily seeking to make room for God and ironic about those whose occupations were at risk. But he himself faced that night sky in resolute fashion.

It was to the basic Hebrew understanding of faith in God that he turned. 'I don't think it is Christian', he wrote, 'to want to get to the New Testament too soon and too directly; you cannot and must not speak the last word before you have spoken the next to the last.' He questioned the long course of Christianity's word to the world. On what foundation did that word rest? Dare one answer that it rested on anti-semitic disdain? The Church had carried the Gospel of Jesus to men who in ever-increasing numbers knew little of its rootedness in Israel's calling and whose contempt for the Jews was a measure of their unreadiness to receive the Gospel in more than name. In time the Gospel thus preached was super-imposed upon whatever political, social or philosophical assumptions were present among those approached. The Christian religion was treated as if it could be known in much the same way as other human knowledge. The basic encounter with God that had stamped its beginnings in Israel's life was thus lost to sight. It was not enought to use Old Testament stories to illustrate New Testament faith, for the faith of Jesus Himself was misrepresented if He was cut off from His people's election and meeting with God, from the basic relationship with God believed in and unconditionally affirmed as Creator and Lord.

Bonhoeffer saw that despite their access to the Old Testament most Christians had become ignorant of any fundamental relationship with it. They knew of it but did not regard it as their own history sufficiently strongly to use it in the religious interpretation of life in the world. They therefore lacked the Hebrew dimension of faith. The Exile, the prophetic demands, the times of darkness, did not become an integral part of Christian education. Such things were seen as being in the past. The edging of God out of the world therefore came not as a test of the spiritual responsibility of the Church but as a weakening of stamina, or confusion and loss of direction. Bonhoeffer looked in vain for Christians who had grown up in the ancestral household of Christ's faith. The search lost its point if it was not set firmly in the ongoing process of spiritual growth whose beginnings lay in the summons of God to this people to participate in His work. Real renewal of faith meant renewal of a sense of purpose. In the words of Teilhard de Chardin it is 'expectation, anxious, collective and operative expectation, of an end of the world, that is to say of an issue for the world, that is the supreme Christian function and the most distinctive characteristic of our religion'. Such an expectation of the coming of God's kingdom had, as we have seen earlier, faded from Christian belief, lacking as it did rootedness in the Old Testament hope.

No less important therefore was Bonhoeffer's warning in *Letters to a Friend* that God was not to be used as 'a stop-gap for the incompleteness of our knowledge'. Recovery of a basically Hebrew understanding of faith meant firm rejection of every form of gnosticism, however tricked out. A God of the gaps would be a ludicrous substitute for the Majesty of the Creator. Better darkness compelling men to wait patiently for His hand than such enfeeblement of His Godhead. What the Old Testament insisted upon was experience of the presence of God in the relationships into which men and women were called in the history of this people. It spoke of historical redemption rather than of salvation in timeless terms. 'Isn't this a cardinal error, which divorces Christ from the Old Testament and interprets him in the light of the myths of salvation?'

Bonhoeffer returned to the Hebrew assertion. Israel had seen man's destiny and spiritual task embedded in history and time. In becoming estranged from its Jewish sources Christianity had allowed the sense of God's relation to the world to be drained of creative reality. The eclipse of the light of life was foreshadowed when men ceased to find Him at work in their midst. Lacking such light men could not but find that every advance of knowledge made Him appear more irrelevant to man's world. Yet if men were to survive as creatures made in God's image they must learn to live wholly to Him in the world, recovering the Biblical sense of the heart's devotion as that of the whole man in relation to God. The Bible must still teach them that God redeemed slaves from Egypt to give direction to all human history and reality to man's handiwork on the earth. In the strength of that faith they might joyously ponder the news of Christ's life being raised from the dead.

Bonhoeffer's writings were made in conditions which signified how far the Christian churches had failed to embrace this Jewish conviction, how far as a consequence of such failure they had lacked the will to oppose the Caesarism of worldly powers and the ability to create wholly different patterns of living. In the darkness which he experienced to the full, having learned to see it as an ordeal of a whole people as well as a person, he grew more convinced of the nature of Christian intention. The true test of Christian faith lay in the 'worldliness' it called for and the participation in suffering that it entailed. Only so could men be caught up in the way of Christ, in the messianic event. Faith in Christ must commit them to the work of transforming the world through the relationships they themselves were ready to make. In all that men spoke or did to 'the least of these my brethren' they received or rejected the Christ. Every act, every thought, every word, had thus become crucial. To know this was to enter the night of expectation. 'The day will come', he wrote, 'when men will be called again to utter the word of God with such power as will change and renew the world. It will be a new language which will horrify men, and yet overwhelm them by its power. It will be the language of a new righteousness and truth, a language which proclaims the peace of God with men and the achievement of His Kingdom.'

'Worldliness' of the kind envisaged by Bonhoeffer in no way detracts from the importance of the spirituality of the Dark Night of the Soul. The road is one and the same. The mystical writer has focussed attention on the darkness that invests man's journey not only at reaches much further along the road than most men have as yet imagined they will be asked to tread but in all times of crisis.

'Worldliness' of this kind became furthermore the informing vision of Teilhard de Chardin's work. Though the great body of it was taken up with the presentation of his theme of the evolution of life upon earth his attention was always directed towards the future, to the Christification of all things to come. Though he made little reference to the Hebrew insights into that theme he was at all times occupied with the significance of the Creation, with the dust out of which man was fashioned, the earth he was called on to help bring to its consummation. *Le Milieu Divin* was dedicated to 'those who love the world'.

Such 'worldliness' found its voice also in Buber's insistence upon the pursuit of community in the relations of mankind. The great threat that disclosed itself in the political pressures of the new age was that of collectivity, the enforced mass-life of meaningless individuals, dehumanized by the manipulation of their lives from cradle to grave, and living only for vicarious satisfaction in the great Idol's triumph. In the face of such threats the people of God must renew and hold fast by their calling as persons, free and willing to build up the body of true community in which each member honoured the others.

Over all such convictions the shadow has fallen. The darkness may deepen in years ahead. There is as yet little to show that mankind in a wholly new spirit is seeking to build a quite different world, that the churches and faiths of mankind are possessed of a vision and will of a different kind from that which they manifested in the Holocaust years. Christianity's days of the eclipse of God may only now be beginning to be truly known. Times of great deprivation and of the purging away of futile and corrupted things may well lie ahead. It may very well be that the elder brother who has gone through such bitter times often before, the despised and rejected brother, may be needed the more to hold out a scarred yet sustaining hand.

The time nonetheless is pressing. We cannot afford to let the truth of the Holocaust be obscured or forgotten. It must be permitted to purge out the dross and the sin of the Church's life. It must compel them to hear all over again the question so often asked by the Jews: 'Why do they hate us so?' and in turn ask their own question 'Why the Jews?'. Only so will the mystery of Israel's presence in the world be accorded its rightful place. Without it we lose our way. Perhaps we must learn to see the whole epoch of Christendom until now as something of a false start. Mighty works were done by it in His Name but the ash of the Holocaust fires lies too deeply upon them today. Buber spoke of our time as a time of darkness but he also rejoiced to call it a night of expectation. It will only be so as far as Christians are humbled enough to realize and admit that it was precisely in their wrongdoing to the people of Israel that they helped to darken the skies and went far to surrender God's world to the terror of the Abyss. They did so because they believed a lie and because they made it their business to maintain it, rejecting the people whom God had called. 'Thou dravest Love from thee who dravest Me' (Thompson, *The Hound of Heaven*).

The new beginning will only be made when those who committed this hideous wrong and those who were wronged learn to speak to each other in love. It is a formidable task, to take part in the redemption of a world that put into effect Operation Night and Fog, a world that had chosen for many centuries of its history to harbour the evil springs of that act. It is a task which will be undertaken only if men read the lesson of Golgotha-Auschwitz aright. Both Christian and Jew are therefore involved in presenting that lesson in all its truth to tomorrow's world. Those who ask God to deliver them must want to be free, to be freed from their own misdoing, their blindness and pride in the past. They can only do that in truth when they seek out those whom they wronged and seek reconciliation with them. How much do Christians want to be free?

On the 1st of December, 1862, in the darkest hours of a great civil war during which this question of freedom was slowly and painfully discerned by some who took part in that war, Abraham Lincoln used these words: 'We can succeed only by concert. . . . The dogmas of the quiet past are inadequate to the stormy present. The occasion is piled high with difficulty and we must rise with the occasion. As our case is new, we must think anew, and act anew. We must disenthrall ourselves.'

It has been said that there can be no poetry after Auschwitz, only silence. Silence alone can set things right between God and man. But, in a last talk given by Rabbi Nachum Yanchiker to Jewish students on the eve of the German invasion of Lithuania, he counselled them not simply to try to stay alive but to 'pour forth your words and cast them into letters.... For words have wings; they mount up to the heavenly heights and they endure for eternity.' But time is needed for the words of poetry to be found, to be refined by fire and washed clean by water that they may so endure. From the camps and cellars there have come to us haunting lines like the now often quoted Cologne fragment:

> I believe in the sun even when it is not shining.
> I believe in love even when feeling is not.
> I believe in God even when He is silent.

There are other words too of still profounder insight, still surer grasp of what was being enacted. The time must come when words can be written and spoken that can inform human flesh anew and cause men's hearts to burn with new hope and love, with the faith that God goes with them as they journey together.

Bibliography

Abrahams, I., *The Glory of God*. Humphrey Milford 1925.

Acton, Lord, *History of Freedom and Other Essays*. Macmillan 1907.

Arendt, Hannah, *The Human Condition*. Cambridge University Press 1958 and Anchor Books 1959.

—— *Men in Dark Times*. Penguin, Pelican 1973.

Baeck, Leo, *The Essence of Judaism*. Schocken Books 1948.

—— *The Pharisees and Other Essays*. Schocken Books 1966.

Baldwin, James, *The Fire Next Time*. Michael Joseph 1963.

—— *Notes of a Native Son*. Michael Joseph 1964.

Barrett, W., *Irrational Man*. Heinemann 1961.

Barth, Karl, *Commentary on the Epistle to the Romans*. Oxford University Press 1969.

Beckwith, J., *Early Christian and Byzantine Art*. Penguin, Pelican 1970.

Bellow, Saul, *To Jerusalem and Back*. Penguin 1977.

Benjamin, W., *Illuminations*. Fontana 1973.

Bentwich, N., *Judaea Lives Again*. Gollancz 1944.

Bergman, S., *Faith and Reason*. Schocken Books 1963.

Berrigan, D., *America is Hard to Find*. S.P.C.K. 1973.

Bettelheim, B., *The Informed Heart*. Thames and Hudson 1961.

Blanshard, P., *Paul Blanshard on Vatican II*. Allen and Unwin 1967.

Bloch, Ernst, *Man on His Own*. Seabury 1971.

Blue, Lionel, *To Heaven with Scribes and Pharisees*. Darton, Longman and Todd 1975.

Bonhoeffer, D., *Letters and Papers from Prison*. Collins, Fontana 1975.

Bosanquet, M., *Life and Death of Dietrich Bonhoeffer*. Hodder and Stoughton 1968.

Brandon, S.G.F., *Man and his Destiny in the Great Religions*. Manchester U.P. 1962.

—— *Jesus and Zealots*. Manchester University Press 1967.

—— *The Trial of Jesus of Nazareth*. Paladin 1971.

Brasch, R., *The Unknown Sanctuary*. Angus and Robertson 1969.
Bronowski, J., *The Ascent of Man*. B.B.C. 1973.
Buber, Martin, *I and Thou*. T. and T. Clark 1937.
—— *Between Man and Man*. Kegan Paul 1974.
—— *Tales of the Hasidim*. Schocken Books 1948.
—— *Two Types of Faith*. Routledge and Kegan Paul 1951.
—— *The Eclipse of God*. Harper Torchbooks 1957.
—— *Moses*. Harper Torchbooks 1958.
—— *The Knowledge of Man*. Allen and Unwin 1965.
—— *Israel and the World*. Schocken Books 1963.
—— *The Way of Response*. Schocken Books 1971.
—— *Biblical Humanism*. Macdonald 1968.
Carlebach, J., *Karl Marx and the Radical Critique of Judaism*. Routledge 1978.
Carmichael, J., *The Death of Jesus*. Penguin, Pelican 1966.
Chesterton, G.K., *The New Jerusalem*. Hodder and Stoughton 1920.
Cohen, A., *The Natural and the Supernatural Jew*. Mitchell Valentine 1967.
Cohn, N., *The Pursuit of the Millennium*. Paladin 1970.
Collingwood, R.G., *An Autobiography*. Oxford University Press 1939.
—— *The Idea of History*. Oxford University Press 1946.
Creighton, L., *Life and Letters of Mandell Creighton*. Longman's, Green 1904.
Cupitt, Don, *Christ and the Hiddenness of God*. Lutterworth Press 1971.
Davies, W.D., *The Setting of the Sermon on the Mount*. Cambridge University Press 1964.
—— *Paul and Rabbinic Judaism*. S.P.C.K. 1970.
Dawidowicz, L., *The War Against the Jews*. Penguin, Pelican 1977.
—— *The Jewish Presence*. Harcourt Brace Jovanovich 1977.
Dodd, C.H., *The Founder of Christianity*. Collins 1971.
Dugdale, B., *Arthur James Balfour*. Hutchinson 1936.
Dumas, A., *Political Theology and the Life of the Church*. S.C.M. 1978.
Eckardt, A.R., *Elder and Younger Brothers*. Schocken Books 1973.
Epstein, I., *Judaism*. Penguin, Pelican 1970.
Fleg, E., *Why I Am a Jew*. Gollancz 1943.
Frankl, V., *The Will to Meaning*. Souvenir Press 1971.
—— *The Doctor and the Soul*. Penguin, Pelican 1973.
Friedlander, A., *Leo Baeck*. Routledge and Kegan Paul 1973.
Friedman, P., *Their Brothers' Keepers*. Holocaust Library 1978.
Fussner, F.S., *The Historical Revolution*. Routledge and Kegan Paul 1962.
Gardavsky, V., *God is Not Yet Dead*. Penguin, Pelican 1973.
Gay, Peter, *Freud, Jews and Other Germans*. Oxford University Press 1978.
Geyl, P., *Encounters in History*. Collins, Fontana 1967.
Ghilan, M., *How Israel Lost its Soul*. Penguin, Pelican 1974.
Ginsberg, M., *Reason and Unreason in Society*. Longmans', Green 1947.

Glatzer, N., *Franz Rosenzweig*. Schocken Books 1961.
—— *Hillel the Elder*. Schocken Books 1966.
Goldman, L., *The Hidden God*. Routledge and Kegan Paul 1964.
Goldmann, N., *The Jewish Paradox*. Weidenfeld and Nicolson 1978.
Green, J., *Diary 1928–1957*. Collins 1967.
Guignebert, C., *Jesus*. Kegan Paul 1935.
Gutteridge, R., *Open Thy Mouth for the Dumb*. Blackwell 1976.
Happold, F.C,, *Religion, Faith and Twentieth Century Man*. Penguin, Pelican 1966.
Herford, C.H., *The Post-war Mind of Germany*. Clarendon Press, Oxford 1927.
Heschel, A., *Who is Man?* Oxford University Press 1965.
—— *A Passion for Truth*. Secker and Warburg 1974.
Hitler, A., *My Struggle (Mein Kampf)*. Hutchinson 1972.
Hochhuth, R., *The Representative*. Methuen 1963.
Hodes, A., *Encounter with Martin Buber*. Penguin, Pelican 1975.
Houlden, J.L., *Explorations in Theology 3*. S.C.M. 1978.
House, E., *The Intimate Papers of Colonel House*. Benn 1926.
Hugel, F. von, *The Mystical Element in Religion*. Clarke 1961.
—— *Letters from Baron von Hugel to a Niece*. Dent 1929.
Jacobs, L., *Hasidic Prayer*. Routledge and Kegan Paul 1972.
Janouch, G., *Conversations with Kafka*. Deutsch 1971.
Jones, D., *Epoch and Artist*. Faber 1973.
Kilpatrick, G., *Origins of the Gospel According to St Matthew*. Clarendon Press, Oxford 1946.
Klausner, J., *Jesus of Nazareth*. Allen and Unwin 1925.
Klein, C., *Anti-Judaism in Christian Theology*. S.P.C.K. 1978.
Koestler, A., *The Thirteenth Tribe*. Hutchinson 1976.
Kung, Hans, *On Being a Christian*. Collins 1977.
Laqueur, W., *The Israel-Arab Reader*. Weidenfeld and Nicolson 1969.
Lods, A., *Israel*. Kegan Paul 1932.
Maccoby, H., *Is the Political Jesus Dead?* Encounter 1976.
Machovec, M., *A Marxist Looks at Jesus*. Darton, Longman and Todd 1976.
Macmurray, J., *The Clue to History*. S.C.M. 1938.
—— *Search for Reality in Religion*. Allen and Unwin 1965.
Mann, P., *Golda Meir*. Mitchell Vallentine 1972.
Martin, M., *Jesus Now*. Collins 1975.
Milman, H.H., *The History of the Jews*. Everyman Edition 1909.
Montefiore, C.G., *The Synoptic Gospels*. 1909.
Mooney, C., *Teilhard de Chardin and the Mystery of the Church*. Collins 1966.
Moore, G.F., *Judaism in the First Centuries of the Christian Era*. Harvard 1970.

Moore, S., *No Exit*. Darton, Longman and Todd 1968.

Namier, L.B., *Conflicts*. Macmillan 1942.

Nef, John, *Cultural Foundations of Industrial Civilisation*. Cambridge University Press 1958.

Oliver, Roy, *The Wanderer and the Way*. East and West Library 1968.

Parkes, J., *The Conflict of the Church and the Synagogue*. Meridian Books 1961.

Petuchowski, J., *Theology and Poetry*. Routledge and Kegan Paul 1978.

Plowman, Max, *Bridge Into the Future*. Andrew Dakers 1944.

Poliakov, L., *History of Anti-Semitism*. Routledge and Kegan Paul 1974.

Post, L. van der, *Jung and the Story of Our Times*. Hogarth Press 1976.

—— *The Seed and the Sower*. Hogarth Press 1963.

Potok, Chaim, *In the Beginning*. Penguin 1976.

Prinz, J., *Popes from the Ghetto*. Schocken Books 1968.

Rideau, Emile, *Teilhard de Chardin*. Collins 1968.

Robert, M., *From Oedipus to Moses*. Routledge and Kegan Paul 1977.

Robinson, J.A.T., *The Human Face of God*. S.C.M. 1974.

Rosenstock-Huessy, E., *The Christian Future*. S.C.M. 1947.

—— *Judaism Despite Christianity*. University of Alabama 1969.

Rosenzweig, F., *The Star of Redemption*. Routledge and Kegan Paul 1971.

Roszak, T., *The Taking of a Counter-Culture*. Faber 1970.

—— *Where the Waste Land Ends*. Faber 1973.

Roth, Leon, *Judaism*. Faber 1960.

Rothschild, F.A., *Between God and Man*. Free Press 1965.

Rynne, Xavier, *The Fourth Session*. Faber 1966.

Sandmel, S., *We Jews and Jesus*. Gollancz 1965.

—— *The First Century in Judaism and Christianity*. Oxford University Press, N.Y. 1969.

Schenk, H.G., *The Aftermath of the Napoleonic Wars*. Kegan Paul 1947.

Scholem, G., *Major Trends in Jewish Mysticism*. Thames and Hudson 1955.

—— *Sabbatai Sevi*. Routledge and Kegan Paul 1973.

Schurer, E., *History of the Jewish People*. T. and T. Clark 1885.

Segal, R., *Whose Jerusalem?* Penguin, Pelican 1975.

Sharf, A., *Byzantine Jewry*. Routledge and Kegan Paul 1971.

Simon, Ulrich, *A Theology of Auschwitz*. S.P.C.K. 1978.

Singer, C., *The Christian Approach to the Jews*. Allen and Unwin 1937.

Smith, R. Gregor, *The New Man*. S.C.M. 1956.

Stanley, A.P., *Lectures on the History of the Eastern Church*. Everyman Edition 1907.

Steiner, G., *Language and Silence*. Penguin, Pelican 1969.

—— *After Babel*. Oxford University Press 1975.

Stendahl, K., *Paul Among Jews and Gentiles*. S.C.M. 1977.

Torrance, T.F., *Israel: People of God*. Lecture to Anglo-Israel Friendship League, 6 February 1978.

228 THE NIGHT SKY OF THE LORD

Troeltsch, E., *The Social Teaching of the Christian Churches*. Allen and Unwin 1931. MEDIAEVAL FOUNDATIONS

Ullmann, W., ~~The Social Teaching~~ of Renaissance Humanism. Elek 1977.

BUTTERFIELD H. ~~Vellacot, P.~~, *The Whig Interpretation of History*. Fontana 1931.

Vermes, G., *Jesus the Jew*. Collins 1976.

—— *The Dead Sea Scrolls*. Collins 1977.

Weil, S., *Selected Essays*. Oxford University Press 1970.

Whiteley, D., *The Theology of St Paul*. Blackwell 1975.

Whyte, L.L. *The Next Development in Man*. Cresset Press 1944.

—— *Focus and Diversions*. Cresset Press 1950.

Wouk, H., *This is My God*. Collins, Fontana 1976.

Zaehner, R.C., *Concordant Discord*. Oxford University Press 1970.

Index